Islam in Contemporary Egypt

Civil Society vs. the State

Denis J. Sullivan
Sana Abed-Kotob

LYNNE
RIENNER
PUBLISHERS

BOULDER
LONDON

Published in the United States of America in 1999 by
Lynne Rienner Publishers, Inc.
1800 30th Street, Boulder, Colorado 80301

and in the United Kingdom by
Lynne Rienner Publishers, Inc.
3 Henrietta Street, Covent Garden, London WC2E 8LU

© 1999 by Lynne Rienner Publishers, Inc. All rights reserved

Library of Congress Cataloging-in-Publication Data
Sullivan, Denis Joseph.
　Islam in contemporary Egypt : civil society vs. the state / by
Denis J. Sullivan & Sana Abed-Kotob.
　Includes bibliographical references and index.
　ISBN 1-55587-448-7 (hc : alk. paper)
　ISBN 1-55587-829-6 (pbk : alk. paper)
　1. Islam—Egypt—History—20th century. 2. Islam and state—
Egypt—20th century. 3. Islam and politics—Egypt—20th century.
4. Egypt—Politics and government—1981–　5. Islam—Social aspects—
Egypt—20th century. 6. Egypt—Social conditions—1952–　I. Abed-
Kotob, Sana. II. Title.
BP64.E3S85　1999
297.2'72'0962—dc21　　　　　　　　　　　　　　　　　　98-42797
　　　　　　　　　　　　　　　　　　　　　　　　　　　　CIP

British Cataloguing in Publication Data
A Cataloguing in Publication record for this book
is available from the British Library.

Printed and bound in the United States of America

∞　The paper used in this publication meets the requirements
　of the American National Standard for Permanence of
　Paper for Printed Library Materials Z39.48-1984.

5　4　3　2　1

Islam in Contemporary Egypt

To JoAnna Noor and Grace Catherine
and
To Husni Shunnar Abed and Naameh Ismail Abed

Contents

Acknowledgments ix
Note on Transliteration xi

1 Civil Society and Islamism in Egypt   1

   Research Questions 2
   Political Occupation and Societal Independence 6
   Islamic Egypt: The Arab Conquest, Muhammad Ali,
      and the Reformist Movement 7
   Egypt First 10
   Conclusion 12

2 The Plural Nature of Islam in Egypt   19

   The Multifaceted Nature of the Islamic Movement
      in Egypt 21
   A Militant Face 22
   Islamic Society Resurgent 24
   Law 32 of 1964 25
   Islamic Associations 26
   Islam—The "Other Path" 32
   Nationally Organized Islamic Services 33
   Corrupt and Self-Serving Organizations 35
   Conclusion 36

3 The Muslim Brotherhood   41

   Evolution of the Movement 41
   Islam and the Political Realm 45
   Strategies for the Establishment of an Islamic State 51
   Conclusion 65

4   Militant Islamist Groups   71

The Believer President and the Birth of Militancy   *72*
Militancy Entrenched   *75*
Al-Takfir wa al-Hijra   *77*
Tanzim al-Jihad   *78*
Al-Jama'a al-Islamiyya   *82*
Government Response   *86*
Conclusion   *89*

5   Gender, Islam, and Civil Society   97

State Opposition to Women's Activism   *99*
Advancing Women's Rights: A Century of Feminism and
   Debate in Egypt   *100*
Malak Hifni Nasif: Feminism with an Islamic Face   *101*
Huda Sha'rawi: Daring to Liberate Woman and Nation   *103*
Zaynab al-Ghazali: Islamist Feminist?   *104*
Women in Public and Private Spheres   *109*
Gender and Islam   *110*
A Nonessentialist View of the Veil   *113*
Conclusion   *116*

6   State and Civil Society in Conflict   121

Islam . . . "Resurgent"?   *124*
Government Attacks   *126*
Laws of the Land   *127*
Government Confronts the Press   *130*
Society Resurgent   *130*
Elections   *131*
The Potential for State-Society Cooperation   *134*

Bibliography   139
Index   151
About the Book   159

Acknowledgments

As with any work that takes years to produce, we are indebted to a number of people who have contributed to the publication of this research. We thank Lynne Rienner for seeing a book before one was even written and then for staying with the project throughout the four years that it took to research, write, rewrite, and produce. We also wish to thank a number of colleagues who have contributed their thoughts, comments, and critiques to various drafts of the manuscript, including Charles E. Butterworth, Mamoun Fandy, Ibrahim Karawan, Salwa Sharawi Gomaa, Mustafa Kamel Al-Sayed, Carrie Rosefsky Wickham, and the anonymous reviewers. Thanks also to Abdullah Al-Faqih, Rania Atieh, and Paul Beran II, graduate students at Northeastern University, who helped with the research on several chapters, and to Wendy Scranton, intern at the Middle East Institute, who helped compile the bibliography. Early drafts of some parts of this book were presented at conferences of the American Political Science Association and the Middle East Studies Association. The comments from the audiences at these conferences have helped to improve the arguments, rethink the conclusion, and generally update and strengthen the data presented here.

We have received institutional support for our research from the Office of the Provost at Northeastern University and from the Earhart Foundation. Special thanks go to Antony Sullivan of the Earhart Foundation for his strong moral and intellectual support and for facilitating the funding of much of this research.

The most important support for our efforts has come from our family members, who have been patient with the travels and travails associated with our research. Our spouses, Stephanie and Shaban, bore the brunt of this. We also thank our children and parents for their understanding as we engaged in a project that took us away from them.

This book seeks to put Egyptian society generally in a favorable light, one in which its tradition of openness and tolerance provides hope for the development of a civil society, a progressive society. Still, we warn of the dangers to that tradition that stem from militant factions of Islamists and others who ignore Egypt's culture of civility. We hold accountable the government that is responsible for maintaining Egypt's traditions, its power, its critical position in the Arab world, and its prominence in the international community. We welcome the comments of critical readers, colleagues, and students, and look forward to continuing the debate on Egypt's future.

Note on Transliteration

Many of the works referred to in this study were published in Arabic. In transliterating from the Arabic we used the basic outlines of the system used by the International Journal of Middle East Studies, with minor changes. We used the apostrophe (') to indicate the hamza, and the open single quotation mark (') to indicate the 'ayn. For the purpose of simplification other diacritics were not used. In most cases, we tried as much as possible to approximate the standard Arabic words and names. In a very limited number of personal names, we opted to use spellings that have become common in the English language, such as Gamal Abdel Nasser instead of Jamal 'Abd al-Nasir, and Muhammad Naguib instead of Muhammad Najib.

1
Civil Society and Islamism in Egypt

This book has an ambitious agenda: to describe the various Islamist[1] movements in contemporary Egypt with an eye on their historical evolution; to discuss issues of civil society and the role Islamist groups play in society as a whole; and to examine the conflict between the state and the society it seeks to control, not just govern. To be sure, we cannot fully cover all of these important topics in one short volume. However, neither can we attempt any one of them without including as much analysis of the others as possible. Islamist movements, civil society, and state-society relations are so intertwined that all must be addressed when analyzing contemporary Egyptian politics as well as contemporary Islam in Egypt.

In particular, we examine the pluralism and diversity of contemporary Islamic Egypt. Pluralism suggests multiple parties or institutions within the Islamic trend; by diversity, we mean various ideologies and tactics to achieve Islamic (or Islamist) ends (e.g., spiritual renewal, political power, or economic development). This *plural diversity* must be recognized by anyone interested in understanding politics and society in Egypt at the end of the twentieth century; it is a result of centuries of development and tradition, of progress and retrenchment, of cosmopolitanism and dogmatism[2] on the part of Sunni Muslim Egyptian Arabs. There is no single Islamist group or movement in Egypt that represents the entire society, even if there is one group, *al-Ikhwan al-Muslimun* (the Muslim Brotherhood), that is more popular than others.

Our focus is on political subcultures[3] and countercultures,[4] primarily those of the Islamist movements, as well as on state-society relations. Our method of investigating Egypt's Islamist movements has not been that of traditional research projects of the political culture genre—that is, there has been no extensive survey research conducted to ascertain the beliefs, values, and attitudes of contemporary Egyptians—because the Egyptian government discourages such efforts.[5] Although many Egyptian scholars have been allowed to conduct such research, government control continues to limit both Egyptian and international scholars' efforts in this realm. Some efforts (by us and others) have been made in the past to ascertain public opinion, attitudes, and beliefs, but these are largely unrepresentative of society as a whole and are thus not generalizeable beyond their limited samples or populations.[6]

Therefore we base our analysis of civil society on (1) extensive field research and interviews (open-ended, oral) conducted by both authors over the past decade; and (2) content analysis of the written works of leading Egyptian philosophers, intellectuals, activists, and policymakers.[7] Egyptian scholars have engaged in civil society and political-culture studies, and these too have been important sources.[8]

Research Questions

This book seeks to address, and to answer as much as possible, the following questions:

- What is civil society?
- Who or what make up the "Islamist movement(s)" in Egypt?
- Are Islamists a part of civil society in Egypt?
- Even if the constituent parts of civil society exist and attempt to work toward a liberal experiment, can a civil society exist if the governing forces sufficiently restrict these efforts?
- What is the nature of the conflict between the state and some Islamist (and other) groups in Egyptian society?

Implicit in all these questions is the assumption that "civil society" is an appropriate concept and framework of analysis to apply to Egypt. We argue that this is a valid assumption. In reading sociological, political, and philosophical analyses of civil society, the public sphere, and the state, it is clear that Egypt fits solidly within this framework.

Augustus Richard Norton applies the framework to the Middle East generally. Civil society is found in the public sphere "where a melange of associations, clubs, guilds, syndicates, federations, unions, parties and groups come together to provide a buffer between state and citizen."[9] Norton assumes that "a vital and autonomous civil society is a necessary condition of democracy (though not a sufficient one)"[10] and that "citizenship, with associated rights and responsibilities, is part and parcel of the concept. Citizenship underpins civil society. To be a part of the whole is a precondition for the whole to be the sum of its parts. [But] [c]ivil society is more than an admixture of various forms of association, it also refers to a quality, civility, without which the milieu consists of feuding factions, cliques, and cabals. Civility implies tolerance, the willingness of individuals to accept disparate political views and social attitudes; to accept the profoundly important idea that there is no right answer."[11] Egypt is no democracy, and its people are more like subjects than citizens, but it is a viable candidate for boasting a civil society based on other reasons. Its vibrant public sphere and thousands of associations, clubs, publishing houses, presses, and other groups serve as a buffer between society and state. Also, Egyptian culture does value civility and tolerance.

Despite these characteristics, many scholars reject Egypt's designation as a "civil society" primarily on philosophical grounds. Such scholars—Western and Eastern, Northern and Southern—characterize the civil society concept and analytical framework as a Western (i.e., alien) notion that is inapplicable to Egypt or other non-Western societies.[12] Some Western scholars argue this case by asserting that non-Westerners simply cannot develop along European trajectories. Many scholars from the South share this conclusion, but for different reasons. For them, the concept stems from the provincialism of European social philosophy, which cannot account for social groups or institutions that form the basis of non-Western societies. This does not mean that Western and Eastern societies cannot be compared; it does mean that scholars must expand their frameworks and theories. Chatterjee, for example, argues that although civil society is quite limited to the Western experience, it is nevertheless "a particular form of a more universal concept": community.[13] As we expand our theories of political development, we can advance and revitalize political thought with new insights, new evidence that we bring from studying non-Western states. This is far more interesting and productive than simply trying to incorporate the evidence we find in "non-Western" settings into preexisting categories (developed largely from Western experience) and arguing whether they fit or not.

In addition to the need to be more expansive in our frameworks and views of state-societal interactions, especially to include the more general role of "communities," it also is important to question how much "civil society" has evolved in the Western experience (or elsewhere). There is no doubt that civil society developed within and is applicable to that experience, but there are doubts about whether it has been achieved. Examine the claim that civil society already exists in the West. Yes, there is in Western societies a web of autonomous associations, independent of the state, and these have an effect on public policy. But there has also been a tendency for these to become integrated into the state, the tendency towards what has been called . . . "corporatism." . . . But in fact what occurs is an interweaving of society and government to the point where the distinction no longer expresses an important difference in the basis of power or the dynamics of policy-making. Both government and associations draw on and are responsive to the same public. . . . So the idea that civil society is something we have in the West needs to be nuanced. In one sense we do, in another sense this is a goal which has to be striven for against the grain of modern democratic government.[14]

Mindful of the limitations of the civil society concept in the Western context, we acknowledge further the arguments against its application to Egypt and the Middle East.

Carrie Rosefsky Wickham suggests that "recent developments in Egypt and several other Arab states do not fit comfortably within the democratization paradigm. [Rather] they suggest an alternative trajectory, one that reveals the specificity of the democratization model and challenges its utility as a general model of political change."[15] She demonstrates the emergence of Islamist social, economic, and political activities independent of Egypt's authoritarian state but shows that this is "not the same as the emergence of civil society, at least not in its liberal conception. . . . Civil society is not merely a sphere outside government but rather one endowed with a legally mandated autonomy, involving legal rights and protections backed by the law-state." Islamists who struggle to attain power and transform state and society "aim not to establish a civil sphere separate from and coexistent with the secular state, but gradually to extend the Islamic domain until it encompasses the state itself."[16]

If qualification for participating in civil society is limited to secularism, Islamists by definition would be excluded.[17] We contend, however, that such disqualification and exclusion of Islamists or other politically active religious groups are as inappropriate for academics as they are dangerous for governing officials. Secular attitudes are but one attribute of civil society, which encompasses a variety of concepts, including civility as well as citizenship, civil liberties, and *civisme*, a participant culture of activism, reason, and political engagement.[18] Civisme also suggests to many the notion of secularism. Questioning whether Islamists are (or can be) part of "civil society" seems to arise when *some* Islamists turn to violence to demonstrate opposition to a regime.[19] For if a group, especially one representing a majority of society, is not tolerant of other groups, or at least respectful of others' rights to participate (even if the group competes against these others), then there can be little hope for the effective, long-term functioning of civil society as a whole.

Even though we appreciate this concern over appropriate conceptions and theory building across cultures, a concern that seems as much about continuing Western cultural imperialism as it is about good social science, we nevertheless employ civil society as a conceptual framework and apply this term to nonviolent religionists and secularists alike.[20]

"Civil society"[21] not only helps frame an argument for social scientists, but may also help students, journalists, politicians, and the lay public better understand political systems and social networks in Egypt, the Arab world, and beyond. Students and others are more likely to "connect with" (and understand) Arab, Turkish, Persian, Kurdish, Berber, Israeli, and other publics when they can relate to the feminist movements, business associations, human rights organizations, labor unions, professional associations, charitable works programs, religious activities, student organizations, and other social networks thereof.

Eva Bellin tells us that the term should be used, indeed *embraced,*

> because it focuses our attention on despotism in all its incarnations and because it captures an ideal that Middle Easterners are actively struggling over (and for) themselves. . . . By retaining the term civil society we will combat the tendency toward Middle East exceptionalism and invite comparative, cross-regional analysis of this dynamic process.[22]

Egypt is an especially important, significant, and useful case to focus on in bridging the Middle East to other regions in that comparative analysis.

There is one last, perhaps best, reason to employ this concept: an increasing number of Egyptian scholars and political activists rely on it in their own communications. As Egyptian human rights workers and leaders of nongovernmental organizations (NGOs) seek legal reform, an end to government repression and torture, and a general liberation from state control over private and nonprofit activities, they do so under the rubric of "setting civil society free."[23]

With a more universal understanding of civil society, public space, and "communities," we continue this analysis with a historical sketch of Egypt's political and social evolution. It is clear that Islamic reform efforts of the nineteenth and early twentieth centuries continue to influence the course of contemporary Egyptian society and politics.

Political Occupation and Societal Independence

Egypt has been conquered all too frequently by outside powers since Alexander founded his city on the Mediterranean in 331(332) B.C., centuries before Cleopatra's suicide precipitated Rome's occupation in 30 (27) B.C. Yet Egyptians themselves, while falling victim to untold numbers of outside conquerors and occupiers, have maintained their own culture and traditions—and are known for having far greater influence on their conquerors than vice versa. Romans, Greeks, Byzantines, Arabs, Shi'ites, Turks, British, French, Israelis—all have come and all are gone.[24] And even as Egyptians are part of the Arab world, they identify themselves as Egyptians first, Muslims or Copts second, and then as Arabs.[25]

This combination of rich history and tradition, invasion and occupation, and a keen sense of national identity are crucial elements in the political culture of contemporary Egypt. What we seek to examine are the qualities of Islamic Egypt and how they manifest themselves in a variety of ways: from accommodationist reformism (Muhammad Abduh; Muslim Brotherhood) to antistate militancy (*Jihad; al-Jama'a al-Islamiyya*); from cosmopolitan secularism (Faraj Fuda; "the left") to chauvinistic Islamism (*al-Takfir wa al-Hijra; al-Shawqiyyun*); from apolitical to antipolitical Islamism (Sufism and liberal Islamists such as Judge Muhammad Said Al-Ashmawi). We seek to demonstrate that there is an abiding and perhaps unresolvable alienation between ruled and rulers, between Egyptian society and the state controlling it. This alienation has not ended just because Egyptians are once again ruled by fellow Egyptians. Writing before Egypt won its independence from Britain, Ahmad Lutfi al-Sayyid (1872–1963), a disciple of Muhammad Abduh and a professor of philosophy, criticized the Egyptian ruling class and Egyptian government officials when he characterized

> the relationship of the government to the nation [as] that of the predator to the victim. We are convinced that it is impossible for such a relationship to create anything between these two sides but perpetual distrust. The strength of the nation reveals itself under the guise of crude social behavior, while its weakness disguises itself with the mask of peacefulness and submission to force. And so distrust of the ruling class on the part of the nation has become one of its permanent characteristics.[26]

State-societal conflict remains a basic element of the contemporary political landscape.

Yet, alongside this alienation, which is certainly not unique for the vast majority of Middle Eastern communities, Egyptian national identity is a powerful and enduring reality. This sense of identity with a historical, political entity known as Egypt is a rarity among national communities in much of the world, and especially in the Middle East, where national boundaries and their resulting identities are in most cases a twentieth-century phenomenon. Combining these themes with a look at the evolution of Islam in Egypt, this book focuses on the multifaceted nature of Islamic Egypt as well as on the "uniqueness" of Egyptianized Islam. In paraphrasing Rifa'a Tahtawi (1801–1873), the liberal-reformist Islamist, Albert Hourani, maintains that

> Egypt is part of the Islamic *umma* [community], but she has also been a separate *umma*, in ancient and modern times alike, and as such is a distinct object of historical thought. Although Muslim she is not exclusively so, for all who live in Egypt are part of the national community.[27]

For Tahtawi, there is a "national brotherhood" between Egyptians "over and above the brotherhood in religion. There is a moral obligation on those who share the same *watan* [nation; country] to work together to improve it and perfect its organization in all that concerns its honour and greatness and wealth."[28]

Ahmad Lutfi al-Sayyid also recognized an Egyptian patriotism above all other affiliations: Egyptians' "love for Egypt must be free from all conflicting associations, and their self-sacrifice in its service must take precedence over every other consideration. . . . Let no one think that we are calling for any division among the various elements which form the bloc of the Egyptian population."[29] The appeal is generally directed toward Jews, Lebanese, Syrians, and Greeks—all important parts of the Egyptian nation in years past—plus a reassurance to Coptic Christians that Egypt is big enough for all of these communities as long as they commit themselves to the "fatherland."

This patriotism and nationalism is an important element in understanding Egyptian politics across time, whether during periods of occupation, anticolonialism, postcolonialism, or the current epoch. It is as important to secular nationalists as it is to Islamists, as demonstrated by a similarity of visions shared by the diverse likes of Tahtawi, Muhammad Abduh, Ahmad 'Urabi, Ahmad Lutfi al-Sayyid, Sa'd Zaghlul, Hasan al-Banna, Malak Hifni Nasif, Huda Sha'rawi, Gamal Abdel Nasser, and Anwar Sadat, among others.

Islamic Egypt: The Arab Conquest, Muhammad Ali, and the Reformist Movement

Egypt's Pharaonic past and especially its Coptic-Christian community are important to the country's social fabric. Still, Egypt remains over

90 percent Sunni Muslim. Conquered in 639–641 by 'Amr ibn al-'As on behalf of 'Umar, the second caliph, Egypt became one of the leading economic, intellectual, and, of course, political centers of the Islamic world. Its leaders (Ibn Tulun, Salah al-Din, Qalawun, Qait Bey, Muhammad Ali), dynasties (Fatimids, Mamluks), and popular movements (Sufism, Salafiyya, Muslim Brotherhood) are among the greatest found in the Islamic world.

Egyptians, once converted to Islam, stuck to this belief system despite the fact that new rulers came in with a variety of markedly different sets of beliefs. Still, it took at least three centuries to get a majority of the population to adopt the new religion. Just as the *Islam*ization of the country took centuries, so too did the *Arab*ization process. And the latter has not fully succeeded in replacing Egyptian national identity with a primarily Arab identity. This is due not only to the fact that "religions" are more easily adopted than are "ethnicities"; it is also because Egyptians "have always identified themselves, from Pharaonic times, as inhabitants of a fixed and unchanging entity known as Egypt."[30] A succession of Egyptian leaders, whether of Egyptian stock or not, took great pains to promote Egypt as an independent state and even an empire.

Reading through the history of early Islamic Egypt, what is readily apparent is the strength of Egyptian society—when it chose to demonstrate it—as well as the society's more frequent bouts of noninvolvement, disengagement, and/or detachment from politics. Strength need not be in the form of a show of force, and has often been demonstrated by ignoring political leaders without evincing any mass concern about retribution. For example, when the army of the Fatimids (a Shi'i dynasty of North Africa that ruled Egypt until 1171) conquered the Egyptian capital in July 969, "the population of Egypt accepted without protest the rule of a Shi'ite, even though they [Egyptians] were Sunni, for his rule brought plenty and security. Moreover the Fatimids did not try to impose their beliefs on the population."[31]

Salah al-Din (Saladin), a Sunni Kurd who was sent to rule Egypt in 1169 on behalf of the Fatimids, in fact replaced this anomalous Shi'i dynasty, one that could not defend Egypt or Jerusalem from Crusaders. Salah al-Din made it his own crusade/*jihad*/struggle to return Egypt to Sunni orthodoxy. His efforts to promote education and stimulate intellectual debate returned Egypt to the center of Muslim civilization. Indeed, his Ayyubi dynasty (1171–1250) based in Egypt also expanded into Syria to liberate the Holy Land from the Crusaders, and then into Iraq.

The Mamluks (1250–1516) likewise ruled Egypt as if it were an entity separate from the rest of the Muslim world. The members of this alien ethnic and linguistic group, who had been slaves of and then successors to the Ayyubid rulers, thus became a "slave elite." Nevertheless, even though Egyptians could not identify with these Turks, Kurds, Circassians, and Greeks, they came to accept and appreciate the Mamluks for their abilities to defend the nation and efficiently administer the government. And the Egyptians "retained an identity as pertaining to a land, Egypt, which was an independent kingdom, and at times was the centre of a Mamluk empire with all that that implies in terms of prosperity, prestige, and patronage of artisans and of intellectuals."[32]

Although the Mamluks were defeated in battle by Ottoman forces in January 1517, the end of their rule was only temporary because the Ottomans found it necessary to turn again to the Mamluks to administer Egypt. The Mamluk-Ottoman rule lasted until 1798, when Napoleon Bonaparte occupied Egypt. It had a brief but unstable reprise from 1801, when an Anglo-Ottoman force ousted the French, until 1805, when Muhammad Ali was sent to govern on behalf of the Ottoman sultan. Muhammad Ali, perhaps the best-known alien ruler who promoted Egyptian national development, instead ruled on his own behalf until his death in 1848 and established his own dynasty that lasted until 1952.

Coinciding with much of this dynasty was a societal movement, the reformist movement of the late nineteenth century led by Jamal al-Din al-Afghani (1838–1897). Al-Afghani came to Egypt with a message of activism and "this-worldly Islam" as he "exhorted Muslims to realize that Islam was the religion of reason and science—a dynamic, progressive, creative force capable of responding to the demands of modernity."[33] Al-Afghani's disciples, most notably Egypt's Muhammad Abduh (1849–1905) and Syria's Rashid Rida (1865–1935), had a significant impact on the unique features of Islam in Egypt as it is observed today. Abduh especially helped transform Islam, as practiced in Egypt, into an activist and nationalist force for progressive change. He was a leading member of the *'ulama*, a reformer of al-Azhar University, and the mufti of Egypt (the chief judge of the *shari'a* [Islamic law] court system).[34] Abduh also was a leader of the nationalist opposition to British control of Egypt. As chief editor of Egypt's official gazette, he helped form public opinion and lobby for reform of public education. His support of the 'Urabi Revolt (1882) led to his exile from Egypt until 1888.

Abduh's goal, for Egypt and for all Muslim societies, was *revival*—spiritual, scientific, educational, legal, political, linguistic, and other. Strengthening Islamic societies' moral roots could not be done by a return to the past but "by accepting the need for change, and by linking that change to the principles of Islam."[35] He felt that devout Muslims must accept the institutions and ideas of the modern world and he wondered "whether someone who lived in the modern world could still be a devout Muslim."[36] Abduh sought to

> prove that . . . religion must be accounted a friend to science. . . . There is still another matter of which I have been an advocate. People in general are blind to it and far from understanding it, although it is the pillar of their social life, and weakness and humiliation would not have come upon them had they not neglected it. This is, the distinction between the obedience which the people owe the government, and the just dealing which the government owes the people. I was one of those who called the Egyptian nation to know their rights vis-a-vis their ruler, although this nation has never had an idea of it for more than twenty centuries. We summoned it to believe that the ruler, even if it owes him obedience, is still human, liable to err and to be overcome by passion, and nothing can divert him from error or resist the domination of his passions except the advice of the people in word and deed.[37]

Abduh helped found the Muslim Benevolent Society to establish private schools and in 1895 set up an administrative council for al-Azhar. His disciple, Rashid Rida, led the more conservative *Salafiyya* movement, the primary source of opposition to secularism throughout the 1920s and 1930s. Rida and the *Salafiyya* group influenced Hasan al-Banna, who founded the Muslim Brotherhood in 1928. Al-Banna also found that he shared one goal with the secular nationalists: to end British rule in Egypt. Yet that was virtually the only shared goal. Al-Banna called for the return to *shari'a* and the establishment of an Islamic government.

Egypt First

A common theme among these contrasting and conflicting movements and leaders is the focus on Egypt as a nation-state. Egypt is first in their collective thoughts; then the focus turns to how to promote Egypt, to develop Egypt, and to make Egypt a leader in the region, the Islamic community (*umma*), and/or the world at large. Other "Egypt-firsters" include Ahmad 'Urabi,[38] Sa'd Zaghlul,[39] and Anwar Sadat. This is Egyptian nationalism played out across ideological lines; although Islamist in many cases, it also plays out across secular, modernist, and even Arab-nationalist lines.

Gamal Abdel Nasser, who led the Free Officers' coup against the monarchy in 1952 and established the current regime, was unquestionably an Egyptian nationalist first and foremost, but he certainly had grander designs. Although his reputation as an Arab nationalist and the preeminent Arab leader is his legacy, he saw Egypt as the center of three overlapping circles—the Arab, Islamic, and African worlds—and he sought to place himself and his nation as the leaders of all three.

Although the more famous "Egypt-firsters" have generally, if simplistically, been described as "secular nationalists," there are a great many Islamists who have equally strong nationalist credentials. "Islamist nationalism," however, is often considered an oxymoron because a fundamental tenet of Islam is its universalism: Islamist movements generally espouse pan-Islamism (and Egyptian Islamists are no exception to this ideal). But most Islamist leaders, such as Ayatollah Ruhollah Khomeini of Iran, Sheikh Ahmed Yassin of Palestine, Hasan Turabi of Sudan, and Rachid Ghanouchi of Algeria, invariably promote nationalist causes first and foremost, and only later, if at all, do they concern themselves with transnational salvation and liberation from secular governance.

Perhaps the best known of Egyptian Islamists is Hasan al-Banna. Al-Banna fought hard against Zionist expansion in Palestine in the 1940s out of religious conviction, but he remained an "Egypt first" partisan. His successors have largely retained that nationalistic emphasis, as do virtually all Egyptian Islamist activists, whether militant antigovernment types or mainstream accommodationists: for Egyptians and their society unfortunately, there is a seemingly endless number of problems, so that such activists must confine their attention to the Egyptian nation-state.

Among these problems is the Egyptian government, which is currently led by Hosni Mubarak. For years indistinguishable from "the state," this government has maintained a campaign of repression against its own subjects throughout the 1990s. It justifies its actions to its subjects and the world community as necessary evils in the fight against "Islamic terrorism," but there appears to be little hope for a unilateral reprieve or even a negotiated settlement between state and society in Egypt. The government makes little effort to distinguish between Islamist militants and peaceful Muslim activists: any opposition is a threat and must be countered. With this attitude, instead of one that might welcome dialogue and cooperation, the government exploits the existence of Islamist militancy, which it uses to thwart virtually all credible opposition.

Regardless of current politics and policies, our examination of Egyptian history indicates a permanence to Islamic activism, even with the episodes of terror and militancy incorrectly ascribed to

Islam the faith or way of life. Islam remains and will remain an inherent part of Egypt's social and political realm. The public sphere, in between the state and society, and civil society, the institutions that inhabit the public space, are vital in Egypt not *despite* the increasing number of Islamic activists and institutions but *because* of them.

Conclusion

Reform efforts of the nineteenth and early twentieth centuries continue to influence the course of politics in Egypt today. That period was one of reform (Islamic, economic, social, political); but it also was one of conflict—between secular forces and Islamist movements. And the latter movements themselves were far from united in purpose.

Contemporary Islamist activism is no less important than its historical antecedents. Islamism today is a widespread phenomenon, gaining momentum and recruits throughout the Near and Middle East and North Africa, and particularly in Egypt. It is vital that scholars, students, journalists, and politicians make an attempt to understand the objectives and strategies expressed by the groups within this rather broad movement. It is also imperative that Islamic resurgence be acknowledged as anything but a monolithic phenomenon. The resurgence is characterized by factions and voices that diverge on their approach to major themes such as the nature of society, the preferred relationship between Islamist activists and the political system, the methodology for alleviating socioeconomic frustrations and spiritual laxity, and the worldly framework within which Islamist goals are to be achieved. The more "radical" or militant of these groups insist upon revolutionary change that is to be imposed on the masses and political system, while the more moderate groups, epitomized by Egypt's Muslim Brotherhood, call for gradual change that is to be undertaken from within the political system and with the enlistment of the Muslim masses.

Despite the fact that many scholars routinely acknowledge that Islamism is not monolithic, actual discourse on the phenomenon too often lumps all groups together without differentiating among the ideological trends. This failure to distinguish among groups leads to a uniform categorization of "the movement" as an antidemocratic threat to political stability. Fairly typical uninformed "expert analysis" warns that "terrorism, intolerance and revolution for export" are "the revival movement's three scourges."[40] Amos Perlmutter stresses "the very real threat of Islamic fundamentalism." In his view, "there is no spirit of reconciliation between Islamic fundamentalism and the modern world—that is, the Christian-secular universe."[41]

The problems with such an approach are that (1) analysts fail to recognize fundamental differences within the Islamist trend; (2) analysts apply secular notions of the proper role of religion to cultures that may cherish their own ideas of religion's role; and (3) such analyses discourage any attempts at rapprochement or mutual coexistence with ideologies that do not conform with such secular perceptions. Pragmatism thus requires us "to demystify the phenomenon of Islamic fundamentalism and to see it for what it is: a movement that is both historically inevitable and politically 'tamable.' Over the longer run it even represents ultimate political progress toward greater democracy and popular government."[42]

There is much in this book to demonstrate this progress and the potential role Islamists have in maintaining civil society and promoting democratization, including popular government. This book is not about Islamic militancy but about Islamist movements *within which* militant Islamists operate. Whether these Islamists also exist within civil society is a fundamental question. There is no question, however, that they have an impact on civil society. In particular, as the Egyptian government acts firmly against the militants it tends also to strike hard against nonviolent Islamists and other elements of civil society, thus endangering the latter in its fight against a tiny minority of militants. In short, the method is "collective punishment," penalizing the whole for the sins of the few.

To fully examine the struggle between the Egyptian state and its struggling civil society, we explore in greater detail the development of contemporary Islamism in Egypt. Chapter 2 examines the plural nature of Egypt's Islamic movement, with a focus on those elements of this varied movement that can rightly be described as "civil" and thus be included as Islamic foundations of civil society in Egypt. Chapter 3 focuses on the most important part of this foundation, the Muslim Brotherhood. Chapter 4 addresses the more infamous and less civil component of the Islamist trend in Egypt, the history and ideology of various movements, and the impact of these groups on the otherwise peaceful relations that make up Christian-Muslim coexistence in Egypt. Chapter 5 examines women in civil society in Egypt and their prominent role in both Islamist and secular-feminist movements. And Chapter 6 argues that much of the violence that occurs between state and society in Egypt is a result of government-initiated legislation, human rights abuses, and other methods of control and repression.

Notes

1. An "Islamist" is one who combines his or her devotion to Islam with a commitment to political activism; we also discuss Islamic groups, such as Sufi orders, that do not fit into this category given their lack of political or social activism.

2. In addition to dogmatism, chauvinism might be used to describe some of the intolerance mixed with religious zeal often heard from militant Islamists. Generally defined as excessive or blind patriotism, chauvinism suggests a narrow and intolerant devotion to one's own cause (in this case "Islamism") to the exclusion of "the other."

3. Larry Diamond suggests that a detailed assessment of political subcultures is much more useful than attempting to determine a more general political culture for any given nation, particularly those in the developing world. See his "Introduction: Political Culture and Democracy" in Diamond, ed., *Political Culture and Democracy in Developing Countries* (Boulder, Colo.: Lynne Rienner, 1993).

4. Gregory Starrett suggests that the "Islamic Trend [*al-tayyar al-islami*], far from being a fringe movement, is pervasive, persistent, and normal, an immense counterculture whose effects on individuals and society do not remain confined to its immediate adherents." *Our Children and Our Youth: Religious Education and Political Authority in Mubarak's Egypt* (Mimeo., 1993), pp. 13–14. See also his *Putting Islam to Work: Education, Politics and Religious Transformation in Egypt* (Berkeley: University of California Press, 1998).

5. When government permission is granted to conduct field research in Egypt, an international scholar generally receives a letter from the Ministry of Higher Education stating that no questionnaires may be administered, no notes may be taken during interviews, and no tape recordings of interviews may be made (Ministry of Higher Education, October 1990).

6. See, for instance, Raymond A. Hinnebusch, "Children of the Elite: Political Attitudes of the Westernized Bourgeoisie in Contemporary Egypt," *Middle East Journal* 36, no. 4 (Fall 1982): 535–561, and Salwa Sha'rawi Gomaa, Ken Menkhaus, and Denis J. Sullivan "Egyptian Public Opinion during the Gulf War" (unpublished research, 1991). Of course, various Egyptian scholars, journalists, and activists find ways to conduct opinion research. This is done through official channels and/or with permission from government ministries.

7. We rely on translations of historical writings as well as on the vast array of secondary accounts that include analysis of speeches by leading nationalists, including Islamists and feminists. For the current era, we rely on Arabic sources, including books by Islamists and by critics of the Islamist trend and newspaper and periodical articles from *Liwa' al-Islam, Al-Sha'b,* and *Al-Ahram,* among others

8. See for example, Afaf Lutfi al-Sayyid Marsot, "Popular Attitudes Towards Authority in Egypt" *Journal of Arab Affairs* 7, no. 2 (1988): 174–198; and Gehad Auda, "The Islamic Movement and Resource Mobilization in Egypt: A Political Culture Perspective" in Diamond, *Political Culture.*

9. Augustus Richard Norton, "Introduction" in Norton, ed., *Civil Society in the Middle East,* vol. I (Leiden: E. J. Brill, 1995), p. 7.

10. Ibid., p. 9.

11. Ibid., p. 11.

12. Gehad Auda has shared with Denis Sullivan his concern about the concept at a meeting in New York, March 1993. Mustapha K. al-Sayyid discusses other scholars' similar concerns in "A Civil Society in Egypt?" *Middle East Journal* 47, no. 2 (Spring 1993): 228–242. See fn. 7. Sami Zubaida discusses contrasting views of "civil society" in "Islam, the State, and Democracy: Contrasting Conceptions of Society in Egypt," *Middle East Report* 22, no. 6 (November/December 1992): 2–10.

13. Partha Chatterjee, "A Response to Taylor's 'Modes of Civil Society,'" *Public Culture* 3, no. 1 (Fall 1990):120.

14. Charles Taylor, "Modes of Civil Society," *Public Culture* 3, no. 1 (Fall 1990): 96, 98. See also Geoff Eley, "Nations, Publics, and Political Cultures: Placing Habermas in the Nineteenth Century," in Craig Calhoun, ed., *Habermas and the Public Sphere* (Cambridge, Mass.: MIT Press, 1992). Eley acknowledges the "pessimistic" Habermas, who spoke of "a degraded public life, in which the substance of liberal democracy is voided in a combination of plebiscitary manipulation and privatized apathy, as any collectivity of citizenry disintegrates" (Eley, p. 290).

15. Carrie Rosefsky Wickham, "Beyond Democratization: Political Change in the Arab World," *PS* (September 1994): 507–508.

16. Ibid, p, 508.

17. Except those Islamists who are more from the "reformist" school of Islamic thought and activism. This group is often associated with the maintenance of the separation of "mosque" and state. In Egypt, this movement can be identified with retired Supreme Court Judge 'Ashmawi who is considered a "liberal Islamist."

18. Eva Bellin, "Civil Society: Effective Tool of Analysis for Middle East Politics?" *PS* (September 1994):510.

19. Carrie Rosefsky Wickham, "Are the Islamists in Egypt Part of Civil Society?" American Political Science Association annual meeting, Washington, D.C., 2–5 September 1993.

20. Western cultural hegemony is a reality and must be taken seriously by scholars, especially when it comes to concepts such as Islamic "fundamentalism," which we resist using. In many ways, our resistance to the term is due more to the negative connotation that term conjures up and the obfuscation of facts and analyses it generates than to our own concerns about the reality of cultural imperialism.

21. "Political culture" is another "neutral" term that is a useful heuristic or framework, except when this term gets applied in a negative (i.e., negating) fashion against Arab and/or Islamic culture. See especially Elie Kedourie, *Democracy and Arab Political Culture* (London: Frank Cass, 1994). Lisa Anderson reminds us that "the inclination toward quasi-cultural explanations probably grows at least in part out of the Orientalist tradition in Western studies of the Middle East, in which unfamiliar or unexpected political institutions or inclinations are attributed to the influence of Islamic tradition." "Policy-Making and Theory Building: American Political Science and the Islamic Middle East," in Hisham Sharabi, ed., *Theory, Politics and the Arab World: Critical Responses* (New York: Routledge, 1990), p. 56.

22. Bellin, "Civil Society," p. 510.

23. See Egyptian Organization for Human Rights, The Group for Democratic Development, and Cairo Institute for Human Rights Studies, "Setting Civil Society Free: A Draft Law on Civil Associations and Institutions"

(Cairo, 1998). These groups and other NGOs seek the amendment or abolishment of Law 32 of 1964, Egypt's restrictive law controlling NGO and other group activities. See Chapters 2 and 6 in this book.

24. An argument could be made that Americans and a host of other external donors (Saudis, Kuwaitis, Japanese, British, French, Canadians, Dutch) are in economic "occupation" of Egypt because these donors and the multilateral institutions (International Monetary Fund, World Bank) they control are determining the direction of economic policymaking in the Egyptian government.

25. In various public opinion surveys, this order has remained consistent. See Hinnebusch (1982) and Gomaa, Menkhaus, and Sullivan (1991). Egyptians have long continued "some form of self-identity—a recognition of an Egyptian self—other than the greater identity belonging to a Muslim Arab empire." Afaf Lutfi al-Sayyid Marsot, *A Short History of Modern Egypt* (Cambridge: Cambridge University Press, 1985), p. 7.

26. "The Egyptian Official" in *Al-Jarida* newspaper, 16 March 1909, taken from *The Evolution of the Egyptian National Image,* Charles Wendell (Berkeley: University of California Press, 1972), p. 310.

27. Albert Hourani, *Arabic Thought in the Liberal Age, 1798–1939* (New York: Cambridge University Press, 1983), p. 80.

28. Ibid., p. 78, quoting from Tahtawi's work *Manahij al-Albab al-Misriyya fi Mabahij al-Adab al-'Asriyya* (Cairo, 1912).

29. Excerpt from *Ta'ammulat* (Cairo: Dar al-Ma'arif, n.d.), reprinted in John J. Donohue and John L. Esposito, eds., *Islam in Transition: Muslim Perspectives* (New York: Oxford University Press, 1982), p. 71.

30. Marsot, "Popular Attitudes," p. 7. Elie Kedourie takes a much different view from Marsot's and our own argument when he asserts that "until Mohammed Ali consolidated his rule, and long afterwards, the majority of the inhabitants of Egypt considered themselves first and foremost as Muslims and subjects of the Ottoman Sultan. Mohammed Ali and his successors endeavored, with some success, to imbue those whom they ruled with the idea that they were first and foremost Egyptians." *Democracy and Arab Political Culture* (London: Frank Cass, 1994), p. 63.

31. Marsot, "Popular Attitudes," p. 13.

32. Ibid, p. 39.

33. John L. Esposito, *Islam: The Straight Path* (New York: Oxford University Press, 1991), p. 127.

34. Ibid., p. 129.

35. Hourani, *Arabic Thought,* p. 139.

36. Ibid.

37. Ibid., p. 141 quotes from fragments of Abduh's autobiography, as published in his student's work, *History of Professor Imam Sheikh Muhammad Abduh* (Cairo, 1931), p. 11.

38. 'Urabi was one of only four native Egyptian colonels in the army in the 1880s. He led the army movement in opposition to the monarchy's unchallenged authority and to European domination. His movement's slogan was "Egypt for the Egyptians."

39. Zaghlul led the Egyptian delegation (*wafd*) to the Paris Peace Conference in 1919 and fought to achieve at least nominal independence from Britain. He became the first prime minister in the "liberal age" of Egypt (1922–1952) when his Wafd Party won a landslide victory in the 1924 elections.

40. James Walsh, "The Sword of Islam," *Time International,* 15 June 1992, pp. 18–22.

41. Amos Perlmutter, "Wishful Thinking About Islamic Fundamentalism," *Washington Post,* 19 January 1992.

42. Graham E. Fuller, "Islamic Fundamentalism: No Long-Term Threat," *Washington Post,* 3 January 1992.

2

The Plural Nature of Islam in Egypt

For far too long numerous misconceptions about Islam have prevailed in the minds of many in the West. Labels such as "militant," "fundamentalist," "extremist," and "terrorist" remain the dominant adjectives used to describe one of the world's most heterogeneous socioeconomic and political-religious ways of life.[1] This chapter addresses some of these misconceptions as we seek to dispel some myths and provide a more detailed picture of the diverse nature of Islam, in particular by examining various Islamic organizations in Egypt.[2]

The current phenomenon of Islamist activism in Egypt (just as in Algeria, the Occupied Palestinian Territories, Lebanon, Iran, and elsewhere) should be seen in historical perspective. These movements are connected to, though different from, episodes of religious activism of the past century (see Chapter 1). Contemporary Egypt differs markedly from early twentieth-century Egypt in the plethora of institutions and trends now pervading the society. Egypt has a complex "Islamic picture." Islam, in accordance with its holistic nature, permeates politics, society, and the economy. Islam in Egypt is thus *plural* (if not always liberal) and *diverse* (if not necessarily heterogeneous). Egypt enjoys an Islamic homogeneity in that approximately 90 percent of the sixty-two million Egyptians are Sunni Muslim (there is a tiny minority of Shi'i Muslims, and 7–10 percent of the population is Coptic Christian). Still, this homogeneous Sunni population is diverse in its approach to politics.

State-sponsored Islam and state control of Islam in the early and mid-twentieth century are also important aspects to understand as we witness the current clash between state and society in Egypt. In the 1950s and beyond, Egyptian President Gamal Abdel Nasser sought to transform Egypt into a modern (read, secular if not a "Western") society. Largely successful in dismantling the power of the *'ulama* (religious-scholarly elite), Nasser could not destroy the power of either Islam or Coptic Christianity, the two dominant religious forces in Egypt then as now.

There are two major events that are essential to our understanding of the revival of Islamist movements in Egypt, as throughout the region. The June 1967 Arab-Israeli War was a tremendous victory for the Jewish state. Beyond the military loss sustained by the Arab states, their defeat also dealt a political blow to a particular type of Arab leadership and ideology: the socialist, secular, authoritarian regimes of Nasser in Egypt and the Ba'thists in Syria.[3] Leadership within the Arab regimes began an unmistakable shift *toward* Saudi Arabia and the conservative Arab regimes that use Islam as their basis of political legitimacy.

The Iranian Revolution (1978–1979) was the next significant event that further invigorated Islamist forces in the Middle East. Although generally at odds with the Shi'i theology of the Iranian *'ulama,* Sunni Arab *'ulama* and popular groups were emboldened by the possibilities of religious forces overthrowing seemingly invincible military dictatorships that also were clients of and/or "propped up" by the United States. The shah was in this category and he was defeated. Anwar Sadat, Egypt's president after Nasser's death, also fit this bill. Could he not be defeated?

If Islamist groups tend to agree on their ultimate objective—establishing Islamic rule—the way in which they approach this goal varies across a wide spectrum of groups. As we will see in detail in the next chapter, the Muslim Brotherhood (*al-Ikhwan al-Muslimun*), is noted for its *accommodationist* (nonviolent, cooperative) approach. It seeks to achieve its objectives—focusing as much on the state as on society—through education, nonviolence, consciousness raising (especially during political campaigns), and example. In contrast, *al-Jihad* and *al-Jama'a al-Islamiyya* (see Chapter 4) take a decidedly *militant* approach in their campaigns, which are aimed primarily against the governmental structures of the current regime. Yet another example and a different approach is found in groups such as *al-Takfir wa al-Hijra* (which was led in the past by Shukri Mustafa) whose approach is first and foremost to transform society and then move on to the political system. In stark contrast to the antisocietal groups is a very significant movement, one with a long tradition in Egyptian society—Sufism. This is a mystical, apolitical (even antipolitical) force in Egyptian society that has no part in political activism or violence.

As these few examples demonstrate, Islam is far from a monolithic movement in Egypt (or elsewhere). Egypt's fifty-six million[4]

Sunni Muslims find a variety of philosophies, theologies, and partisan groups with which to identify and/or affiliate as the members of this population express their political and religious beliefs. This chapter and subsequent chapters elaborate on this point.

The Multifaceted Nature of the Islamic Movement in Egypt

Egypt's contemporary Islamic social and political activity grew out of the work of Muhammad Abduh (d. 1905), the *Salafiyya* movement of the 1920s and 1930s, and especially *al-Ikhwan al-Muslimun* led by Hasan al-Banna.[5] Despite King Faruq's and Nasser's attempts to smash the latter organization, it has survived and has even become a part of the political process of Egypt with its support becoming the primary basis of any successful opposition in the *Majlis al-Sha'b* (People's Assembly, or Parliament).

In the early 1970s, when socialism was the reigning ideology thanks to President Nasser, a new president found himself at odds with this trend. Sadat, by most accounts a devout Muslim, manipulated Islam for his own political purposes. Billing himself as *al-Ra'is al-Mu'min* (the believer president), Sadat used television and other media to enhance his religious image in an attempt at building political legitimacy by contrasting himself to his predecessor.

> Sufi brotherhoods and the Muslim Brotherhood, suppressed by Nasser, were permitted to function publicly. The creation and growth of Islamic student organizations on campuses was promoted to counter the opposition of Nasserites and leftists who opposed Sadat's pro-Western political and economic policies. Sadat used Islam to legitimate key government actions and policies . . . and to denounce as extremism the increasing challenges to the regime by Islamic activists during the late seventies.[6]

Sadat also practiced divide-and-rule tactics: he "was well aware of the rivalries between these [various Islamic] groups, particularly of the radicals' contempt for the 'collaborationism' of the Ikhwan and the 'reformism' of the [Islamic charitable organizations]. Nevertheless, he thought it useful to portray fanatical fringe groups such as al-Takfir wa al-Hijra as making up the 'secret army' of the Muslim Brotherhood."[7]

When Hosni Mubarak succeeded Sadat as president in 1981, he continued an openness toward the Muslim Brothers (*Ikhwan*) while cracking down on militancy. This legitimized the *Ikhwan* and allowed it to resurface and to promote openly its political and economic agendas. (Mubarak's crackdown on the *Ikhwan* is a more recent trend.)

The Muslim Brotherhood has long been involved in national politics and social welfare in Egypt. The group is, in fact, both a political movement and a social welfare agency and is the single most important opposition group to Mubarak's ruling National Democratic Party (NDP). Although not legally registered as a political party, the group's participation in national and other elections was tolerated by Mubarak between 1984 (the first of the more open elections) and 1995, when the regime reversed its earlier tolerance. In alliances with the New Wafd Party in 1984 and then the Socialist Labor Party in 1987, support for the Brotherhood translated into a sizeable number of seats for these parties. The Brotherhood's members are also quite successful in union elections: their candidates have dominated (until the government began to reverse this trend in the early 1990s) the executive boards of lawyers', doctors', and engineers' unions.

The Muslim Brotherhood has been very active in promoting social welfare, particularly in the areas of health care and education. The organization and its supporters run schools, hospitals, day care programs, job training centers, tutoring programs, Quranic instruction programs, after-school programs, and numerous other development and social programs. Its members also are very much involved in capitalist enterprises, such as factories, investment companies, and agricultural enterprises. But Islam in Egypt is about much more than the *Ikhwan*.

A Militant Face

The Brotherhood's involvement with an increasingly unpopular regime (i.e., Sadat's) led to the rise of other, more radical, militant, and revivalist groups in Egypt.[8] In the 1970s, the primary groups were *al-Takfir wa al-Hijra* (Denouncement and Holy Flight, which refers to its ideology) and Egypt's *Jihad* (Struggle), members of which assassinated Sadat in 1981.[9] In addition to these two most prominent groups, a host of other militant organizations arose that shared a general goal of achieving an Islamic Egypt; but these groups were organizationally distinct in terms of leadership and tactics. They include *Jund Allah* (God's Troops), *Jaysh al-Tahrir al-Islami* (the Islamic Liberation Army), *Jam'iyyat al-Tabligh*[10] (Society of Denunciation, or of Fulfilling One's Mission), among others. In the mid-1980s, social scientists viewed these groups as the most extreme elements of the "Islamic movement" in Egypt. Moreover, these groups found a large following that supported their aims but that largely rejected their tactics.

Jama'at Islamiyya, or Islamic (student) associations, "became the dominant force on Egyptian university campuses during Sadat's presidency."[11] Although Sadat himself encouraged their growth, one month before his death in 1981 he ordered these groups disbanded, their infrastructure destroyed, and their leaders arrested. But these groups still remain quite active. From the mid-1980s through 1991, such groups seemed to have lost their "appeal," or at least their "ability to constitute a movement that might serve as the mouthpiece of civil society in its confrontation with the state."[12] The personification (i.e., Sadat) of that confrontation was, afterall, gone, and President Mubarak adeptly used, confronted, and perhaps manipulated the various subgroups that make up an Islamic "force" in Egypt.

By 1992, Mubarak's government itself had become the new target of Islamist groups in the continuing struggle between Islamism and secular nationalism and governance. With the reemergence of *militant* Islamist activity after 1992 and the even more ferocious violence perpetrated by the government against suspected militants, their families, and others, the question arises: Has the government gone too far (in police and military terms) in trying to stop violence? Another, more important, question is this: Has the government not gone far enough (in political terms—through liberalizing the system) to try to stop the violence? These questions will be revisited in the last chapter of this work.

Militant Islamist activity over the past few decades is aimed primarily against the state; frequently, militants also target international entities (tourists especially) as symbols of foreign support of the regime.[13] The most horrific of the attacks on tourists was in November 1997 in Luxor when militants killed fifty-nine tourists. As support for such activity remains consistently low among the Egyptian population, the *Ikhwan* maintains mass appeal. "Islam" is vital to the vast majority of Egyptians, but *militant* Islam is anathema to them. With the illegitimacy and unpopularity of militant Islamist groups, the Brotherhood and other mainstream, nonviolent Islamic organizations receive popular support. And they remain popular and legitimate not because Egyptians have suddenly been "born again" but for two other reasons:

1. The failures of government: Egyptian authorities and the institutions they run are renowned for corruption, mismanagement, inefficiency, authoritarianism, repression, and political exclusion.

2. The willingness of Islamist groups, led by the Brotherhood, to step in and help local communities suffering from unemployment, poverty, inflation, and government neglect.

Islamic Society Resurgent

The Islamist groups, whether Brotherhood-affiliated or otherwise, that provide for the needs of local communities are frequently mosque-based NGOs. These groups recognize the problems society faces and do something to fix them. The groups also see that many of society's problems stem from government officials and their policies, for even when government is not responsible for the problems, the popular view remains that government leaders either do not care to fix things or just cannot do anything to solve them.

Islamist groups, along with thousands of Christian and secular NGOs, are doing for their societies what the government has long promised but has not fulfilled. They have developed efficient social services, most notably schools, trade skill centers (carpentry, sewing), day care and health-care centers, and hospitals out of frustration with the government's inability to recognize the needs of specific communities and to target these communities with development projects in response to those needs.

Voluntarism, *tatawwa'iyya*, (including that of an Islamic nature) has a long history and solid reputation in Egypt. Islamic associations originated in the nineteenth century, were legitimized with the successes of the *Ikhwan* and the Young Men's Muslim Association, had a rapid growth after World War II and in the late 1950s, and began to be transformed in the Nasser era as the government sought an increasing role in the daily private lives of its subjects.[14] Yet with the failure of government to efficiently or effectively displace private initiative, there has been a gradual reassertion of voluntarism and "self-help" in Egypt that is directed toward needy and impoverished communities. This voluntaristic impulse has developed over the past century from a predominantly elitist sense of noblesse oblige to a more middle-class willingness to help communities in need. Also, there is the overwhelming impulse for survival among impoverished and neglected subjects of the authoritarian state.

Such community organizations are a primary component of Egyptian civil society: there are approximately fourteen thousand NGOs alone that are *registered* with the government of Egypt. Roughly eleven thousand of these are actively working throughout the country to provide health care, education, job training, child care, elder care, welfare, legal assistance, human rights monitoring,[15] access to credit (especially for women), water, irrigation, and environmental and other social and economic services to a largely poor population. Community development associations, Islamic and Christian charitable groups, feminist organizations, student groups, and, more recently, capitalist associations are active in satisfying their own markets, their own community needs.

Use of the terms "private voluntary organizations" and "nongovernment organizations" to describe charitable, development, nonprofit, and other organizations is done with some skepticism in Egypt. Virtually all participants in and observers of NGO activity in Egypt recognize that these organizations are far from being independent of the government, and many in fact are government creations.[16]

This is hardly unique to Egypt. NGOs are established in many developing countries by governments themselves or by officials of those governments. However, the relationship between NGOs and the state can be tentative and conflictual as much as it can be cooperative, or even co-optative, and there are numerous examples from Egypt about this distrustful and conflictual nature of state-NGO relations. One of the more prominent cases of government control over nongovernment activities is the 1991 disbanding of the Arab Women's Solidarity Association (AWSA) led by physician and author Dr. Nawal el-Saadawi.[17] The Egyptian government closed down this NGO more as a reaction against Dr. el-Saadawi's criticisms of President Mubarak's policies (e.g., the 1990–1991 Gulf War) than any violation of "NGO etiquette." The government then took AWSA's assets and gave them to a little known "GONGO" (government-oriented NGO), Women of Islam, a group run by a government official (also see Chapter 5). The government's refusal to register the *Ikhwan* as either a political party or an NGO (as a charitable association) is further evidence of the way this regime controls civil society institutions.

Many NGOs are involved in both socioeconomic development and political activism, the latter being specifically illegal under Law 32, Egypt's 1964 Law of Association.

Law 32 of 1964

The legal and bureaucratic structures that regulate NGO activity in Egypt are enshrined in Law 32 of 1964. The Ministry of Social Affairs (MOSA) is entrusted with sweeping powers of registration, control, supervision, regulation, oversight, management, direction, and appointment.

MOSA may refuse an association permission to be formed (see Law 32, Book One, Chapter One, Article 12 [I,1,12]); prevent money from coming to an association from abroad (I,1,23); appoint a temporary board of directors (I,1,28); dissolve an association and transfer its money to another (I,4 is devoted entirely to this); merge two or more associations performing similar activities (I,1,29); and deny permission to raise funds through donations "and other methods of collecting money for social purposes" (I,1,25). The authorization granting such control and oversight goes on and on throughout the text of the law.

In general, Law 32 discusses how "the respective administrative entity has the right to" do such and such; how MOSA can, may, or shall do thus and such; how associations "cannot," "are prohibited from," and "shall not" do this or that; and how they "are subjected to authority of" MOSA and its subunits. In short, the government gives itself rights and puts constraints on members of the public from freely associating to promote their own individual and collective rights (e.g., basic human rights, community development.)

For years, Egyptian and international NGOs and aid agencies have tried to persuade the government of Egypt to amend this restrictive law. Unfortunately, they might succeed: that is, the government may react to this pressure by moving in the opposite direction of what is needed and intended. In spring 1998, the government allowed the *Majlis al-Sha'b*, People's Assembly, to consider a new draft law of associations to replace Law 32. However, this proposed new law was quickly condemned by international human rights organizations as unsatisfactory. Human Rights Watch of the United States condemned the draft as it engendered "fear" within Egypt's NGO community and argued that it would permit "excessive government interference in the affairs of NGOs and their management structures. The draft law's provisions combine to shift the levers of control over key aspects of NGO operations—such as structure, programs, management, and financing—from membership bodies and boards of directors to the state."[18]

Islamic Associations

Private Islamic associations are evident throughout Egypt. They range from small organizations of five people or so operating out of satellite villages to large "societies" (even corporations) employing scores of health care professionals, educators, and clerical personnel in middle-class suburbs of Cairo. In general, these Islamic NGOs are *jam'iyyat khayriyya,* or charitable associations that are registered by MOSA. There is an important question as to whether the Islamic NGOs' services are determined by their own members or, as in the case of other NGOs (e.g., some community development associations, or CDAs) by the government or its agencies. The answer varies with the individual NGO. There is considerable disdain shown by many NGO managers and boards for government interference; there is often appreciation among others for whatever governmental assistance they can receive, even if it is accompanied by bureaucratic control or irrelevant programs.

As mentioned, the focus of many NGOs is on education and job training, providing health care to mothers and infants, and, in many cases, day care services. In a village near al-Minya, job training consists of a small room with several Singer sewing machines operated by mothers whose children attend school in the room next door. Other such training, geared mostly toward males, includes carpentry centers in which men are instructed on the use of certain machines.

As with Islam in general, the plethora of Islamic NGOs is by nature far from monolithic or homogeneous. Some NGOs are GONGOs, some amount to Islamic corporations (Mustafa Mahmud Society, below), some are state-supported but privately run CDAs ('Izbat Zayn, below), and some eschew any reliance on government support (though they must succumb to government regulation, if not full control) and are the more entrepreneurial. Many of these latter utilize the concept of "Islamic NGO" more as a cover or a marketing tool.

The Community Association of 'Izbat Zayn

'Izbat Zayn, on the southern edge of Cairo, provides an important case study in the development of Islamic associations.[19] Originally a squatter community that grew up around a factory in the early 1960s, 'Izbat Zayn still had no public sewage system and no public schools as late as the mid-1980s. In the late 1970s, leaders of the community approached MOSA for financial support to make their mosque a more permanent structure. MOSA officials responded that their public funds could not be used for mosques and suggested that the residents form a CDA to which MOSA could contribute some human and financial resources. After 1979, the CDA of 'Izbat Zayn began a nursery school and a vocational training program. The mosque was rebuilt as a two-story building, the upper level to be used for community services: teaching the Quran, providing day care and medical care, and offering remedial tutoring. Members of this community are responding to the challenge of earlier government neglect and provide themselves with educational, health, and other services. They are developing community participation in decisionmaking and promoting self-reliance. In this case, the government is supporting these efforts and encouraging "Islamic development."

Al-Mustashfa Sayyida Zaynab

Connected to the mosque of Sayyida Zaynab in Cairo is a hospital (*mustashfa*). Founded in the late 1970s, this hospital has four beds, treats up to two hundred patients per day, and there is a doctor on duty 24 hours a day. In 1989 a patient paid two Egyptian pounds (£E 2) for a physical exam (the cost used to be twenty-five piasters and increased gradually to this level; by the mid-1990s, other Islamic NGO hospitals were charging an average of £E 5 for initial visits). The mosque of Sayyida Zaynab pays the doctors for operations as well as the cost of medicines and other treatments that are beyond the capacity of the patients to pay. The doctors work for government hospitals in the mornings and come in the evenings to Sayyida Zaynab or one of the other mosque-hospitals around Cairo that are affiliated, loosely, with Sayyida Zaynab (e.g., Rud al-Faraj, Shubra, Qalya). These eighteen mosque-hospitals are developing, among other services, an informal network of sharing doctors and referring patients elsewhere for more appropriate treatment.

Mustafa Mahmud Society

Perhaps the most widely noted of the urban Islamic NGOs is the Mustafa Mahmud Society in Mohandisin, a middle- to upper-class section of greater Cairo. Mustafa Mahmud is a widely known and generally respected Islamist. Trained as a physician, Mahmud has gained prominence as an Islamic entrepreneur: scientist, television personality, author of over sixty books, cardiologist, and founder of a successful charitable organization. He is dedicated to the precept that Islam and science are completely compatible and mutually supportive, and so he founded his society in 1975, in the name of Islam, to promote the general welfare through a highly skilled medical staff at his health center (a polyclinic) and hospital.

In 1979, the Office of Social Services began providing sociomedical services. By the early 1990s, approximately eight thousand families annually were receiving financial aid: monthly stipends, medical services (related to kidney, chest, cancer, cardiac, and leper illnesses), and aid to poor students and to blind and disabled individuals.[20]

Similar to the Sayyida Zaynab operation—but on a much grander scale—the Mustafa Mahmud Society links a mosque with a hospital, the former raising the funds, the latter providing such health services as physical exams, blood testing, urinalysis, diagnoses, kidney dialysis, appendectomies, and heart treatment. Dental and psychological services are also provided.[21]

This capitalist enterprise founded in the name of Islam is hardly representative of the vast number of Islamic NGOs in urban or rural settings, but it is a model of achievement with financial benefits accruing to the staff and low-cost health care for thousands of patients.

Young Men's Muslim Association

The Young Men's Muslim Association (YMMA), *Jam'iyyat al-Shaban al-Muslimin*, is a national NGO with branches throughout Egypt. The branch in Tanta, Egypt's third largest city in the middle of the Nile Delta, has a membership (age 18 years and over) of one thousand. In addition, this NGO has twelve hundred members (12- to 30-year-olds) in a Cultural and Social Club, *Nadi Thaqafi wa Ijtima'i*. The Association also includes an elementary school (6- to 12-year-olds), two day care centers (3.5- to 5-year-olds), two libraries, sports facilities (karate, volleyball, swimming pool, soccer), computer training, English-language instruction, a video collection and television, a lecture series (religious figures' presentations as well as those by agricultural engineers and sports teachers), and job training centers for men and women. The YMMA organizes trips to Alexandria and beaches on the Mediterranean for its members and helps community members make the *hajj* (pilgrimage to Mecca).

> Many of our activities—films, trips, sports, job training—are to keep kids off the streets and give them something to do, something that they can enjoy and learn from. The kids want to watch a lot of American and Japanese films, especially karate movies. We give them religious and other films, like Indian movies.[22]

The YMMA operates a *mustawsaf tibbi*, medical center, next to the Sayyid Badawi mosque, Sayyid Badawi being the patron saint of Tanta and his shrine the site of an annual pilgrimage for tens of thousands of Egyptians. The YMMA's health center's location next to the mosque places the health care facilities at the center of community activity in Tanta. The center has three doctors providing general medical services.

At YMMA headquarters, some distance from the Sayyid Badawi area, the NGO's schools and clubs operate year round, providing training programs to men and women, college graduates without jobs, for free. "We used to charge £E 10—which was nothing, really—but no one came. So we offer carpentry and sewing and other training for free and we get many applicants. The government has stopped hiring graduates so this is now our most important activity—to provide training and help graduates find jobs or become self-employed."[23] The association also provides courses in the Arabic language and the Quran without charge to primary and secondary students; its English-language course has a nominal fee.

The significant contributions by Tanta's YMMA to the poor, unemployed, and youth in its community is an indication of why the national YMMA is so highly regarded throughout Egypt, even though national reputations are not as important to Egyptians in need as is active, caring, community service. There are over two hundred such nationally registered NGOs—Islamic, Christian, and other—many of which do provide a vast array of desperately needed services. The national Islamic organizations, like the national YMMA, perhaps pose the most critical challenge to the failing state system that is nominally secular and socialist.

Islamic Medical Associations

The Islamic Medical Society at Faruq Mosque in Ma'adi is one of fourteen branches of the society, which was established in 1973 and with headquarters in downtown Cairo. The Faruq branch, set up in late 1990, is a hospital with fourteen doctors with three shifts daily of general practitioners plus a number of specialists who come at night. The Faruq society is a CDA registered with MOSA.

Ma'adi also is home to a very successful and visible Islamic hospital, the Fath Complex. Moreover, there are several other smaller NGOs (Islamic and other) in the Ma'adi area that provide medical services, again suggesting a large market that has not been saturated by health care (or other) providers. MOSA overlooks this violation of its own regulations, which prohibit so much NGO activity in a concentrated area, probably because the government itself cannot provide all the medical services that communities need.

The Faruq mosque-hospital prides itself on being cheaper than the Fath society and thus sees the latter as its principal rival. As far as a general coordination of the Islamic medical societies, Dr. Muhammad of Faruq asserts that there is no cooperation between hospitals or between the branches of this *jam'iyya*.

The coordination that does occur is often individually motivated since doctors do continue to work at various hospitals. Dr. Muhammad, for example, works in Faruq, Fath, and Qasr al-'Aini (run by Cairo University) hospitals. Also, doctors come from Qasr al-'Aini and other hospitals to provide services at night to patients at Faruq. This double and triple workload is typical for Egyptians from all walks of life: for instance, government employees moonlight as taxi drivers, medical students double as health care providers, and doctors travel from government hospitals (their day job) to private clinics (usually their own) and to NGO hospitals catering to the poor and middle class. Such moonlighting is quite lucrative and is in many cases the main source of a doctor's income.

Most doctors interviewed tended to criticize the government-run hospitals and to praise the private and NGO hospitals and health centers, Islamic or otherwise. The perception that public-sector hospitals are poor in quality and private centers are relatively superior is certainly the norm in Egypt among patients and doctors alike. This notwithstanding, there are numerous examples of poor treatment at private and NGO hospitals as well as the endless examples from public-sector hospitals.

Patients at Islamic NGOs stated they prefer to use the "Islamic" hospitals rather than those of the "public" or "private" sectors for one main reason. For them, the public hospitals are not an option because of their poor quality and reputation, and the private hospitals are far too expensive and elitist and arrogant toward these working-poor patients.

Qalyub Islamic Hospital and School

NGOs may use Islam as a legitimate "cover" as well as a sincere impulse to help communities in need. Doctors at many of the Islamic medical associations acknowledge they come to work at Islamic NGOs in the evenings because of the supplement to their income. Others say such income is an added bonus to the satisfaction they get from serving the community, a drive that is inspired by their faith.

The leader of a community development association in the Nile Delta, in a village north of Cairo, admits that calling his NGO an

Islamic hospital and school has helped it become more successful. "I'm not a fundamentalist," he says, and he attempts to prove it to his visitors. "But Islam has helped us to get organized and become successful in our attempt to improve health care and education for our community."[24]

This NGO is attached to a mosque in Qalyub and will be referred to as *Dar Muhammad* (House of the Prophet Muhammad, not its real name). This society was founded in 1980—the mosque and the school were started at the same time; the hospital and day care center came later. The driving force behind its creation was the head of the *majlis al-mahalli* (village council). Given what the village generally regarded to be the poor quality and insufficient services of the government,

> we built our own hospital, day care, and primary school. The government can't or won't help us so we do for ourselves. Here, in the village, the government is ignored or even hated. What counts for these village people is what is here for them, not the government but their own community. "The Government" means the central government and they are far away and only care for themselves or care only to stop us from doing as we wish.[25]

The society is not a for-profit organization; it operates for the benefit of the poor, and yet is run on sound principles of welfare economics, including the rational decision to keep prices low so as not to price itself out of the market. It is well placed in the market because it can promote itself as nongovernmental (i.e., private) and, as in this case and thousands of others, further promote itself as Islamic (and thus more trustworthy, caring, and honest.)

The success of this NGO in providing services in health, education, and training is apparent to the community at large. Even with overcrowded classrooms, parents say they prefer to send children to this "private," "Islamic" school. The NGO's oversubscribed health services suggest that due to a perception of better quality in services, equipment, and attention from physicians, patients are willing to pay fees higher than what government hospitals charge.

This case demonstrates that organizing an NGO around Islamic principles and with an "Islamic cover" may significantly enhance the reputation and chances of success of a community service, non-profit organization.

Islam—The "Other Path"[26]

These last examples indicate that the perception of the public at large[27] is that Islamic (and other) NGOs provide services superior to those of the government. Many patients come to Islamic hospitals because the hospitals are Islamic—"Islamic" being seen as something between "public" and "private," and having the positive elements of both. Islamic institutions have the concern for the poor that the public sector is supposed to have and the efficiency and quality attributed to the private sector. For example, a maid visits Fath Hospital for family planning services and pays several Egyptian pounds for services she could receive for free from a public-sector hospital because, she says, "it is Islamic and therefore better."

The doctors who serve in both public and Islamic/private settings have varying reasons for wanting to work in the Islamic centers at night. Dr. Muhammad of Faruq, for instance, is very religious. He praises the glories of Islam generally, not simply those of Islam in the context of health care. In addition to his religious devotion, Dr. Muhammad wants to specialize in cardiology "to be proud of myself. As a generalist I can do everything but I want to show that I can do one thing especially well. Then I will feel happy in my career." So, his three jobs provide him with personal satisfaction (both careerwise and spiritually) as well as with necessary income.

Others are not as motivated by personal growth and religious commitment as Dr. Muhammad. At the main branch of the Islamic Medical Society[28] (*al-Jam'iyya al-Tibbiyya al-Islamiyya*) there are more than thirty-five doctors who serve the hospital throughout the week. The doctors receive from 40 to 60 percent of service fees, depending on their seniority and the treatment they provide. One doctor, a cardiologist who retired from the army as a general and who worked at Ma'adi Military Hospital, puts it quite bluntly: "We come for the extra income." There is no overwhelming selfless interest to help the poor or promote Islamic medicine or care for the sick. The interest is self-interest, to enhance the insufficient salaries provided by the government or from one's own private practice. This is not the same for the founders of these organizations who serve as volunteers and who are motivated by a variety of factors, such as faith, family, community service, or frustration with government neglect.

Nationally Organized Islamic Services

Although some of the Islamic NGOs discussed here are autonomous or independent, some of the others are part of a network. Most NGOs in Egypt must be registered in a single community, yet there are over two hundred that are nationally registered. *Al-Jam'iyya al-Shar'iyya li al-'Amilin bi al-Kitab wa al-Sunna al-Muhammadiyya*, or The "Lawful/Religious" Association for "Those Who Behave" According to the Book and the Muhammadan Sunna, is one of the nationally registered NGOs. It has a branch in each of the nation's twenty-six governorates and 123 branches in Cairo. It is the more political of the various Islamic associations, better organized and more centralized than most of the others. There is reportedly a relationship between the NGOs and the student *Jama'at Islamiyya* (see above) and other groups, such as the *Ikhwan* (Muslim Brotherhood).

In many ways, the *shar'iyya* NGOs represent the trend in Egypt toward private Islamic organizations in society. That is, through their relationship with the *Ikhwan* and student societies, they are developing a network of connections in political, educational, social, and economic fields. Groups like *al-Jam'iyya al-Shar'iyya* perhaps represent a new class vis-à-vis the state, a largely "unincorporated"[29] class even though some of it is incorporated through MOSA registration and regulation by the government's other agencies (health, education, labor). *Al-Jam'iyya al-Shar'iyya* has hospitals and health clinics, day care centers, orphanages, schools, libraries, and other service centers throughout Egypt. It also publishes two magazines: one for public consumption that comes out monthly, *Majallat "I'tisam"* (*Preservation, Adherence*), and one for internal use and distribution only, *Majallat "al-Jum'a"* (*Friday, Gathering*). This *shar'iyya* group is perhaps the most famous of the national Islamic organizations.

Jam'iyyat al-'Ashira al-Muhammadiyya, the Muhammadan Family Association, led by Shaykh Wahba, is another of the big, centralized associations, with branches throughout Cairo, if not throughout Egypt. This group is more focused on religious service and less on political issues than is *al-Shar'iyya*.

Jam'iyyat al-Muhafitha 'ala al-Quran al-Karim, Society for the Preservation of the Quran, is a common name used by many mosques, but the various associations under this name are not centralized or organized under any specific leadership, as are *al-Shar'iyya* and *al-'Ashira*. Although they are not an obvious threat to the social order, there has been concern over their activities in the past. In 1964 (the year Law 32 was enacted), Nasser's MOSA issued a special report on these groups. Of the then 291 societies, 55 percent of which were found in villages throughout Egypt, there were 388 branch agencies, most of which did in fact teach the memorization of the Quran. Yet, these societies did much more than the activities in which they were legally registered to engage. They also established mosques, schools, training centers, day care centers, libraries, and athletic clubs. MOSA found many of them to be in violation of their charters, delivering poor-quality services and being run inefficiently (in terms of high administrative costs).[30] Skeptics should consider the source for these criticisms, but MOSA nevertheless was making some positive critiques and suggestions for improvement. Still, the end result was increased subsidization of these societies by MOSA and increased control over their activities.

The ultimate fate, as witnessed by Berger in the 1960s and still evident in the 1990s, of many such NGOs

> that the government had taken over from voluntary associations [was one of] much poorer service because they now received no private funds and the government was unable or unwilling to support them on the previous scale, and the spirit of spontaneity and service declined considerably under government operation. . . . [T]he general level of services declined as the government took them over or assisted in them. Many of the agencies welcomed government aid of various sorts, realizing they needed it. But such aid was given with little imagination and not much respect for the achievements of the associations, which had been carrying out these functions before the government took so great an interest in them.[31]

Corrupt and Self-Serving Organizations

We do not intend to present simply a one-sided, overly optimistic view of the potential and power of Islamic NGOs. Indeed, there are many examples of corrupt and ineffective NGOs in Egypt. *Huda and Nur,* an Islamic society in Giza, was highlighted by the semiofficial press for its corrupt practices. The president of the *majlis al-idara* (board of directors) of the benevolent society was arrested for embezzling funds and pocketing money collected to help people make the hajj: he stole over £E 100,000 and opened accounts in the names of his children.[32]

There have been numerous examples cited by *Al-Ahram, Al-Jumhuriyya,* and other print media highlighting the corrupt practices of enterprises functioning as Islamic institutions. Even though the government tolerates and even encourages criticism of these enterprises, it will also continue to use these enterprises when it is deemed useful.

Islamic investment companies are perhaps the most infamous of nongovernment, for-profit Islamic organizations that have circumvented laws, as well as ethics, as they bilked Egyptians, Christians and Muslims alike, of billions of dollars. The pyramid schemes of and commodity speculation by these companies led to nearly one-half million investors losing their savings. Of course the 1988 government crackdown on these companies demonstrates the appropriate exercise of regulation and monitoring toward private activities. Unfortunately, the government shows no restraint over other groups that obey the law even as they anger government officials.

The government's disbanding of AWSA and transferring its assets to the Women of Islam NGO (see above) highlights how the regime manipulates both the law and Islam for political control over civil institutions. The government can promote a conservative view of women's rights and it can undermine progressive women's organizations that also criticize government practices. In other instances, the government promotes secular organizations to compete against Islamic forces, which, by demonstrating the power and potential for socioeconomic development that Islamic organizations are indeed good at, might challenge the secular nature of the state.

It is the latter issue of an emerging and demonstrably efficient and effective Islamic sector that worries the government most. This is not a recent concern. "It was the troubles with Islamic associations in the early '60s that led the government to inaugurate Law 32 of 1964 to regulate and monitor associations. Now, CDAs are encouraged by the government over benevolent societies (*jam'iyyat khayriyya*) because the latter are usually associated with a church or mosque. It is easier to register . . . CDA[s] than a *jam'iyya khayriyya* because they ostensibly do not do religious work. Plus, CDAs are semi-governmental."[33] Thus, the government has greater control over their activities.

Conclusion

This chapter highlights the various types of Islamist organizations—political, social, developmental; violent, nonviolent, and nonpolitical—that exist in Egypt. It does not gloss over the failings of some Islamist groups (e.g., corruption, violence, social repression), but demonstrates the positive contributions Islamists do make to social and economic (if not fully political) development in Egypt. And the chapter suggests that the government is anxious about the successes of Islamist social (and political) organizations whose reputations grow daily with their successes.

Perhaps the one organization the government is trying its utmost to either co-opt or destroy is *Jam'iyyat al-Ikhwan al-Muslimin*, the Society of Muslim Brothers. Since its founding in 1928 and its registration as a society in 1929, its goals have been both social and political, promoting the cause of benevolence, charity, and development on the one hand and the cause of nationalism, independence, and

Islamism on the other. Even though various governments, whether monarchical or republican, have outlawed its activities, the very success and continuing popularity of the *Ikhwan* demonstrates to Egyptians and their government that Islamic NGOs are legitimate, positive influences on the daily lives of the population. If allowed to operate openly and freely, this NGO/party/movement could demonstrate perhaps all by itself—if in fact it does not do so already—that a national Islamic organization can challenge the very basis of the secular republican form of government in Egypt.

We turn now to examine this most popular of the Islamist organizations and the way in which the regime has sought to offset or limit the impact the *Ikhwan* has had on social, economic, and political development in Egypt.

Notes

1. This way of life is better understood as a multicultural, cross-national, diverse, and internally divided global phenomenon.

2. Jordan's King Hussein, who had little choiohn L. Esposito, *The Islamic Threat: Myth or Reality?* (New York: Oxford University Press, 1992); Dale F. Eickelman and James Piscatori, *Muslim Politics* (Princeton: Princeton University Press, 1996); and John L. Esposito and John O. Voll, *Islam and Democracy* (New York: Oxford University Press, 1996).

3. Jordan's King Hussein, who had little choice but to join Nasser in the war, also was a big loser.

4. This is 90 percent of a population of 62 million.

5. Needless to say, Richard Mitchell's *The Society of the Muslim Brothers* (London: Oxford University Press, 1969) is the most enlightening account of the founding, development, and program of the *Ikhwan*. For more recent accounts of the *Ikhwan*, see Gilles Kepel's *Muslim Extremism in Egypt* (Berkeley: University of California Press, 1985), in which the author compares the neo-Muslim Brotherhood with not only the original leadership of the *Ikhwan* but with leaders of other contemporary Islamic organizations in Egypt; Saad Eddin Ibrahim, "Egypt's Islamic Activism in the 1980s," *Third World Quarterly* 10, no. 2 (1988): 632–657; and Emmanuel Sivan's *Radical Islam: Medieval Theology and Modern Politics* (New Haven, Conn.: Yale University Press, 1985) for a general comparison between the Egyptian and Syrian Muslim Brotherhoods.

6. Esposito, *The Islamic Threat*, p. 94. See also Raymond A. Hinnebusch, Jr., *Egyptian Politics Under Sadat: The Post-Populist Development of an Authoritarian-Modernizing State* (updated edition) (Boulder, Colo.: Lynne Rienner Publishers, 1988), p. 84.

7. Robert Bianchi, *Unruly Corporatism: Associational Life in Twentieth Century Egypt* (New York: Oxford University Press, 1989), p. 199.

8. There continues to be much debate over the term "fundamentalist" in reference to Islamic and Jewish revivalist movements. Some argue that in a strict sense, this term refers solely to a movement within the American Protestant churches and thus is applicable neither to non-Protestant nor

non-Christian movements. Others, such as Bruce Lawrence, seem to have little aversion to using the term; see his *Defenders of God: The Fundamentalist Revolt Against the Modern Age* (San Francisco: Harper & Row, 1989). In this book, Lawrence discusses fundamentalism as a religious ideology in the contexts of Judaism, American Protestantism, and Islam. See also Martin Marty and R. Scott Appleby, *Fundamentalisms Observed* (Chicago: Chicago University Press, 1991). This is undoubtedly the most ambitious project to date seeking to describe and analyze, in cross-national and cross-religious contexts, the global phenomenon of religious revival.

9. For an excellent account of the ideology, leadership, and organization of *Tanzim al-Jihad*, see Guenena, *The Jihad: An Islamic Alternative in Egypt* (Cairo: American University in Cairo Press, 1986). Hamied Ansari also discusses *al-Jihad* briefly in Chapter 10 of *Egypt: The Stalled Society* (Albany: SUNY Press, 1986). See also his "The Islamic Militants in Egyptian Politics," *International Journal of Middle East Studies* 38, no. 3 (1984): 123–144.

10. This group should not be confused with *Tablighi Jamaat*, which is one of the South Asian subcontinent's most important Islamic movements and which is concerned with the moral and spiritual uplift of individual believers and does not focus on establishing an Islamic state under *shari'a*. Although such establishment would be acceptable, *Tablighi Jamaat* adherents focus on *da'wa*, the invitation or call to Islam. It is a grass roots organization and thus resembles more the Islamic NGOs described in this work rather than the Society of Denunciation, *Jam'iyyat al-Tabligh*, of Egypt.

11. Kepel, *Muslim Extremism in Egypt*, p. 129.

12. Ibid., p. 241. See Chapter 5 for a complete analysis of the student *jama'at*.

13. Egypt's militants have made threats against and have killed some foreigners. Still, most of the dead are Egyptians: innocent victims, government officials, and Christians (especially in Upper Egypt). Others killed in this ongoing battle between militants and the government include suspected and "convicted" militants as well as their families.

14. Morroe Berger, *Islam in Egypt Today: Social and Political Aspects of Popular Religion* (Cambridge: Cambridge University Press, 1970).

15. Since the government has not allowed the Egyptian Organization for Human Rights to register as a charitable organization, it and other human rights groups have sought to go around the restrictive clauses of Law 32 by registering their groups under the commercial code, normally used by for-profit private companies.

16. Similarly, there is a great deal of criticism of American PVOs working in the United States and especially in the international arena for being nearly totally dependent on the U.S. government for their financial survival. See Brian H. Smith, *More Than Altruism: The Politics of Private Foreign Aid* (Princeton: Princeton University Press, 1990), especially Chapter 6.

17. For some of the details, see Middle East Watch "Egyptian Government Moves to Dissolve Prominent Arab Women's Organization" September 1991.

18. Kenneth Roth, Executive Director of Human Rights Watch, letter to His Excellency Hosni Mubarak, 5 June 1998.

19. Most of the information on 'Izbat Zayn taken from Louise White, "Urban Community Organizations and Local Government: Exploring Relationships and Roles," *Public Administration and Political Development* 6 (1986): 239–253.

20. Iman Roushdy Hammady, *Religious Medical Centers in Egypt*, (Master's thesis, American University in Cairo, 1990) p. 42.

21. Ibid., p. 45. Hammady speaks of a £E 600 cap per month for medical analysis unit personnel but does not mention any particular cap for the specialized physicians. In our own interviews with some of these physicians there did not appear to be a cap on income. Some doctors said that they could make up to £E 2,000 in a month depending on the services they provided.

22. Interview with *mudir* (director) of YMMA, 14 August 1991.

23. Ibid.

24. Interview with *mudir* of *Qalyub* association, 19 April 1991.

25. Interview with village head, April 20, 1991.

26. Borrowed from Hernando de Soto, *The Other Path: The Invisible Revolution in the Third World* (New York: Harper & Row, 1989). Although Islamic and other legally registered NGOs are not technically part of the informal sector, the underground economy highlighted by de Soto, there are parallels between the two. NGOs in Egypt, while ostensibly part of the formal sector, nevertheless continue to skirt legality by bending some of the regulations in Law 32 of 1964. This and many other characteristics of these organizations place NGOs in a tenuous situation between formal and informal.

27. Based on interviews with patients at NGO hospitals and two large private hospitals and on discussions with medical students and physicians in and out of university settings.

28. *Al-Jam'iyya al-Shar'iyya bi-Masjid al-Sahah,* The Shar'iyya Society of Al-Sahah Mosque (al-Sahah being a street name, also known as Rushdie Street).

29. See Bianchi, *Unruly Corporatism.*

30. Berger, *Islam in Egypt Today*, p. 115.

31. Ibid., pp. 116–117.

32. *Al-Ahram,* 14 March 1991, p. 8.

33. Interview with Egyptian development specialist, February 12, 1991.

3

The Muslim Brotherhood

Evolution of the Movement

In this chapter we identify the major goals and strategies of the *Ikhwan al-Muslimin,* or Muslim Brotherhood—the largest Islamist opposition group in Egypt.[1] In so doing, we will continue to address the primary focus of this study, the development of Islamic pluralism and the applicability of the term "civil society" to Islamist associations in Egypt. As a corollary, and of fundamental importance to the study of civil society, a major objective of this analysis is to determine the group's views on the topic that is too often portrayed as the raison d'être of political Islam: violence as the means of attaining political power.

The Muslim Brotherhood is the Islamist group that most felt the wrath of Gamal Abdel Nasser, and that has continued to play a large role in the Egyptian opposition movement, both under Anwar Sadat and his successor, Hosni Mubarak. The Brotherhood was founded in 1928 by a small group that included Hasan al-Banna, a twenty-two-year-old teacher working for the state school system in Isma'iliyya. He called for mass mobilization of Muslims to return to the faith. Al-Banna, responding to colonial rule of the developing world in general, and the British occupation of Egypt in particular, argued that the Muslim world had been assailed by the West's "abuses that have done injury to their [Muslims] dignity, their honor, and their independence, as well as commandeered their wealth and shed their blood."[2] He argued that Egypt's Islamic culture and heritage had been supplanted by Western traditions. Egypt should not import foreign political ideals because the Islamic state is "more complete, more pure, more lofty, and more exalted than anything that can be found in the utterances of Westerners and the books of Europeans."[3]

Moreover, al-Banna asserted, it was not only the West that had harmed the Muslim East; the latter's own political leaders were largely to blame for the presence of imperialism in their midst. For this reason, al-Banna preached that Muslims must stand up to the dictators of the Islamic world: "One of the loftiest forms of *jihad* [religious struggle] is to utter a word of truth in the presence of a tyrannical ruler."[4] Toward this effort, al-Banna wrote a letter of advice to King Faruq of Egypt in 1947. In the letter, al-Banna attempts to maintain a modicum of respect for the king as he gives him suggestions for the pursuit of a better system of government patterned upon Islamic ideals. Faithfully referring to the king as "Excellency," al-Banna asks him to release Egypt from Western influence and apply Islamic jurisprudence, Islamic military spirit, Islamic health traditions and scientific studies, Islamic morality, and an Islamic economic system. "Finally, when the nation possesses all these reinforcements—hope, patriotism, science, power, health, and a sound economy—it will, without a doubt, be the strongest of all nations."[5]

In al-Banna's view, imitations of the West and the replacement of God's law (*shari'a*) with Western law had poisoned Muslim society. In demanding the regulation of every aspect of life with Islamic values, al-Banna was asserting the Islamic belief that state and religion are inseparable.

> Every nation has a body of law to which its sons have recourse in their legal affairs. This body of law must be derived from the noble Qur'an, and in accordance with the basic sources of Islamic jurisprudence. For the Islamic Sacred Law and the decisions of the Islamic jurists are all-sufficient, supply every need, and cover every contingency.[6]

Al-Banna's organization grew quickly in both rural and urban areas, with membership totaling one to two million people by 1949. In the early days of the Brotherhood, its effective membership came from the "discontented city proletariat and the struggling lower middle class of the white-collar worker."[7]

The growth of the Brotherhood, coupled with al-Banna's calls for the replacement of secular law with Islamic law, led the monarchy of King Farouk to ban the organization in 1948. In response, the Brotherhood later that year assassinated Prime Minister Mahmud Fahmi al-Nuqrashi. In retribution, the regime arranged for al-Banna's assassination by the secret police on 12 February 1949. The ban was lifted in 1951, and the Brotherhood helped the army's Free Officers, led by Nasser and Muhammad Naguib, successfully overthrow King Farouk in 1952. The Brotherhood's expectation was that it would have a share of the power in the new government. The new government quickly dissolved all political parties in 1953, but allowed the Brotherhood to continue its activities because it was not a party but an association. As the Brotherhood made demands for changes in the legal code, Nasser acquiesced on minor matters.

He did not, however, welcome the protests and political demands made by the Brotherhood and refused the group's demands for the full application of *shari'a*. An attempt on Nasser's life in Alexandria in October 1954 led to a clampdown on Brotherhood activities: more than one thousand members of the group were imprisoned and tortured, and its leaders were executed. Government repression forced what was left of the Brotherhood underground; but by 1965 the group had regained its strength, resulting in another assault by the government, this time with twenty thousand arrests, replete with torture and executions.

Among those imprisoned in 1954 was Sayyid Qutb,[8] a leader and ideologue of the Brotherhood. Qutb had lived in the United States during the 1940s, an experience that left him convinced of the imminent failure of Western civilization. Qutb was bothered by what he considered a lack of values in the West, and, upon his return to Egypt, observed the same distance between man and spirituality. Qutb endured severe torture in prison and was hanged on 29 August 1966 for inciting the masses to revolt.

While in prison he wrote five books, most prominent among them *Ma'alim fi al-Tariq* (*Signs Along the Path*),[9] which was soon to become the source of inspiration for the growing Islamist movement. In this book, Qutb charged that Egyptian society was living in a *jahiliyya*, or a state of ignorance similar to that which predated the coming of Islam. Qutb's book called on Muslims to undertake *jihad* against their leaders because they had replaced God's *shari'a* with their own man-made laws. He defined *jihad* as "a complete armed rebellion" against rule by secular laws,[10] and as a "declaration of the freedom of man from servitude to other men."[11]

Qutb's militancy had been shaped by the hardship endured in Nasser's prison. Twenty-one of his prisonmates had been massacred in prison in June 1957, making a deep impression on Qutb, who "was horrified by the barbarism of the camp guards, by the inhumanity with which they had let the wounded die. Various witnesses report that it was then that he lost his last remaining illusions as to the Muslim character of the Nasser regime."[12] Whereas al-Banna had urged reform of the Egyptian political and legal systems by making recommendations to leaders to implement Islamic law, Qutb declared religious war against the Egyptian state. *Signs Along the Path* was written as an indictment of the contemporaneous Arab and Egyptian regimes; but, with subsequent Egyptian leadership maintaining the secular trajectory of these regimes, the Islamist movement was to use the book thereafter as an inspiration against the regimes.

Nasser made several attempts to rid Egypt of the Brotherhood, which, however, regrouped after every such endeavor. Although Nasser's attitude toward the movement was antagonistic, his pronouncements after Egypt's military defeat in 1967 increasingly created an aura of religiosity. Religious activities were encouraged and hundreds of the *Ikhwan* were released from prison. As if to rationalize the defeat by Israel in the Six-Day War, he resorted to Islamic slogans in his addresses to the masses. Egypt's military weakness had created fertile ground for the growth of religious ideals because the defeat was perceived as a punishment for Egypt's pursuit of socialist, rather than Islamic, ideals. Only when Egypt returned to Islam would God support the nation's war against Israel. In the defeatist postwar climate, Islamist groups presented a religious alternative to Nasser's secular, socialist political style.

The atmosphere of religiosity continued under Sadat.[13] In the early 1970s, he responded to Brotherhood overtures for a rapprochement with the state. Salim Nijm, an exiled leader of the organization, sent a message to Sadat saying that "the Brothers want to return [to Egypt] and are willing to cooperate with Anwar al-Sadat."[14] At the same time 'Abd al-Qadir Hilmi, a Muslim Brother held in Tura Prison, also sent a message recommending a reconciliation.[15] Upon Sadat's instruction, his private advisor, Mahmud Mu'awwad Jami', met with exiled Brotherhood members, who included Yusif al-Qirdawi, Ahmad al-'Asal, and 'Abd al-Mun'im Mashhur. They offered to let bygones be bygones in return for the release of prisoners, and soon after these overtures Sadat proceeded to release imprisoned Brethren. Upon the release of Salih Abu Raqiq and 'Abd al-Qadir Hilmi, they were taken to Sadat's house, where they had lunch together and made plans to mutually normalize their relations.[16]

In this climate, and in line with Sadat's appeals for a more democratic state, the government did not interfere when the Muslim Brotherhood rebuilt its organization. Sadat did not grant the group the legal recognition it requested, but in 1976 he did allow it to temporarily resume publication of its old monthly magazine, *Al-Da'wa* (*The Call*). Until the publication was banned again in 1981, the Brotherhood used it to editorialize and expound its Islamist views.

Since the release of *Ikhwan* members from prison in the 1970s, the Brotherhood has once again been able to consolidate its power and influence, but the theme has now become one of accommodation of, not struggle against, the political system, of course with an eye toward reforming the system. The calls by Qutb for *jihad* against the *jahiliyya* state have been supplanted by calls for the enactment of political change through cooperation with the ruling regime.

Islam and the Political Realm

Understanding the objectives of the Brotherhood requires an understanding of Islam as a religion that transcends the relationship between an individual and his or her God. In fact, an accurate definition of Islam would necessarily interpret the oft-quoted phrase that it is "religion and state" *(din wa dawla)*. 'Umar al-Tilmisani, General Guide of the Muslim Brotherhood until his death in 1987, characterized Islam as "creed, worship, homeland, citizenship, creation, the physical, culture, law, forgiveness, and power."[17] Islam is thus a complete system governing all aspects of life. It encompasses all things material and spiritual, societal and individual, political and personal. It is the vastness of the territory covered by Islam that lends to the dramatic resurgence of calls for Islam as the solution to worldly societal issues. Whether the problem is Egypt's defeat by Israel in 1967 or the lack of affordable housing in 1998,[18] activists promote Islam as a political, social, economic, and spiritual embodiment of the solutions. Certainly, argue the Islamists, the failure of both socialism and capitalism to address Egypt's (and the entire Muslim world's) grievances indicates that a return to Islam, at both the individual and collective levels, is imperative for the success of the nation.

In accordance with this comprehensive doctrine members of the Muslim Brotherhood describe their organization as more than either "a political party or a charitable, reformist society." Rather, it is a spiritual worldwide organization that is (1) a *da'wa* from the Quran and the *sunna* (tradition and example) of the Prophet Muhammad; (2) a method that adheres to the *sunna;* (3) a reality whose core is the purity of the soul; (4) a political association; (5) an athletic association; (6) an educational and cultural organization; (7) an economic enterprise; and (8) a social concept.[19]

Toward an Islamic State

Such an all-encompassing organization necessarily has very broad goals, and these essentially have not changed since the founding of the Brotherhood in 1928. The major focus of the Brotherhood, in the initial stages of reform, is the individual as a member of society. Today's Brethren reiterate al-Banna's objective of building a new generation of believers who will support the *da'wa* and become models for others, such that ultimately the Islamic nation will be liberated from foreign domination and a free Islamic state will be established. Al-Banna's ideal Islamic nation was to be built upon the reform of individual hearts and souls.

Individuals must become more pious and more observant of their religious obligations. This would be followed by the organization of "society to be fit for the virtuous community which commands the good and forbids evil-doing, then from the community will arise the good state."[20] This fundamental goal of the Brotherhood was also pursued by ideologue Sayyid Qutb, who called for the establishment of a nation whose foundation is Islam. Ahmad S. Moussalli defines Qutb's goal as an Islamic system "where Islamic law is executed, where the idea of Islam rules, and where its principles and regulations define the kind of government and the form of society."[21]

The central objective of the contemporary Brotherhood continues to be the establishment of an Islamic state that is governed not by man-made laws, but by *shari'a*. Whereas the former system of legislation implies the sovereignty of man over man (interpreted as man's servitude to man), the latter testifies to the sovereignty of only God over man. This is equivalent to man's liberation and therefore must be enforced if the state is to be other than nominally Islamic. It is critical to most Muslims that sovereignty cannot be assumed by man. As Charles Butterworth notes, "Insofar as a Muslim literally surrenders himself to God he can recognize no other being or entity as sovereign." Therefore "none but God can be lawgiver."[22]

Because only God is the sovereign lawgiver, God's law, or *shari'a*, must necessarily be applied to man's pursuit of worldly affairs. The Brotherhood's objective of applying *shari'a* in the Egyptian state raises the question of rule *(hukm)* in an Islamic state. If sovereignty is the realm of God only, whose responsibility is it to govern in God's name on earth? That is, who shall be given the authority to preside over the nation? This question is vital to discourse on the goals of the Brotherhood because scholars and political practitioners tend to view political opponents, whether secular or religious, as power seekers whose true goal (even if unspoken) is rule over the political system. It is thus important to determine the Brothers' viewpoint on political governance.

In this regard, an essay by 'Umar al-Tilmisani, who became the Brotherhood's General Guide in 1973, is informative. With regard to power as an objective of the Brotherhood, he states:

> The first level of power is the power of creed and belief. The second is the power of unity and belonging. And third comes the

power of weapons and strength. If the power of creed and belief is lost and there is no unity, reliance upon weapons results in destruction. The Brethren do not consider revolution, nor do they depend upon it, nor do they believe in its utility or its outcome. As for rule, the Brethren do not request it for themselves. If they find among the nation one who can handle this burdensome responsibility, . . . who can rule following Islamic and Quranic mores, . . . [the Brethren will be] his soldiers, his supporters, and his assistants. If they do not find such a leader, [then rule will follow the Brotherhood's program].[23]

Shaykh Muhammad 'Abdallah al-Khatib, a columnist for the Brotherhood's *Liwa' al-Islam (The Banner of Islam)*, expresses the same sentiment:

[The Brethren] are not concerned with who rules because they do not seek the worldly; they are missionaries for the good. It is known that the Muslim missionary does not think of fame, nor does he work to gain power. The Muslim Brothers use neither legal nor illegal methods to gain power, because their foremost concern is the system of rule and not the ruler.[24]

Zaynab al-Ghazali al-Jubayli, an early and long-time supporter of the Brotherhood, asserted in an address to female Muslims: "I know that you long to have the world opened up, not so we can rule it, but so that we can improve it and establish God's rule over it."[25] The Brethren's stated goal, therefore, is not power for power's sake, nor is it rule by the Muslim Brotherhood. The Brotherhood's leaders stress that the Islamic state need not be governed by the Brethren, but must be governed by one who will uphold Islamic precepts. This emphasis on the nature of governance and not on who governs is in agreement with the philosophy of al-Banna, who stressed that the goal of the Brethren is to build Islamic individuals who will then build an Islamic state. As John Voll notes about al-Banna, "Although he believed that the power to reform was inextricably linked to the power to rule, al-Banna insisted that the Muslim Brotherhood was committed to broad-based social reform, not to the direct exercise of political power."[26] The philosophy of the Brotherhood has therefore not changed in this regard. Their only criterion for a ruler is the ability to govern in accordance with the Islamic principles they wish to see applied.

Islamic Democracy and Pluralism

The Muslim Brotherhood has not specified the definitive technical dimensions of the anticipated Islamic state, but it must be noted that the terms "democracy," "liberty," and "freedom" are used freely and repeatedly by Brethren, suggesting a conviction that democratic institutions can function within a system of Islamic legislation. While Western scholars and many in the Muslim world are debating the compatibility of Islam and democracy, the Brethren consistently dismiss the argument that the two are incompatible. Muslim Brother 'Isam al-'Aryan, for example, calls the charge that the Brethren are against democracy "a great lie," stressing that "the Brothers consider constitutional rule to be closest to Islamic rule. . . . We are the first to call for and apply democracy. We are devoted to it until death."[27] Similarly, Muslim Brother Fahmi Huwaydi comments, "The Brothers support pluralism and reject violence; moreover, Imam al-Banna did not reject democracy." Huwaydi asks, "Who antagonized whom? Has democracy antagonized the Brethren or have the Brethren antagonized democracy? I confirm to you that it was democracy that antagonized the Muslim Brothers."[28]

According to the Brotherhood members' published statements, they not only do not reject democracy, but in fact encourage its expansion, as stressed by Muhammad Ma'mun al-Hudaybi, son of former General Guide Hasan al-Hudaybi and head of the Brotherhood delegation in the Egyptian People's Assembly. Speaking about democracy in Egypt, al-Hudaybi observes that "there is a certain degree of democracy; we guard and hold on to it. We work to confirm and develop it until rights are complete. It is important to confirm the democratic pursuit in practice."[29]

The younger al-Hudaybi identifies various attributes of democracy he deems important, such as respect for the constitution, an independent judiciary, freedom of the press, party independence, and people's protection from torture.[30]

There is an appreciative acknowledgment among the Brotherhood that despite some setbacks, Mubarak's regime has broadened the democratic process. Writing in the aftermath of the 1987 People's Assembly elections, which brought thirty-six Islamists to Parliament, Muslim Brother Al-Sadiq 'Abduh commends the "relative democratic relief" enjoyed in Egypt under President Husni Mubarak. 'Abduh insists that the Brethren support the relatively democratic process that gained them representation in the Assembly.[31]

'Abduh's comments are made despite the fact that the Egyptian state continues to bar the Brotherhood from assuming the full role of a legitimate political party. Restrictions on the Brotherhood's involvement in the political system have certainly not gone uncriticized. Sayf al-Islam Hasan al-Banna, son of the founder of the Brotherhood, urges the government to "open the doors to all to participate in decision making. . . . [This] will therefore guarantee that all will execute it [democracy] and abide by it."[32] The call for greater democracy is also made by Muhammad 'Umara of the Brotherhood:

> If Mubarak opens the doors and windows to listen to thinkers and leaders of Islam and their struggles and views on the Islamic renaissance [nahda], his picture of the Islamic solution would change. . . . This encourages us to ask President Mubarak, whom we recognize as having transferred the relationship between the state and Islam from a clash with the Islamist movement to a period of truce [hudna], . . . to transfer this relationship to a period of reconciliation [musalaha]. . . . If he opens the doors to the thinkers and leaders of the Islamist movement, he will find a new color of men who give without considering the cost.[33]

With a pragmatic appreciation of the benefits the group might derive if the political system were more democratic and pluralistic, the Brotherhood considers it imperative that democratic freedoms be expanded and an open multiparty system established, such that their group will be able to operate independently and not necessarily in an alliance with other political parties.

Muslim Brotherhood leaders representing both the older (e.g., Ma'mun al-Hudaybi) and younger (e.g., 'Isam al-'Aryan) generations of Brethren speak often of liberty and democracy; however, perhaps most significant is the emphasis on the actualization of freedom made by Muhammad Hamid Abu al-Nasr in his capacity as General Guide of the Brothers. Until his death in 1996, Abu al-Nasr highlighted the importance of liberty to the Muslim Brotherhood by featuring the concept repeatedly in his writings. For example, in an editorial criticizing the Egyptian government's failure to enforce civil liberties, Abu al-Nasr argues that, in contrast to the government's view that national security is gained by repression,

> Security, in the perception of legal and social scholars, is actualized when freedom is coveted, when justice takes its course and allows the general activities of groups and organizations in the shelter of laws that judge each transgression and give each citizen the opportunity to defend himself.[34]

In another editorial, Abu al-Nasr speaks of the collapse of communism and the spread of democracy in the former Soviet bloc in almost wistful terms. In a critique addressed to Arab and Muslim governments that are not moving quickly enough toward the realization of liberties, especially "the freedom to elect representatives of the people," Abu al-Nasr warns:

Freedom is dear and it is preferable for you to avoid your nations' anger and riots. It cannot be imagined that any people will remain under subjugation and repression after hearing and witnessing surrounding nations achieve their freedom and dignity.... A nation's power is derived not from material power, but from the entire citizenry's liberty, the people's trust in the government, and the government's trust in the people. A government that lacks the people's trust due to the government's domination, subjugation, and denial of the people's rights and freedoms has no weight among states; nor will it achieve stability.[35]

No doubt, much of the affirmation of democracy is due to the desire of the Brotherhood to participate fully in the political system. The lowering of barriers to participation will enable the Brotherhood, and other political parties, to engage the dominant National Democratic Party on a more equal footing. While some radical factions of the Islamist movement decry democracy as a Western construct that is alien to their political philosophy, the Brotherhood embraces the concept, not as Western, but as a set of ideals that is compatible with Islamic constructs.

Socioeconomic Justice

The all-encompassing nature of Islam makes it necessary for Islamist groups to address issues that transcend the religious and political realms. The group is often criticized for not having formulated a detailed program of reforms; however, the Brotherhood does advance a commitment to the rectification of Egypt's economic decline and the population's low standard of living. Foremost in the current writings of the Brethren is the importance of socioeconomic justice as a foundation of the Islamic political system. In their references to this ideal the Brethren emphasize that a society based on Islamic precepts would necessarily promote social security for all citizens, narrow the socioeconomic gap between classes, undertake welfare spending to assist those in need, encourage economic solidarity among citizens, respect private property, and enforce the requisite that each able-bodied person must be economically productive.[36]

The Brotherhood's economic program makes both the individual and the state active and responsible participants in the pursuit of social justice. It is also the responsibility of all able individuals to alleviate the suffering of others by practicing the Islamic principle of *zakat* (almsgiving). Muslims are thus mutually responsible for one another, and the wealthy are required by Islamic principles to help the poor.

The state's role is to encourage economic productivity and, despite privatization as a general rule, to own and manage some enterprises that should necessarily remain in the public domain. Citing the program of the 1987 tripartite electoral alliance (Muslim Brotherhood, Labor and Liberal Parties), Ann Lesch identifies the following as the Islamists' requirements for economic development: (1) shrinking of the government bureaucracy and public sector; (2) official adherence to standards of high productivity; (3) the private sector as the backbone of the economy; (4) a non-interest-bearing banking system; (5) *zakat;* and (6) independence from foreign economic intervention. In this latter concern, the Brotherhood hopes to promote integration of the Egyptian economy with other Muslim economies as an alternative to the present reliance on, and interference by, "foreigners from the West."[37]

Even though much of the Brotherhood's economic framework has been identified as comparable to the economic thought of socialism, the Brethren's respect for private property and insistence on downsizing the public sector make their platform notably different. Significantly, the Brethren did not oppose Anwar Sadat's plans to privatize the Egyptian economy through the policy of *Infitah* (Opening). In fact, it has been observed that many members of the Brotherhood were beneficiaries of *Infitah,* having become wealthy through foreign connections and the establishment of lucrative economic enterprises in Egypt.[38]

The socioeconomic principles advocated by the Brotherhood are, as Lesch notes, not ends in themselves. "They ideally would lead to the creation of a harmonious Islamic society in which the upper class would not exploit the poor, the manager would not oppress the worker, and the profit would be tempered by piety and good works."[39] The goal of social justice is thus part of the overall objective of establishing an Islamic society, governed in its totality by Islamic precepts.

Strategies for the Establishment of an Islamic State

'Umar al-Tilmisani was quoted above as saying, "The Brethren do not consider revolution, nor do they depend upon it, nor do they believe in its utility or its outcome." Such statements should be reassuring to the Egyptian government, for there is the suggestion that the Brotherhood does not intend dramatically and violently to uproot all things un-Islamic, which in the view of more radical Islamists include the entire political system. If revolution is not the Brotherhood members' preferred means for establishing the Islamic state, what form of action does their program entail?

Accommodation and Constitutional Change

To date, the Brotherhood's most significant strategy is its willingness to work within the existing political system for the advancement of its goals. This, in fact, is the major defining trait differentiating the Brotherhood's activities from those of Egypt's more militant Islamist groups. Political accommodation is not a new strategy in terms of Brotherhood ambitions, although it is a new phenomenon in terms of actual practice. John Esposito and James Piscatori remind us that, as early as 1941, the Muslim Brotherhood advocated participation in the political system. "Early in its development the Muslim Brotherhood accepted that it had to contest elections if it was to exercise real influence. . . . [I]t resolved to field candidates in any forthcoming national election." The group was unsuccessful, however, due to corrupt elections, boycotts of elections, and/or prohibition against operating as a political organization.[40]

Although the contemporary political election in Egypt has yet to be proclaimed totally open and fair, the Brotherhood has since 1984 experienced participation in the campaign and election circuit, and has thereby won a role in the People's Assembly. In particular, despite the fact that the government continues to deny Brotherhood requests for recognition as a legitimate political party, the group has aligned itself with authorized parties to gain access to the political system. In 1984 the Brotherhood formed a tactical alliance with the New Wafd Party, thereby winning eight seats in the 360-member Parliament. In 1987 it formed a tripartite alliance with the Labor and Liberal parties, gaining thirty-six seats for Islamists in the People's Assembly and constituting the main parliamentary opposition group.

The coalitions forged by the Brotherhood with secular political parties have been a necessary strategy enabling the group to bypass the legislative restrictions on its participation in the electoral system. A previous Egyptian law requiring individual parties to get at least 8 percent of votes cast to gain representation in Parliament, coupled with the law preventing nonparty organizations from entering elections, meant that coalition was the only mechanism that could both get the Brethren into the elections and give them a chance at gaining the necessary 8 percent. The situation changed in 1990 when, to counter the electoral gains made by Islamists, the election law was changed to allow only individuals, not parties, to participate. To protest what was perceived as the government's attempt to maintain political control of the People's Assembly, the Brotherhood and its coalition partners, along with all other opposition groups except *Tajammu'*, boycotted the 1990 elections.

The boycott did not indicate an abandonment of the accommodationist strategy; this was equally true of the secular parties that also boycotted the elections. In fact, after the boycott Muslim Brothers continued to contest seats at the local level, and later reentered the national contests. In the 1992 local elections the Brotherhood and the Labor Party intensified campaigning under their coalition slogan, "Islam is the solution." Voter turnout, however, was very low, reaching a high of only 15 percent in rural areas and a low of 5 percent in urban areas.[41]

As tensions grew between the government and militant Islamist groups, the government began to regard the Brotherhood with the same apprehension that it had reserved for militant groups. An attempt on President Mubarak's life on 26 June 1995 in Ethiopia, for which the *al-Jama'a al-Islamiyya* declared responsibility one week later, greatly exacerbated the security concerns and led the government to crack down on Islamists. The strong measures included moves against the Muslim Brotherhood in the months before the November 1995 People's Assembly elections, which the group had decided not to boycott despite the government's adherence to the individual candidacy system that had resulted in the 1990 boycott. Brotherhood members were arrested in waves; in one such episode two hundred members were apprehended in a single operation spanning several cities. Many of those arrested were referred for trial by military courts, indicating that they were security threats and arousing criticism from other opposition parties, including, among others, the Nasserist Party, the New Wafd Party, and the *Tajammu'*. These parties are political opponents of the Brotherhood, but they protested the military trials on the grounds that the Brotherhood was committed to dialogue. The Brotherhood fielded candidates in the 1995 elections under severe conditions, demonstrating further its resolve to take advantage of constitutional mechanisms of political participation. Fifty-four Brotherhood members, many of whom were candidates for the People's Assembly, were sentenced by military courts to three to five years in prison in the days prior to the elections on charges that the group had engaged in "unconstitutional activities." Also, the group's Cairo headquarters were closed by the courts. On 24 November Minister of Interior Hasan al-Alfi announced that the Brotherhood, Islamic *Jihad*, and the *al-Jama'a al-Islamiyya* were all part of the same organization, and, on the eve of the elections, over one thousand Brethren were arrested. In the tense and controversial elections that followed most of the Islamist candidates were defeated.

No doubt, the activities of the militant groups in Egypt have led the battered government to suspect the activities and motives of all Islamists. Despite the government's relentless efforts to marginalize the Brotherhood, there is significant evidence that the group has become even more inclined to use the political system. The most important indication of the group's proclivity to accommodate the system is its emphasis on elevating the organization to the status of a recognized political party. Ma'mun al-Hudaybi notes that, despite the 1990 boycott, "the Brothers are the main political power in the state. . . . We are prepared to operate within the realm of political party pluralism and the declaration of the Muslim Brotherhood Party."[42] Mustafa Mashhur, General Guide of the Muslim Brotherhood since 1996, argues that legal party status and removal of restrictions on the group's activities "will help spread the spirit of good relations" among Egyptians and unite the nation.[43]

This position on party status is markedly different from that of founder Hasan al-Banna, who had believed that the *da'wa* could not be confined to a party aligned with patrons of the ruling authorities. The *da'wa*, according to al-Banna, was to address the general interest of the entire *umma* (worldwide Islamic community), and not just an organized segment of it. Today, the Brethren still believe in addressing the *umma*, but they concede that organization must begin at the local level. Furthermore, they argue that if the state in which they must organize has rules that limit political participation only to parties, then they are compelled to form a party. With the government rejecting Brotherhood demands for party status, a small group established a new political party, *Hizb al-Wasat*, or Party of the Center. Interestingly, founders of the Center Party included Islamists, Christians, leftists, and Nasserists. Muslim Brother Abu al-'Ala Madi, former deputy secretary-general of the Engineer's Syndicate, was arrested in April 1996 with two other founding members of the Center Party. Madi was charged with using the new party as a cover for Brotherhood activities, while the party's founders insisted that the Center Party was meant to occupy the middle ground between militant Islamists and the government.

In addition to their demands for full party status, and as a strategy that bypasses the restrictions the government has placed on their participation in national elections, the Brethren have intensified their involvement in politics at the professional association and syndicate level. By the late 1980s, the Brotherhood had gained control of the doctors', engineers', and pharmacists' professional associations, all significant indicators of political participation at the grassroots, or civil society, level. In 1992, Brotherhood control reached one of the oldest and most prominent of the syndicates—the lawyers' association—after winning two-thirds of the seats in that syndicate's administrative assembly. The victory of the Brotherhood allowed it to assume important positions in the association, and, significantly, Sayf al-Islam al-Banna became the secretary-general.

In addition, the Muslim Brothers have competed successfully in student associations and university faculty clubs, winning the majority in the administration of the faculty club of Zagazig University in April 1993. Here, they gained ten of the fifteen seats being contested, making this the first university faculty club to come under the control of the Brotherhood in northern Egypt. Previously, the Brethren had gained majorities in the faculty clubs of Cairo and Asyut Universities. Success in nongovernment associations has given the *Ikhwan* a chance to be heard among the educated in Egypt. At a 1991 conference organized in Zagazig by the Engineers' Syndicate, for example, representatives of the Brotherhood decried the excesses of emergency law and the restrictions on civil liberties.

The increased stature of the Brethren at the syndicate level led the Egyptian government in February 1993 to introduce a new law—Syndicate Law 100—which decrees that 50 percent of syndicate members must vote in order for elections to be considered valid.[44] The government has thus found it necessary to combat the political ascendance of the Muslim Brotherhood, first in national elections by changing the election laws, and then in syndicate elections by introducing a new legislative constraint. Another legislative hurdle was introduced in February 1995, this time giving the judiciary the power to intervene in syndicate elections. In further attempts to discredit and weaken the influence of the Brotherhood, particularly as the November 1995 People's Assembly elections approached, five Islamist members of the Doctors' Syndicate were detained in March and charged with using medical relief operations outside of Egypt as a cover for military training. In April 1996 the government once again maneuvered to reduce Brotherhood control of professional syndicates. The Lawyers' Syndicate, which was under the control of the Brotherhood and had staged political demonstrations against government policies, was charged with financial mismanagement and placed under the control of court-appointed custodians.

It remains to be seen what avenue the Brethren will take to bypass the most recent restrictions, but if earlier patterns are any indication, protests will remain confined to legally accepted channels. This includes communication of the Brotherhood's platform to the population by use of the written word. Both the Liberal and Labor Parties provide the Brotherhood a media platform to disseminate the Islamist message, and Brethren write articles for *Al-Haqiqa* and *Al-'Usra al-'Arabiyya*, both operated by the Liberal Party, and for *Al-Sha'b*, the Labor Party newspaper.

The Brethren periodically issue announcements stating their views, most often condemning violence and calling for liberalization of the political process. Announcements in the aftermath of the 1990 boycott included demands for the freedom to form political parties and freedom of expression for all political tendencies, thus maintaining the Brotherhood's accommodationist strategy. Such themes are discussed in sermons at mosques and at religious celebrations: in 1991 General Guide Abu al-Nasr used a celebration at al-Huda Mosque in Helwan, commemorating the Prophet Muhammad's *hijra* (migration to Medina), to protest the government's denial of party status for the Brotherhood.

Significantly, therefore, newspaper articles, speeches at conferences, announcements issued, and sermons at mosques all suggest that accommodation of the political system continues to be a major Brotherhood strategy, despite the 1990 election boycott. Because the Brotherhood's influence has become too pervasive for it to withdraw from the electoral process, it will continue to seek ways to more firmly entrench its presence. As one scholar says of the Brethren, "They are a part of the political system, not an Islamic alternative to it."[45]

As the Brethren have won representation in the People's Assembly and professional associations, they have also aroused criticism from adversaries both within and outside of Egypt. Western critics are suspicious of the Brotherhood's participation in parliamentary elections, fearing that the Brethren are using elections as a tactic to gain power and subsequently do away with the democracy that gave them their voice. Domestically, other factions of the Islamist movement have criticized the Brotherhood for its apparent willingness to cooperate with the government. In the local elections of 1992 the criticism was evident in Upper Egypt, where the Brotherhood failed to receive significant electoral support. Also, the more militant Islamists charge the Brethren with abandoning the principle of *jihad* and allowing themselves to be co-opted by the ruling regime.

What, therefore, do the Brethren hope to achieve by defying such criticism and becoming part of the system whose very foundation they wish to change? Interestingly, despite their representation and activities in the People's Assembly and despite their critics who attack them for being part of the system, the Brethren do not acknowledge being such. They insist that they are simply changing the system from within. As Ma'mun al-Hudaybi argues:

> I've said many times, we entered elections under the slogan "Islam is the solution." How can it be said that we participate in the existing system when we are trying to change it in the preferred manner—by changing institutions with institutions?[46]

Other Brotherhood leaders insist that because the Egyptian government has declared its constitution to be based on Islam as the official religion of the state, and because the British have long been expelled from Egypt in fulfillment of the Brotherhood's original goal to remove foreign domination, there is no longer a need for a strong confrontation between the Brotherhood and the government. Significantly, leaders argue that antagonism (*mukhasama*) against the government is not an objective in itself and that the Brethren must achieve their goals through the legal channels available through the constitution.[47]

The Brotherhood has thus taken a conciliatory stance, partially in response to the government's move in May 1980 to amend Article 2 of the constitution, making Islamic *shari'a* the only source of legislation. The Brotherhood views this as the first step in the long trek to implementing Islamic law. This political accommodation by the Brotherhood takes on significance when one considers the nature of the government's posture toward Islamic law, which is basically one of promises without subsequent action. Fauzi Najjar notes that

> the Egyptian government has deliberately procrastinated [in] the codification of Islamic laws but always affirmed its commitment to Islam and its religious and cultural values. . . . The Mubarak government has followed a dual policy: it strives to appease the Islamists with equivocal statements while it pursues the normal activities and policies required by its international position.[48]

By suggesting that the government is no longer an enemy because it has changed the constitution in the desired way, the Brotherhood confirms its commitment to work within the present system, despite the government's snail's pace approach to change and obvious hesitation to implement the legislation demanded by the Islamists.

Dissemination of the Message

This therefore brings us back to the original question: Why has the Brotherhood chosen to work within the system instead of battling it through extralegal mechanisms? Primarily, the Brotherhood hopes that an insider status will encourage political and economic reform, and it also views the election *campaign* as an ideal apparatus for promulgating its message of Islam as the solution. As Mustafa Mashhur stresses, election campaigns allow the Brethren to spread the word of God. In campaigns the masses become aware that Islam is not solely for worship, but that it is comprehensive, that it covers life in its entirety, both in this world and the hereafter. Writing before the 1990 election boycott, Mashhur notes that gaining representation in the People's Assembly allows access to a platform that is immune to legal restrictions and from which the Brotherhood "can clarify what is meant by 'Islam is the solution,' and thereby make people at all levels aware."[49]

Furthermore, Muslim Brothers argue, membership in the Assembly allows the Brotherhood to hold the government accountable for its positions and actions in light of Islamic regulations. Brethren recognize that the government's response to their requests will be limited; but, they insist, at least the Brotherhood will have been heard by God and the people, thereby gaining credit and a positive impression among the people while simultaneously detracting from the popularity of the ruling National Democratic Party.[50] Muhammad Ma'mun al-Hudaybi suggests that by participating in the government the Brotherhood is able to gain the support of the masses.[51]

Participation in the existing electoral system thus serves a very basic purpose, whether or not it leads quickly to the changes demanded by the Brotherhood. The electoral platform and seats in the People's Assembly provide a major tool used by the Brethren to advance their *da'wa* by sidestepping the many legislative restrictions that otherwise would prevent promulgation of their message. The boycott of 1990 was not a withdrawal from the entire electoral process; it was a protest against the government's attempts to decrease the Brotherhood presence in the People's Assembly. Political participation is crucial to the Brotherhood, for it provides a mode of communication that promotes awareness at the societal level, thus aiding in the creation of the Islamic society that is at the core of the Brotherhood's long-term ambitions. It is also a method of keeping the ruler in check in accordance with the Islamic belief that rulers are accountable both to God and to the people.

There is more to participation in the system than these instrumental functions, however. Also critical to the Brotherhood is the very essence of Islam as a comprehensive system, governing not only the spiritual but also the material. In response to criticism that the Brotherhood is overly concerned with politics, Dr. Ahmad al-Malt, deputy to General Guide Abu al-Nasr and president of the Islamic Medical Association, notes that politics is part of Islam because Islam is concerned equally with this world and the hereafter. Worldly issues must be addressed as a religious duty. Brotherhood member of Parliament Ahmad al-Bis agrees that working for politics is working for Islam.[52]

The Brotherhood has thus accommodated itself to working within the established system, not as recognition of the inherent virtues of the system, but in hopes of gradually enlightening the masses so that eventually the Islamic nation will be formed. As noted earlier, the group is not content with its de facto recognition by the state, which is by no means a legal recognition of its status as a political party; but the Brotherhood believes it important that the state recognize and cooperate with the Brotherhood, so that misperceptions can be erased and society's ills can be redressed.

Affirmation of Nonviolence

Western scholars often cite the use of violence by Islamists as evidence of the noncivil nature of the Islamic movement. A movement that achieves its goals through the use of violence is, by definition, intolerant of other viewpoints and cannot be considered part of "civil society." Although there are militant groups in Egypt that do use violence, this does not justify lumping together all organizations in the movement and placing the whole outside the civil society paradigm. The Brotherhood, the largest faction in the Islamic movement, has for reasons both philosophical and pragmatic, shown itself to be tolerant of the slow pace of reform and of the numerous government restrictions on its behavior. Its proclamations also affirm a commitment to party politics and constitutionalism, which suggests a tolerance of opposition viewpoints in the political system.

The militant tendencies of some Islamist factions are criticized by the Brotherhood, but, whereas many political analysts lay the blame for the violence on the groups themselves, or even on the *jihad* tenet of Islam, the Brotherhood thinks otherwise. Political violence is considered the result of the government's refusal to acknowledge the legitimacy of the calls for a return to Islam. With a change of orientation and behavior by the state, the Brotherhood argues, more moderate factions in the Islamist movement (i.e., the Brotherhood) will be able to preempt the growth of radicalism and militancy by appealing to the Egyptian people's inherent sense of justice.

The foregoing discussion of the Brethren's major strategy focuses entirely on legitimate, constitutional mechanisms promoted by the group's leadership. Most obvious in its current strategies is the Brotherhood's purposeful repudiation of violence as a means to achieve an Islamic society. Indeed, the contemporary Muslim Brotherhood takes offense at the charge that it engages in violence and terrorism against the state and civilians. In his exposé on the thought of Hasan al-Banna, al-Tilmisani promotes al-Banna's interpretation of *jihad*. Confirming that *jihad* is an important obligation for each Muslim, al-Tilmisani emphasizes that there exists a holy interdiction against aggression *(tahrim al-'idwan)* and offensive attacks. Instead, he asserts, *jihad* prescribes "justice towards enemies and the guidance of Muslims to show mercy in this respect."[53] Similarly, while announcing that *jihad* continues to be the Brotherhood's method and "death on behalf of God is our highest hope," Dr. al-Malt notes that *jihad* requires not violence but words: "We state the word of truth. . . . We summon with every available means, distant from evil, distant from offensive actions. Wisdom and good advice are our religion."[54]

This is reminiscent of al-Banna's moderate tone. Although he insisted that Muslims must stand up to political leaders who colluded with the West, he noted that "one of the loftiest forms of *jihad* is to utter a word of truth in the presence of a tyrannical ruler."[55]

The emphasis on nonviolence contrasts with the image of the Brotherhood that developed from the 1940s to the 1960s, that of a violent organization committed to the forceful overthrow of the political system. In 1948 the "secret apparatus" of the Brotherhood assassinated a judge and a police chief; in 1949 it assassinated Prime Minister Mahmud Fahmi al-Nuqrashi; in 1954 President Nasser was the target of a planned assassination attempt; and in 1965 the Brotherhood was accused of an armed plot against the government.

Acknowledging that in the past members of the organization did employ violence against the state (although the group claims that some of these charges were fabricated), the Brethren argue that such tactics are now history and deny that violence is a method authorized by the contemporary association. The emphasis today, in accordance with their support of constitutional avenues for change, is on a total renunciation of the use of violence. For example, leader Ahmad Hasanayn argues that "the Brethren are given credit for terrorism even if they condemn the act. This is a major injustice. It is wrong to accuse Islam for the activities of an individual who undertakes an action not approved by religion."[56]

Hasanayn insists that terror has never been ordered by the Brotherhood, even when repression by the state was at its highest, as in 1954 and 1965 when the organization was suppressed. He argues that had terror truly been in the nature of the Brethren, they would have taken revenge upon the state when they were faced with its repression.

However, Hasanayn acknowledges that, although the Brotherhood itself is nonviolent, violent offshoots have sprouted from its umbrella. This is due not to the Brotherhood's command, he states, but to the "psychological and social pressures of societal dissolution and to the state's failure to announce its seriousness to change laws that contradict the law of God." Violence at the hands of individual Islamists erupts not because of organizational doctrine, but because of the inability of the Brotherhood to control its followers. And this, he insists, is a result of the restrictive policies of the state in its perpetual nonrecognition of the Brotherhood. Because the group lacks "the opportunity for youth to have general meetings and debates, to straighten misunderstandings, and to unify their methods, . . . there arose a loss of control and disparity between the youth who are overly enthusiastic and those who possess a more rational orientation."[57] The violence that takes place at the hands of Islamists, therefore, occurs not at the directive of the Brotherhood, but as a result of government restrictions that leave legitimate channels of political action closed to those with Islamist tendencies.

Today's leaders of the Brotherhood do not deny that violence has been committed by both Brethren acting on their own and members of more militant groups that might actually have grown out of the Brotherhood. But, despite this acknowledgment, the leaders provide no moral justification for the use of violence in pursuit of religious ideals; in fact, the Brotherhood has often condemned acts of violence undertaken by militant groups. It denounced, for example, the coup attempt of 1974 at the Military Technical Academy by Salih Siriyya's *Hizb al-Tahrir al-Islami* (Islamic Liberation Party) and the assassination of Minister of Islamic Affairs Shaykh Muhammad al-Dhahabi by Shukri Mustafa's *al-Takfir wa al-Hijra* (Denouncement and Holy Flight) in 1977. More recently, Ma'mun al-Hudaybi criticized the Islamist assassination attempt on the life of former Interior Minister Hasan Abu Basha, stressing, "We [the Brethren] condemn and loath this method."[58] According to al-Hudaybi, violence is un-Islamic: "Our position with regard to [violence] is clear and permanent. It contradicts Islamic *shari'a*, the constitution and law, and human rights."[59] Similarly, General Guide Abu al-Nasr stresses that "violence is a result of not understanding Islam."[60]

Significantly, the Brethren's condemnation of violence continues in the aftermath of their 1990 boycott of the People's Assembly elections, indicating that violence will not replace the electoral route. In April 1993, they issued an announcement against the assassination attempt on Minister of Information Safwat al-Sharif in which they stated: "Islam does not permit killing. Islam values the human spirit and made harming it one of the major sins in God's view."[61] In another announcement, issued in response to the assassination attempt on Minister of Interior Hasan al-Alfi, the Brethren state that "the attack was a devaluation of the human soul. . . . Religion cannot justify it."[62]

Similar views on violence were published in *Al-Sha'b* in response to the sectarian conflict that plagued Egypt in the early 1990s. Mustafa Mashhur, for example, writes that "Islam confirms freedom, equality, and security for Muslims and non-Muslims. It condemns each Muslim who attacks a non-Muslim. . . . The true Muslim . . . protects the rights of non-Muslims."[63] In addition, the Brethren's position on violence was featured in a 1993 issue of *Al-Da'wa* magazine, printed in Pakistan. In an article entitled "How Can We Stop the Chain of Violence?" 'Isam al-'Aryan, assistant secretary-general of the Doctors' Syndicate, condemns recent attacks on tourists in Egypt not only on moral grounds but also with reference to the lack of pragmatism involved in violence. He argues that such tactics will not lead to desired changes in the political system. "Rather, the opposite. The political system increases its violence and the situation is transformed to revenge and counterrevenge. . . . I support the state's taking its own revenge by applying the law and judging the guilty through the use of law."[64]

Other Brethren writing in the *Al-Da'wa* article insist that by continuing to leave the Islamist movement out of the political system Egypt will be unable to resolve the issue of violence. Abu al-'Ala Madi, then deputy secretary-general of the Engineers' Syndicate, suggests that the best way to combat the political violence that was becoming increasingly common in the early 1990s is by incorporating all the political parties and groups into the political system. In this manner, "a popular conception that confronts violence" can be created.[65] Thus the Brethren, despite boycotting the elections of 1990, continue to demonstrate their intent to work within the system and continue demanding full entry into the political process. In addition, their discourse argues for participation in the political process by all parties, for recognition of the rights of other religious groups, and for application of the rule of law in dealing with militant organizations. Muslim Brotherhood positions demonstrate respect for a political system based on principles of pluralism.

The political pragmatism, emphasis on institutional reform as opposed to revolution, and condemnation of violence now declared by the Muslim Brotherhood are signs that the group has distanced itself from the more militant views of ideologue Sayyid Qutb in favor of the original, moderate stance of the group's founder, Hasan al-Banna. Theoretically, this also entails a shift away from Qutb's charge of *takfir* (judging others to be unbelievers), which the more militant groups (e.g., *al-Takfir wa al-Hijra, al-Jihad*) have adopted. In his criticism of Egyptian society in *Ma'alim fi al-Tariq*, Qutb applied the concept of *jahiliyya* (paganism or the state of ignorance before the coming of Islam) to both rulers and society, and insisted that any nominal Muslim who did not uphold the Islamic tenets was a *kafir* (unbeliever who was no longer Muslim). This laid the groundwork for Qutb's authorization of active revolution, because *jahiliyya* and Islam could not coexist in the same social order.[66] Indeed, Qutb's very definition of *jihad* was as "a complete armed rebellion" against rule by secular laws,[67] a definition much more militant than the view that *jihad* is a personal struggle for the betterment of self and society.

Qutb's view differed from the thought of al-Banna, who hesitated to judge society so harshly, preferring instead to teach and propagandize until Islamic society was built peacefully. John Voll has dated the contemporary shift away from Sayyid Qutb and back to Hasan al-Banna to the year 1969, when the Brotherhood's General Guide Hasan al-Hudaybi (successor to al-Banna) published his book, *Du'ah la Qudah* (*Missionaries, Not Judges*), written in prison in the 1960s. In this book, al-Hudaybi "rejected the practice of *takfir*, thereby rejecting the rationale for active revolution," and stressed that Egyptians need only to be educated in matters of Islam.[68] Whereas Qutb had believed that true Muslims could not live in a *jahiliyya* state, al-Hudaybi believed that they could survive and that Muslims are held responsible *as individuals* for their adherence to Islamic codes of conduct. This change in Brotherhood ideology is critical, for it no longer holds individuals responsible for the actions of society at large; on the contrary, in a tone much more moderate than that of Qutb, al-Hudaybi stresses the need for society to work collectively to establish an Islamic government, without branding any individual Muslim as a *kafir*, and without calling radically for revolution to uproot the un-Islamic system of government.

In the aftermath of al-Hudaybi's death, the contemporary Brotherhood has not returned to the practice of branding society as unbelievers and consequently has continued to shun the use of political violence in pursuit of the ideal Islamic society. It must be noted that in their condemnation of violence it is not uncommon to find the Brotherhood members accusing the Egyptian government of using that same method often attributed to Islamist fundamentalists—terrorism.

Jabir Rizq, editor in chief of the Islamist *Liwa' al-Islam*, expounds upon both the Brethren's opposition to and the state's resort to violence:

> We do not defend terrorism. Nor do we authorize it; because Islam does not authorize nor approve terrorism. However, we remind writers to be objective and fair, because the Egyptian people have suffered from government terror for half a century, much more than they have suffered from the terrorism of religious groups. . . . We thus ask writers to challenge terrorism in all its images.[69]

Brethren harshly criticize what they view as government terrorism against Islamists, particularly insofar as the Egyptian regime systematically uses arrests and torture.[70] Brethren engage in an ongoing critique of both individual and government violence, but it is the latter kind that is considered the more threatening. 'Isam al-'Aryan, for example, quoted earlier for his opposition to Islamist violence against tourists, states also that "The state is primarily responsible for the violence that occurs, and it must judge itself and make its role consistent with the law."[71] The Brotherhood urges the government to discontinue the tactic of punishing whole families and villages for the actions of militant individuals, arguing that by so doing the Egyptian regime has made an enemy of the citizenry.

Thus, although there is an affirmation of Brotherhood support for the relative democratic opening in Egypt, there is also a strong condemnation of the government's heavy-handed methods of combating the Islamists. Moreover, the Brotherhood fears that the government and its media might promote the view that all Islamist activists are characterized by the same militancy seen in the radical branch of the movement. This, argues the Brotherhood, is erroneous and misleading. Violence has been definitively renounced, and the Brethren are working actively within the established political system out of a conviction that they are thereby promoting their *da'wa* and proceeding toward their goal of an Islamic state.

In fact, the government, although for the most part tolerating the Brotherhood, does arrest members when they overstep the bounds of acceptable criticism of government. For example, Brethren were arrested and tortured in 1990 for their opposition to the peace process. In 1991 Brethren, including some former People's Assembly members and the editor of *Liwa' al-Islam*, were also arrested for opposing the Egyptian government's part in the Madrid peace talks. Middle East Watch has determined that torture in Egypt "is used as a mechanism to define the limits of acceptable political activity."[72] This raises the fear that such attempts at marginalizing the Brotherhood might lead the disillusioned to sprout new militant appendages, as was the case in the Brotherhood's earlier days.

Conclusion

The Muslim Brotherhood shares interests with both its predecessors in the history of Islamist thought in Egypt and with the groups that emerged after the Brotherhood. The efforts of all the Islamist groups have been focused on applying Islamic *shari'a* to the social and political systems of their nation. As explained above, the major goal pursued by the Brotherhood is the establishment of an Islamic state governed by Islamic jurisprudence. Even though this goal is no doubt alien to Western political thought, and perhaps even threatening in the view of many scholars, it is significant that the Brotherhood's vision of an Islamic state encompasses other, less alien objectives: (1) the imposition of democratic ideals such as liberty, representation, and accountability, and (2) the pursuit of socioeconomic justice.

The Brethren's major strategy is a pragmatic accommodation of the existing political system, for the group has become totally focused on constitutional channels to institute the changes they envision. Notably, the election process has become important both in order to gain parliamentary and syndicate representation and, perhaps more important, to gain access to an unrestricted channel through which the group's Islamist message can be disseminated to the Egyptian masses. The government has attempted to curb access to both Parliament and professional associations, but it is worth observing that the Brethren nevertheless continue their calls for constitutional access to the political system. They have thus not abandoned the system that is apparently trying to abandon them. Most critical here is the absolute resort to constitutionally recognized strategies and the equally absolute renunciation of violence as a strategy. Although Westerners and militant Islamists alike often interpret *jihad* as an armed struggle against the state, the Brethren have chosen an alternative interpretation, that of a personal and collective struggle employing social justice, mercy, and communication, so that an Islamic state will be built from the individual upward.

The Brotherhood's emphasis on the accountability of rulers and responsibility of the individual is not new in Islamic thinking; indeed, Taqi al-Din Ahmad Ibn Taymiyya, in the fourteenth century, had demanded that society should engage in *jihad* against a ruler who did not obey the *shari'a*. Accountability is an old Islamic notion, notwithstanding the fact that in most of the contemporary states of the Middle East, there are virtually no mechanisms for the peaceful transfer of power from a head of state to a successor. It is understood, though not out of the preference of the masses, that a head of state will maintain his throne until death. It is this lack of a mechanism for peaceful succession that makes the Brotherhood's calls for accountability both meaningful and timely.

The Brotherhood's demands that rulers be held accountable forces a reevaluation of the perception of Muslim societies as submissive to authority even if the political order is unjust or tyrannical. Too often, Islamic culture has been viewed as nonparticipatory and therefore incompatible with democratic governance. The activist demand that rulers must enforce Islamic law has led to a new image of Islamic society—that of a restive, demanding, unacquiescent, and unsubmissive Muslim population. This changing image requires that we reevaluate the potential fit between Muslim society and democracy. If previous Islamic societies were incompatible with democracy because of their total submission to authority, are today's Muslims more compatible due to their demands to participate in the political system? If so, why are scholars and governments alike so hesitant to encourage unfettered participation by the Muslim masses?

Regardless of our answers to these questions, we are now facing the reality of a movement that will not subside merely because of our reluctance to accept its growth. At the political center of the movement, the Muslim Brotherhood is proving to be a highly pragmatic organization that has rejected violence and that calls for the expansion of democracy in a state ruled by Islamic legislation. Notwithstanding scholarly debate on the compatability of the latter two features, the Brethren have at least given Egypt a moderate platform that pursues the Islamic ideals sought by many other groups in a more militant fashion.

The Egyptian government (and its U.S. and European backers) has shown a preoccupation with the more militant forces within the Islamist movement, leading to repression against even mainstream, peaceful activism. Unfortunately, this might be a self-defeating policy insofar as it threatens to confirm the militants' belief that the government is anti-Islamic and thus must be fought by any means. The regime has consistently pushed the extremes of coercion to battle the Islamist movement. While professing an intent to democratize, thus encouraging political opponents to engage in the political process, the regime unflinchingly cracks down on opposition when it realizes, in the words of Anwar Sadat, that "democracy has fangs." The imperative to maintain political stability (and to preserve

National Democratic Party rule) takes precedence over the public demands for democratization.

Many scholars insist that the Islamist movement in all its parts must be subdued, but we argue that groups with a verifiable commitment to pluralism and constitutionalism might serve some positive functions in Egypt. Indeed, the Brotherhood can function as a legitimate outlet for the grievances of the Egyptian masses and thereby mitigate the growth of support for the radicals. This might require the Egyptian government to grant the Brotherhood the legal recognition it demands so that it can function as a full-fledged political party. By bringing the Brotherhood fully into the folds of government, the state will have isolated the militant trends and given those segments of the population demanding Islamist representation a legitimate alternative to the use of violence. A preoccupation with the separation of church and state, while perhaps appropriate for Western publics, might not be as appropriate in the eyes of Muslims who stress the intricate connections and overlapping between their religion and the preferred role of the state. More important, recognizing the Brotherhood as a party and allowing it—and its secular opponents—to compete in fair elections will help to legitimize the electoral process and promote the long-term stability desired by the regime. A democracy is better able to deal with opposition politics, particularly because it does not intuitively embrace coercive measures that delegitimize its authority and encourage the instability it seeks to avoid.

Notes

1. The contemporary Brotherhood's philosophy is ascertained primarily through an analysis of the themes emphasized by their leadership in the Islamic monthly newsmagazine, *Liwa' al-Islam*. Other organs for the dissemination of the Brotherhood's philosophy, for example, *Al-Sha'b* and *Al-Da'wa* (published in Pakistan), and public announcements are used to supplement this major source. All translations from Arabic to English are made by the authors.
2. Hasan al-Banna, *Five Tracts of Hasan al-Banna (1906–1949): A Selection from the Majmu'at Rasa'il al-Imam al-Shahid Hasan al-Banna*, trans. and annot. Charles Wendell (Berkeley: University of California Press, 1978), p. 48.
3. Ibid., p. 48.
4. Ibid., p. 155.
5. Ibid., p. 118.
6. Ibid., p. 89.
7. Ibid., introduction by Charles Wendell, p. 5.
8. Qutb was first arrested and held for three months in early 1954. After the assassination attempt on Nasser in October 1954, Qutb was arrested

again in the mass arrests that followed. He endured severe torture, resulting in his transfer to a prison hospital, and in July 1955 he was sentenced to fifteen years in prison. After a short release from prison in May 1964, Qutb was again arrested in August 1965 on charges of terrorism.

9. Sayyid Qutb, *Ma'alim fi al-Tariq* (Cairo: Dar al-Shuruq, 1980). The title is also translated as "Signposts" and "Milestones" by different scholars.

10. Ibid., p. 67.

11. Ibid., p. 72.

12. Gilles Kepel, *Muslim Extremism in Contemporary Egypt* (London: Al-Saqi Books, 1985), p. 28.

13. The October War of 1973 has become the symbol of the relevance of religion. Folklore has it that because the war was launched in the climate of religiosity, during the Muslim holy month of Ramadan, and with the code name "Operation Badr," Egypt was able to cross the Suez Canal in a successful attack on Israel. "Badr" was a significant name because of its reference to the Prophet Muhammad's successful war against infidels, in which the Muslims were assisted by an army of angels.

14. This message was delivered through Sadat's private advisor, Dr. Mahmud Mu'awwad Jami', and related in an interview with Ayman al-Sayyad, "'Ala Lisan Munsha'ayha wa Qadatha: Al-Tarikh al-Siri Li Jama'at 'al-Jihad' fi Misr," *Al-Majalla*, 14 May 1994, 28.

15. Ibid., p. 28.

16. Ibid., p. 30.

17. 'Umar al-Tilmisani, "Do the Missionaries for God Have a Program?" *Liwa' al-Islam*, June 1987, p. 7.

18. See Iliya Harik, *Economic Reform in Egypt* (Gainesville: University Press of Florida, 1997).

19. Ibid., p. 7.

20. Hasan al-Banna, *The Reform of Self and Society*, quoted in Sami Zubaida, *Islam. The People and the State* (London: Routledge, 1989), p. 48.

21. Ahmad S. Moussalli, *Sayyid Qutb: The Ideologist of Islamic Fundamentalism*, Abstract from *Al-Abhath*, V. XXXVIII, 1990, p. 60.

22. Charles E. Butterworth, "Prudence Versus Legitimacy: The Persistent Theme in Islamic Political Thought," in Ali E. Hillal Dessouki, ed. *Islamic Resurgence in the Arab World* (New York: Praeger Publishers, 1982), p. 95.

23. Al-Tilmisani, "Missionaries," p. 8.

24. Muhammad 'Abdallah al-Khatib, "Al-Ifta' [Legal Opinion]," *Liwa' al-Islam*, January 1990, p. 60.

25. Zaynab al-Ghazali al-Jubayli, "Complete Joy at the Return of *al-Da'wa*," *Al-Da'wa*, 6 May 1993, p. 38.

26. John O. Voll, "Fundamentalism in the Sunni Arab World," in Martin E. Marty and R. Scott Appleby, ed. *Fundamentalisms Observed* (Chicago: University of Chicago Press, 1991), p. 366.

27. Jihad al-Kurdi, "The Muslim Brotherhood and Democracy: Conference Transformed to Confrontation," *Liwa' al-Islam*, October 1990, p. 15. This article was an analysis of a conference held in Cairo from 29 September to 1 October 1990 on "The Development of Democracy in the Arab World."

28. Ibid., p. 15.

29. "Representatives of the Muslim Brotherhood Respond to the Government's Report," *Liwa' al-Islam*, February 1989, p. 28.

30. Ibid., p. 28.

31. Al-Sadiq 'Abduh, "President Mubarak and the Islamic Movement After Six Years," *Liwa' al-Islam*, September 1987, p. 27.
32. "Representatives of the Muslim Brotherhood Respond to the Government's Report," *Liwa' al-Islam*, February 1989, p. 28.
33. Al-Sadiq 'Abduh, "President Mubarak," p. 27.
34. Muhammad Hamid Abu al-Nasr, "Editorial: Liberties, Between Application and Slogans," *Liwa' al-Islam*, August 1988, p. 5.
35. Muhammad Hamid Abu al-Nasr, "Editorial: Valuable Freedom," *Liwa' al-Islam*, July 1990, pp. 4–5.
36. Al-Sadiq 'Abduh, "What Has the Muslim Brotherhood Offered?" *Liwa' al-Islam*, September 1987, p. 14.
37. Ann M. Lesch, "The Muslim Brotherhood in Egypt: Reform or Revolution?" in Matthew C. Moen and Lowell S. Gustafson, eds. *The Religious Challenge to the State* (Philadelphia: Temple University Press, 1992), p. 201.
38. Ibid., p. 203.
39. Ibid., p. 183.
40. John L. Esposito and James P. Piscatori, "Democratization and Islam," *The Middle East Journal* 45, no. 3, (Summer 1991): 429.
41. Al-Ahram Center for Political and Strategic Studies, "Parties and Political Power," *Arab Strategic Report: 1992* (Cairo: Al-Ahram Center for Political and Strategic Studies), 1993, p. 320.
42. *Al-Safir Newspaper* (Lebanon), 7 September 1993, quoted in Al-Ahram Center for Political and Strategic Studies, "Parties and Political Power," *Arab Strategic Report: 1993*, (Cairo: Al-Ahram Center for Political and Strategic Studies), 1994, p. 334.
43. Mustafa Mashhur, "Islam Calls Us to Unite the Egyptian Nation," *Al-Sha'b*, 1 October 1991, p. 5.
44. Al-Ahram Center for Political and Strategic Studies, "Parties and Political Power," 1994, p. 334–335.
45. 'Abdel 'Azim Ramadan, "Fundamentalist Influence in Egypt: The Strategies of the Muslim Brotherhood and the Takfir Groups," in Martin E. Marty and R. Scott Appleby, eds. *Fundamentalisms and the State: Remaking Polities, Economies, and Militance* (Chicago: University of Chicago Press, 1991), p. 177.
46. Salah 'Abd al-Maqsud, "Ten Charges Against the Society [Muslim Brotherhood]," *Liwa' al-Islam* February 1989, p. 14.
47. Ibid., p. 14.
48. Fauzi M. Najjar, "The Application of Shari'a Laws in Egypt," *Middle East Policy* 1, no. 3 (1992): 72–73.
49. Mustafa Mashhur, "Elections: On the Road to the Call," *Liwa' al-Islam*, June 1987, p. 10.
50. Ibid., p. 10.
51. Majdi Mustafa, "The Muslim Brotherhood in the People's Assembly: Trial and Results; Dialogue with Ma'mun al-Hudaybi," *Liwa' al-Islam*, June 1990, pp. 24–25.
52. 'Abd al-Maqsud, "Ten Charges," p. 13.
53. Al-Tilmisani, "Missionaries," p. 8.
54. 'Abd al-Maqsud, "Ten Charges," p. 16.
55. Hasan al-Banna, *Five Tracts of Hasan al-Banna*, p. 48.
56. 'Abd al-Maqsud, "Ten Charges," p. 14.
57. Ibid., p. 14.

58. "Dialogue Between Ma'mun al-Hudaybi and Hasan Abu-Basha," *Liwa' al-Islam*, January 1991, p. 26.

59. Ma'mun al-Hudaybi, "Muslim Brotherhood Condemns the Assassination of Dr. 'Ala' Muhi al-Din," *Liwa' al-Islam*, September 1990, p. 41.

60. Muhammad Hamid Abu al-Nasr, "Communiqué Regarding the Minya and Asyut Incidents," *Liwa' al-Islam*, March 1990, p. 7.

61. Quoted in Al-Ahram Center for Political and Strategic Studies, "Parties and Political Power," 1994, p. 338.

62. Ibid., p. 338.

63. Mustafa Mashhur, "Who Are the Terrorists? And Who Are Their Accusers?" *Al-Sha'b*, 3 September 1991, p. 5.

64. "How Can We Stop the Chain of Violence?" *Al-Da'wa*, 6 May 1993, p. 21.

65. Ibid., p. 21.

66. Voll, "Fundamentalism," p. 372–373.

67. Qutb, *Ma'alim fi al-Tariq*, p. 67.

68. Voll, "Fundamentalism," p. 373.

69. Jaber Rizq, "Egypt Between the Terror of Governments and the Terror of Groups," *Liwa' al-Islam*, June 1987, p. 5.

70. Al-Sadiq 'Abduh, "President Mubarak," p. 27.

71. "Chain of Violence," *Al-Da'wa*, p. 21.

72. Middle East Watch, *Behind Closed Doors: Torture and Detention in Egypt*, (New York: Human Rights Watch, 1992), p. 72.

4

Militant Islamist Groups

The constitutional strategies employed by the Muslim Brotherhood and the group's disavowal of political violence render them members of Egypt's civil society. In this regard, the methods of the Brotherhood stand in stark contrast to the methods of the militant Islamist groups that have, since the 1970s, tested the patience of the government and undermined the domestic political stability of the state. Militant groups have waged a violent campaign against the Egyptian regime, both directly, against government agencies and officials, security personnel, and public service personnel, and indirectly, by staging bloody campaigns against persons who contribute unwittingly to the Egyptian economy. These include tourists, who bring in over $3 billion in hard currency per year and whose murder frightens other foreigners from contributing to the Egyptian government coffers. Recently, the wrath of the militants has also been felt by literary figures and intellectuals who criticize the militant forces within the Islamist movement. Social and public institutions that diverge from the militants' interpretation of Islam have also come under attack. For example, banks in Cairo have been targeted because they give or collect interest, and video stores and liquor shops have been attacked because they contradict Islamic ethics.

This chapter analyzes the philosophy and tactics of a select group of militant Islamist organizations—those that have gained notoriety as the most prominent and active of the militant wing. Again, it is important to keep in mind that the Islamist movement is no monolith. Declaring a segment of it as militant and violent does not imply that all who call for the creation of an Islamic political and social order share these characteristics. Nor does it absolve the government of responsibility for adopting strategies and policies that might inadvertently have encouraged the increase of militancy among frustrated segments of the public. The government of Egypt has embarked on an iron-fisted, repressive campaign against the Islamists, imprisoning and executing leaders and members of the militant groups. This strategy, however, can succeed only if security forces discriminately round up those who take part in violence, without terrorizing whole neighborhoods and without apprehending moderate Islamists who have vowed to employ constitutional methods. In this regard, the government has fallen short, risking a further escalation of violence.

The Believer President and the Birth of Militancy

President Anwar Sadat, praying regularly in mosques and bearing the dark forehead mark of the devout Muslim, created an aura of religiosity around himself as the "father" or "lord" of the Egyptian family (*rab al-'a'ila al-Misriyya*). The Egyptian media portrayed Sadat as the Believer President (*al-Ra'is al-Mu'min*),[1] and his public projection of piety differed from his predecessor's secular, socialist persona. In an era in which Egyptians and the Arab world at large were mourning the loss of successive wars to Israel, Sadat outwardly showed his faith in Islam by waging the 1973 October War with Israel within the framework of Islamic symbolism and during the Islamic holy month of Ramadan. His code name for the October War, in which Egypt was able to cross the Suez Canal in a successful attack on Israel, was "Operation Badr," after the Prophet Muhammad's successful war against the infidels of Mecca. The success of the crossing brought back the pride that had been shattered following the 1967 defeat by Israel, and the religious overtones of the 1973 war stood in stark contrast to the secular framework within which the 1967 war was fought and lost.

Those who knew him attest to Sadat's authentic personal piety and faith (*iman*). Nevertheless, it is also recognized that Sadat, attempting to fill the presidential chambers held previously by the charismatic Nasser, was trying to carve his own niche in a sea of secular (Nasserist and leftist) opposition. His strategy in this effort involved the tolerance and encouragement of young groups with Islamist inclinations and is said to have resulted in the growth of the militant movement.[2] Although Sadat initially followed Nasser's lead by restricting severely the activities of political opponents, he nevertheless came to find it politically expedient to encourage the development of a more Islamic sociopolitical milieu on university campuses to rally against the ideologies carried over from the Nasser days. This involved both the aforementioned release of imprisoned

Muslim Brothers and facilitation of the activities of the emerging Islamist student associations in universities, *al-jama'at al-Islamiyya*, as a counterforce to the ideologies of leftists and Nasserists, whom he considered his real political opponents. In a lengthy interview, Sadat's private advisor, Dr. Mahmud Mu'awwad Jami', sheds light on Sadat's proactive role in the growth of the Islamist movement in the 1970s.[3] He states that Sadat clearly expressed his intention to encourage the growth of Islamic youth to counter the leftist and Nasserist trends in universities. According to Jami', Sadat said, "I want us to raise Muslim boys, and to spend money on them, so they can become *rakizitna* [our anchor] in the university."[4] Sadat instructed his aides to "create an Islamic *tayyar* [movement]," a mission they tackled by organizing summer camps for university students.[5]

The net result of Sadat's approach, particularly coming on the heels of Nasser's secular regime that had been unable to defeat Israel, was the encouragement of the *al-jama'at al-Islamiyya* on university campuses. Before long, Islamist groups were holding meetings in universities and running successfully in student union elections.[6] As they grew, the groups chose a leader for each university *jama'a* and established one *majlis 'am* (general assembly) that covered *jama'at* throughout the country. The *majlis* had one leader, Hilmi al-Jazzar, a medical student at Cairo University. The *jama'at* created followings on university campuses by preaching Islamic observance and social justice and by providing much-needed social and community services to students. Islamic attire, particularly for women, became common, both out of conviction that one should dress modestly, and in an attempt to protect the women from unacceptable sexual advances and relations. The Islamist groups were disturbed by the fact that males and females in the universities and on university buses were not segregated, and they worked to make alternative arrangements, such as providing separate transportation for women. In the universities of Upper Egypt, the groups' activities were confrontational, with students waging a battle against social gatherings and parties in which opposite sexes mingled and against Christians, who constitute a significant minority in southern Egypt. As Islamist youths clashed with Christian and secular students and faculty members, tensions grew between Muslims and Christians. Sectarian violence thus ensued in the early 1970s, especially in the Upper Egypt province of Asyut, and has continued in Upper Egypt through the 1990s.

The groups' preoccupation with matters of Islamic morality did not preclude the adoption of positions on political matters, for, after all, as Muslims the students believed that Islamic conduct was expected both from the individual and from his or her political leaders.

The Islamist *jama'at* in the early 1970s focused their political protests, as the president had envisioned, against the leftist and secular tendencies. As Sadat embarked on new foreign policy initiatives, however, their attention turned to the policies of the state. It was not long before the new groups were transformed from political allies into political opponents. In particular, as Sadat made peace overtures toward Israel, the groups became increasingly political and critical. They emphasized the illegitimacy, first, of their president's visit to Jerusalem to address the Israeli Knesset and, second, of the Camp David accords and the process of normalization between Egypt and Israel. Also, the student groups gave moral support to Iran's 1979 Islamic revolution and opposed Sadat's offer of political asylum to Shah Reza Pahlavi following his ouster by the new Islamic regime. A demonstration staged by the students in Asyut expressed their anger toward the ailing shah's presence in their country.

The overall aim of the *jama'at* was the same as that stated by other Islamist groups, including the Muslim Brotherhood: they urged the application of Islamic *shari'a* throughout Egypt. They opposed the government's secular laws and identified specific laws, such as the Law of Shame[7] and the National Unity Law, as contrary to Islamic law. The *jama'at* began writing articles critical of Sadat, sectarian strife grew, and the groups came to be seen as a threat to the authorities.

Sadat was initially patient in the face of the criticism, but before long he was often heard repeating the phrase: "Most fires come from the tiniest sparks."[8] Realizing that the groups posed an increasing threat, he unleashed a series of responses that signaled the end of the regime's positive involvement with the groups. He withheld subsidies from the student unions that were dominated by Islamists; in 1979 his regime outlawed the activities of the religious *jama'at;* and the Central Security Forces shut down Islamic summer youth camps in Alexandria, Cairo, and Zagazig. This, as Rudolph Peters notes, deprived the *jama'at* of their legal cover, their organization, and their funds.[9] The dissolution of the student associations forced their members to disperse into the cities and villages, where, Gilles Kepel notes, "Islamicist cadres and agitators went to preach among the people, making new recruits in the poor neighbourhoods."[10]

By the autumn of 1981 several new Islamist groups had formed to challenge what were considered illegitimate political policies and state secularism. As a result, it was no longer Nasser's enemy, the Muslim Brotherhood, that threatened the secular nature of Egyptian politics. As the *jama'at Islamiyya* grew and then were dispersed among the people, Sadat also faced challenges from *Jama'at al-Muslimin*

(The Society of Muslims, better known as *al-Takfir wa al-Hijra*, or Denouncement and Holy Flight), *Jund Allah* (The Soldiers of God), *Hizb al-Tahrir al-Islami* (The Islamic Liberation Party), *al-Jihad* (Holy Struggle or Holy War), and *al-Jama'a al-Islamiyya* (The Islamic Group). The last, soon to become one of the most violent groups in Egypt, is thought to have developed directly from the student *jama'at*. All these militant Islamist opposition groups did not exist during Nasser's regime, but grew actively during Sadat's era. (Similarly, the Society of Repudiation and Renunciation, the Islamic Vanguards, Those Saved From the Fire, and other Islamist forces later developed during Mubarak's regime.)

It is, of course, an understatement to observe that the year 1981 was for Anwar Sadat a dangerous one. His policies were under scrutiny from Islamist and secular opposition forces alike, and political tensions in his country were heightened. Challengers of all political persuasions were seen as grave threats to regime stability. His personal advisor has noted that Sadat was receiving almost daily reports from security forces suggesting that Egypt was about to fall from his hands, and that "around Sadat there were those who were throwing oil on the fire. These included his wife and some of his friends."[11] Sadat's fears culminated in his infamous arrest wave of September 1981, in which he targeted well over a thousand (reported as three thousand in some sources) political opponents for arrest. In addition to Socialists, Nasserists, and Coptic leaders (including Coptic Pope Shenouda III), Sadat's security services rounded up numerous Islamists in police raids, and Sadat issued a warning that "he would arrest five thousand additional opponents if they did not behave."[12] One of those arrested and tortured in 1981 was Muhammad al-Islambuli, a leader of a student *jama'a* at the University of Asyut. One month later, in October 1981, Muhammad's brother, Lt. Khalid al-Islambuli, assassinated President Anwar Sadat. In the 1990s, more than a decade after Sadat's assassination, another of the Islambuli brothers, Muhammad Shawqi al-Islambuli, was carrying on the legacy of antistate militancy.

Militancy Entrenched

The contemporary militant movement, composed of *Tanzim al-Jihad*, *Jama'at al-Muslimin*, *al-Jama'a al-Islamiyya*, and other, smaller groups, makes up a branch, or wing, of the Islamist movement referred to by Egyptian scholars as *al-Tawaqquf wa al-Tabayyun* ("stop and disclose").[13] The major link between the groups is their fierce and hostile opposition to the state. The *Tawaqquf* wing sees the basis of state and society as *kufr*, or apostasy. Members believe it is imperative that the faithful must "stop" in front of each errant individual or group to "disclose" the extent to which *kufr* has been reduced and the subject has returned to Islam. The roots of the wing have been traced to the prisons of Egypt at the end of the 1960s, when the *Ikhwan al-Muslimin* were imprisoned. Shaykh 'Ali 'Abdu Isma'il, one of the incarcerated leaders of the *Ikhwan*, briefly held the conviction that both *hakim* (ruler) and *mahkum* (ruled) were guilty of *kufr*. He also determined that members of society who are oblivious to the *kufr* of the ruler are themselves *kuffar* (apostates). Isma'il soon abandoned these views, but some of his young associates remained convinced of the veracity of these charges against society and went on to establish groups intent on eradicating the *kufr* from Egypt.

Hizb al-Tahrir al-Islami (The Islamic Liberation Party, or ILP), established by Salih Siriyya, a Palestinian from Jordan, was the first group during the Sadat regime to stage a violent attack based on the principle of *jihad*. In contrast to the gradualist convictions of the Muslim Brotherhood, the ILP believed in the importance of immediately establishing an Islamic state. In 1974, following the conclusion of an Egyptian-Israeli disengagement agreement, ILP members attempted a coup d'état through an abortive takeover of the Military Technical Academy at Heliopolis, earning them the name *Jama'at al-Faniyya al-'Askariyya* (Military Technical Academy Group). In November 1976, Siriyya was executed by the state and group members were forced underground. They apparently joined other emerging associations, and the ILP was replaced by several enduring Islamist groups that have lasted well into the current decade.

Experiences in Egypt's prisons during the Nasser regime contributed to the escalation of militancy among Islamists. Incarcerated Muslim Brothers, under the influence of the radical thought of Sayyid Qutb and 'Ali 'Abdu Isma'il, were also influenced by the excessive torture they suffered in prison. Although some Brothers emerged from the experiences with a more moderate and politically accommodating philosophy, others became even more convinced of the illegitimacy of the state. Scholars of the Islamist movement are in agreement that much of the new militancy developed in response to the torture suffered by the *Ikhwan* in Egypt's prisons.

> When the members of the Muslim Brotherhood were released from jail, they harbored even more resentment and bitterness toward the government because the authorities had inflicted torture on them. They could not reconcile their view of the government with their perception of a pure Islamic society. They wondered how government

officials could torture their own Muslim brothers, and concluded that Egypt was not simply a Muslim society in need of reform, but rather a *kafir* or infidel society, just as Said Kotb [Sayyid Qutb] had thought.[14]

These experiences help explain Islamist violence; they are not used here to justify it.

Al-Takfir wa al-Hijra

Agricultural engineer Shukri Ahmad Mustafa, born in 1942, was one of those most convinced of the misguided nature of the Egyptian state and society. Shukri Mustafa had himself been tortured in prison for distributing Muslim Brotherhood leaflets at Asyut University. Although, within the ideology of the Muslim Brotherhood, the militant dogma of Sayyid Qutb came to be replaced by the more reformist and gradualist ideology of the accommodationists, Qutb's philosophy lived on in Nasser's prisons and came to light again in Mustafa's organization. Mustafa began recruiting members to establish the *Jama'at al-Muslimin,* one of the more militant of the new wave of Islamist groups, while in prison from 1965 to 1971. Upon his release in 1971 he established the Society.[15] Recruitment for the group was centered in Upper Egypt, Cairo, and Alexandria. The Society was dubbed *al-Takfir wa al-Hijra* by the Egyptian press for its declaration of *takfir* (charging a person with apostasy) and *hijra* (holy flight).[16] The group denounces present Egyptian society and its leadership as *kufara* (infidels), which thus makes both legitimate targets. The group's program to reinstate an Islamic society involves three stages. First, *tabligh* requires the spread of the group's ideas through the practice of *da'wa* (preaching). Second, *hijra,* the process of withdrawal from the infidel society, establishes and gives military training to a community of believers, just as the Prophet Muhammad did in his *hijra* from Mecca to Medina (*tabligh* and *hijra* were to be undertaken simultaneously). In practice, Mustafa's group practiced its *hijra* by secluding itself from society, not necessarily by physically migrating to a society outside of Egypt but by living in isolation from society within Egypt: in 1973 the group took up its *hijra* by establishing its society in al-Minya, Egypt. Finally, once the community gains enough strength, it returns to society to eliminate the infidel state and establish a truly Islamic state.

Shukri Mustafa's confrontation with the state came prematurely in late 1976, since he had not yet completed his *hijra* as planned. After dissidents from *al-Takfir wa al-Hijra* were murdered by Mustafa's group, police arrested fourteen of the Society's members and issued a warrant for Mustafa's arrest. In response, Mustafa decided to challenge the state directly.[17] This he did by kidnapping and subsequently, on 4 July 1977, assassinating Shaykh Muhammad al-Dhahabi, the former minister of Islamic affairs (1975–1976). Dhahabi was targeted for having criticized Mustafa's group in an official pamphlet directed against the Society of Muslims.

After the murder, the government assumed the offensive and attempted to eliminate the group. Hundreds of the Society's members were arrested. Five, including Mustafa and his close associates, were executed, and thirty-six others received prison terms ranging from three years to life in prison with hard labor. The government's action, although it weakened the group, did not erase *al-Takfir wa al-Hijra* from the Egyptian militant scene. The government's crackdown did lead to a lull in the Society's activities, but more than one hundred members were later arrested in 1982, indicating that the society must have maintained an underground cell. By the mid-1980s, the *Takfir* group had become known as *al-Shawqiyyin* and was based in Fayyum governorate, eighty kilometers south of Cairo. In April 1990, twenty-five members of *al-Shawqiyyin* were killed in a clash with security forces. While Mustafa's original group had called for *hijra* until society was ripe for Islam, the new group believes in undertaking *hijra* and killing the *kuffar* simultaneously. According to Diya' Rashwan of the Al-Ahram Center for Political and Strategic Studies, the *al-Takfir* group was ultimately transformed into a new, permeable wing that accommodates many militant groups—the *Tawaqquf wa Tabayyun* wing discussed above.[18]

Tanzim al-Jihad

Tanzim al-Jihad, which can be translated as either "Holy War" or "Holy Struggle" Organization, was founded in Alexandria in the late 1970s by Salim al-Rahhal, a Jordanian student at Al-Azhar University, and Hasan Halawi.[19] Both had been members of the ILP, the group that staged an attack on the Military Technical Academy in 1974. They adopted the name *Jihad* in 1977, and the group was discovered in August of that year in Alexandria during a raid by security forces in which arms and explosives were seized and eighty *Jihad* members arrested. After the government crackdown Kamal al-Sa'id Habib, a twenty-four-year-old graduate of Cairo University, became the leader of the Alexandria-based organization. Muhammad 'Abd al-Salam Faraj, a twenty-seven-year-old electrical engineer employed at Cairo

University, joined the *Jihad* organization in 1978. In 1979 the group expanded and established a presence in Cairo under the leadership of Faraj. In 1980, pursuant to a decision to infiltrate the military forces as a strategy to combat the state, 'Abbud 'Abd al-Latif al-Zumur joined the group. He was a thirty-year-old military intelligence officer in the armed forces. After October 1981 Zumur became the military and strategic planner for the group, and he urged an overthrow of the Egyptian state and its replacement by an Islamic caliphate.

During this period *Jihad* was able to attract leaders of the Islamist movement then existing in Upper Egypt, which led to the establishment of a branch of *Jihad* in Upper Egypt under the leadership of Karam Muhammad Zuhdi, a twenty-seven-year-old leader in Asyut. Zuhdi was responsible for recruiting and training new members in Upper Egypt. In 1980 *Jihad* established an eleven-member *Majlis al-Shura* (Consultative Assembly). The *Majlis* had executive and legislative responsibilities and encompassed three committees: *i'dad* (preparation), *da'wa* (preaching), and *iqtisad* (economics). The leaders of *Jihad* then selected as their spiritual leader forty-three-year-old blind cleric Shaykh 'Umar 'Abd al-Rahman, a teacher of religion at Al-Azhar University's Asyut branch. His role was symbolic, in that his presence gave a religious justification to the acts of violence committed by the group, but his leadership over *Jihad* was brief. Al-Rahman subsequently became the *mufti* of *al-Jama'a al-Islamiyya*.

In 1982, Faraj established himself as the ideologue of *Jihad* when he penned the outlawed *Al-Jihad: Al-Farida al-Gha'iba*, commonly translated as "Holy War: The Neglected Duty" or "Holy War: The Missing Religious Precept."[20] In his monograph, Faraj examined the principle of *jihad*, which he defined as armed struggle, as an obligatory precept of the Muslim religion, no less important than the five commonly affirmed pillars of the Islamic faith: fasting, pilgrimage, prayer, *al-shahada* (declaration of faith), and *zakat* (almsgiving). Much of the philosophy of Faraj suggests the intellectual influence of the Brotherhood's Sayyid Qutb, who had also stressed the need for *jihad* as an armed struggle against the illegitimate government. Hasan al-Banna, founder of the Brotherhood, had by contrast stressed the civil nature of the concept of *jihad*, seeing it as a personal and social modus operandi in which one uttered the words of truth and persuasion to a misguided ruler while struggling to better one's spiritual and social lot in life. Thus for al-Banna *jihad* was predominantly a personal struggle, but for Faraj, as it had been for Qutb, *jihad* was an armed struggle with the goal of uprooting the evil in the state and replacing it with Islamic rule.

In his book, Faraj expresses two major goals for Egyptian society: (1) Islamic law must replace secular law, even if this means fighting nominal Muslims who profess the faith while resisting the application of *shari'a*; and (2) current leaders of Muslim countries who have adopted the secular ways of the imperialists (who include Christians [Crusaders], Communists, and Zionists) must be killed.

Faraj is critical of any type of association with the Egyptian regime, and he is critical of interpretations of *jihad* that do not directly and militarily confront the state. In response to the Muslim Brotherhood, which repeatedly appeals in vain to the Egyptian authorities for recognition as a political party, Faraj adamantly states that accommodation of the political system by working within the existing political apparatus merely strengthens the state. In fact, Faraj insists that Muslims should not even work for the government nor serve in the military, demands that are extremely difficult to meet for a nation that heavily relies on public-sector employment. And, in response to arguments that the true meaning of *jihad* is liberation of the Holy Land (Jerusalem) from Israel, Faraj stipulates that one is obligated first to undertake *jihad* against the nearer enemy (i.e., the Egyptian government), and only then turn to the more distant enemy. Liberation of the Holy Land under the authority of the infidel Egyptian state would merely strengthen the infidel state. To Faraj, there is no solution to the infidel character of state and society but for both of these to be replaced with Islamic state and society, governed by Islamic law.

Faraj's writing, no doubt more militant than that of al-Banna, is nevertheless reminiscent of al-Banna's thought. Although Faraj wrote during the period of the United States' influence on Egypt and al-Banna during Great Britain's influence, both speak of westernization as the pivotal problem plaguing Egypt. To both Islamists, it is unfathomable that secular Western law, rather than Islamic *shari'a*, governs Egypt, and this unacceptable situation is the fault first and foremost of the infidel Egyptian government. Faraj shuns al-Banna's willingness to employ reformative strategies and declares that Muslims must revolt against and destroy the infidel government in order for imperialism to be uprooted. And, while the support and backing of the masses in this endeavor—a condition on which al-Banna focused—would certainly be welcome, for Faraj it is by no means a precondition to the revolt. Similarly, in contrast to Shukri Mustafa's belief in *hijra* as a prelude to Islamizing the society, Faraj was determined that revolution must be undertaken immediately.

The most notorious act by the *Jihad* organization was an attempt to carry out the radical thought of Faraj. Zumur, the strategic planner from within the military, made plans that led to the assassination of President Sadat, on 6 October 1981, by Lt. Khalid al-Islambuli from al-Minya. Evidence presented during the trials of *Jihad* members after the assassination suggests that killing the president was to be the first step toward an Islamic revolution.[21] Sadat's murder was to be followed by a guerrilla takeover of the radio and television building in Cairo, from which the revolution was to be announced to the nation. Mass support for the revolution was to be mobilized by regional *Jihad* leaders, who were to seize control of major cities as soon as they saw the president's assassination on television.

This stage of the revolution never came to fruition, however, because the government retained control of the radio and television building and immediately silenced the media in the aftermath of the assassination, leaving regional *Jihad* contingents unaware of the status of the operation. Numerous riots took place in Asyut, 250 miles south of Cairo, between 8 and 11 October 1981. But in Cairo, *Jihad* units failed to carry out their role in the plan, which would have involved similar riots in the city. Thousands of *Jihad* backers were arrested following the assassination and the rioting associated with it. More than three hundred *Jihad* members were charged with murder, attempted murder, and attempting to overthrow the government, with the prosecutor demanding the death penalty for all the defendants. On 15 April 1982 the five men directly responsible for the assassination were executed. Subsequent sentences included eighty-nine prison terms ranging from three to fifteen years, and sixteen life prison terms (there were 174 acquittals). These sentences, announced on 30 September 1984, were considered unusually lenient and stirred speculation that the regime of Hosni Mubarak did not want to risk antagonizing the militant *al-Jihad* organization. Immediately after the release of the acquitted, members staged a demonstration outside the prison. Chanting "Islamic revolution is coming," they foreshadowed a drawn-out battle that was yet to be waged against the government.

In December 1986, thirty-three *Jihad* members were arrested and charged with the theft of weapons and intent to undermine public security (four of these were army officers). *Jihad* stepped up its operations in 1987 with four assassination attempts, an unprecedented number following two decades of one attempt, at the most, per year. In 1986, Islamists tried to assassinate Hasan Abu Basha, on 5 May, and Muhammad Nabawi Isma'il, on 13 August, both of them former ministers of the interior who had led the government's battle against Islamists. The message was clear: the Ministry of Interior was responsible for maintaining the state's internal security, and the Islamists had resolved to undermine that security in their focus on unseating the secular rulers. Also targeted for assassination in 1987 were Makram Muhammad Ahmad, editor in chief of *Al-Musawwir* magazine, which had criticized the Islamist movement in its reports, and Dennis Williams, a U.S. Embassy security official. Three other U.S. diplomats were physically assaulted in May, though the attacks were not reported as assassination attempts. The dramatic upsurge in attempted assassinations was attributed to the *Jihad* organization. A new splinter group calling itself *al-Najun min al-Nar* (Those Saved from the Fire) later took credit for the assaults. Arrests resulting from the attacks involved between five hundred (official figures) and five thousand (opposition estimate) Islamists. Although the opposition estimate indicates a rather large following for *Jihad*, even the lower estimate suggests that the assassination attempts were the work of a large organization and not the isolated actions of disgruntled or deranged individuals. In October 1990 *Jihad* was again involved in an assassination, killing Rif'at al-Mahjub, the speaker of the People's Assembly.

Al-Jama'a al-Islamiyya

The roots of the *al-Jama'a al-Islamiyya* (Islamic Group) are presumed to be in the religious student associations (*jama'at Islamiyya*) established in Egypt's universities in the early 1970s. Then, the major concerns were with ethical and moral issues. The increased criticism by the student associations of President Sadat's policy initiatives led him to deprive them of necessary funds, outlaw their campus activities, and include their members in his arrest wave of September 1981. Angered by the state's tough posture, they spread out among the people and carried their message underground.

By the early 1980s, the *jama'at Islamiyya* seem to have formed several tendencies within one broad organization, which became known as the *al-Jama'a al-Islamiyya*. One tendency, centered in the universities of Cairo and Alexandria, supported the philosophy of the Muslim Brotherhood. In fact, according to Tal'at Fu'ad Qasim, a leader and spokesman for the *al-Jama'a al-Islamiyya*, some members of the *Jama'a* in 1978 left the group to join the Brotherhood. These included Muslim Brothers Muhi al-Din, Abu al-'Ala Madi, 'Isam al-'Aryan, Hilmi al-Jazzar, 'Abd al-Mun'im Abu al-Futuh, and Ahmad 'Umar.[22] A second tendency, found in the universities of Upper Egypt, opposed the truce between the Muslim Brotherhood and the government and rejected the constitutional mechanisms preferred by the Brotherhood. They saw cooperation with the existing system as futile and dangerous and they supported the philosophy of the *Jihad* organization. Leaders from Aswan, Asyut, al-Minya, Suhaj, and Qina led the way for cooperation between *al-Jama'a al-Islamiyya* and the *Jihad* organization. A third tendency, limited to Alexandria University, adopted the *Salafy* line.[23]

In September 1981, as Sadat swept up his political opponents nationwide, he also called for the arrest of the *Jama'a*'s leadership. It was during this government seige on the leadership that Faraj, leader of the *Jihad* organization, attempted to harmonize the activities of the *Jama'a* branch in Upper Egypt with those of his own group. A *Majlis al-Shura* was created, allowing the two groups to cooperate while maintaining their separate identities. 'Umar 'Abd al-Rahman assumed the leadership role of the *Majlis*. The assassination of Sadat in October, initially considered the work of the *Jihad* organization acting alone, was according to subsequent court testimony the work of both the *Jihad* organization and the Upper Egypt-based *Jama'a*. Tal'at Fu'ad Qasim argues, however, that the *Jihad* organization had no role in Sadat's assassination and that it was merely caught up in the arrest campaign of 1981.[24]

In the same year, the *Jama'a* staged an armed attack on the state's security headquarters in Asyut, resulting in the deaths of dozens of security personnel. In the aftermath of these violent events, the tendency that supported the Brotherhood disappeared from public view, and the tendency that supported the *Jihad* organization became prominent. Following the assassination and the Asyut rebellion, most of the leadership of the *Jama'a* was arrested, including 'Isam al-Din Dirbala, Najih Ibrahim, 'Asim 'Abd al-Majid, 'Ali al-Sharif, and Karam Zuhdi; all were sentenced to life in Liman Tura Prison. Some leaders, including 'Umar 'Abd al-Rahman, leader and *mufti* of the group, were released—it having been suggested that President Mubarak released 'Abd al-Rahman to avoid making him into a martyr (only in 1994, when he was in New York, was he tried in absentia and sentenced to seven years in prison.)[25] Incarcerated in Tura Prison just two weeks before the assassination of Sadat was Tal'at Qasim, who had led the student union at al-Minya and was a founding member of the *Majlis al-Shura*.[26] He spent seven years in prison and one year under house arrest before fleeing through Sudan to Peshawar, Pakistan to help to establish a *mahkama shar'iyya* (Islamic court), which issued death sentences against Egyptian officials and secularists, including Egyptian intellectual Faraj Fuda. In 1989, Qasim became the deputy to the *amir*, 'Umar 'Abd al-Rahman and, following Rahman's subsequent imprisonment, the leader of *al-Jama'a al-Islamiyya*. He was forced into exile in Copenhagen following Egyptian pressure on Pakistan for his extradition.

While in prison, the leadership wrote monographs explaining the philosophy of the *Jama'a*, the most important of which is the *Mithaq al-'Amal al-Islami* (*Conventions of Islamic Action*), written in 1984 by Dr. Najih Ibrahim, 'Asim 'Abd al-Majid, and 'Isam al-Din Dirbala, under the supervision of 'Umar 'Abd al-Rahman, and published in 1989. The *Mithaq* is a 231-page explanation of the *Jama'a*'s goals, beliefs, and strategies, declares adherence to the tenets of Islam.

The first section of the *Mithaq* discusses what the authors call their *ghaya* (goal), and it proclaims a commitment by the group to follow the commands of God and the Prophet Muhammad in all that they do, so that God will reward them by making their program successful. The second item to be discussed is the *'aqida* (creed) of the group, proclaiming a commitment to action, not rhetoric, and pledging that the *Jama'a* will demonstrate its adherence to the tenets of Islam. Here the authors commit themselves to emulating the deeds of the *Sahaba*, the companions of the Prophet Muhammad. In the *Sahaba*, members of the *Jama'a* see individuals who were willing to give their all to their religion, without regard to sacrifices this might entail.

The third section of the *Mithaq* discusses the group's understanding, or *fahm*, of Islam. This *fahm* is based on the scholarly interpretations of the *'ulama* that display a strict adherence to Islam as originally preached and demonstrated by the Prophet, without the unnecessary influence of ideologies alien to pure Islam. In this discussion, the group notes that the majority of Muslims have a distorted understanding of their religion.

In the fourth section, the authors proclaim their *hadaf,* or aim "to establish Islam as a totality in each soul, and over each *shibr* [handbreadth] of land, in each house, in each organization, and in each society."[27] This will be accomplished if *Jama'a* members succeed on two counts: (1) People must be made to worship their Lord, and (2) A *khilafa* (caliphate, religious-political leadership) on the model of prophethood (*nubuwwa*) must be established. "This requires the ruling political system to proclaim, follow, and rule through Islam."[28]

The fifth section discusses the group's approach, or *tariq*, which involves two processes. The first process is *da'wa* by calling for *al-amr bi al-ma'ruf wa al-nahi 'an al-munkar* ("undertaking the good and eliminating that which is forbidden"), a concept repeated throughout the monograph. The second process is *jihad* in the service of God through the work of a disciplined, organized group that operates under Islamic law. The group must learn from the experiences of those who came earlier and must be active, avoiding complacency.[29] *Jihad,* in the sense used here, is a struggle to change the ways of those who abandoned the good (*al-ma'ruf*) in favor of the forbidden (*al-munkar*). *Jihad* is seen as a two-step struggle. First, it entails gentle preaching, meeting "bad deeds" with "good deeds" to influence reform in the path of Islam. If this does not succeed, *jihad* then requires the use of physical force, and a limited number of weapons, such as swords, are identified as tools to be used in the struggle.[30]

The sixth section addresses what the group refers to as *zad* (sustenance). In an analogy, the authors note that just as a traveler on earth needs sustenance to make it to his destination, so the traveler to heaven needs sustenance. This consists of *taqwa* (fear of God), *'ilm* (knowledge), *yaqin* (trust in God), *tawakul* (dependence on God), *shukr* (gratitude to God), *sabr* (patience), and *zuhd* (disinterest in the material world).

Section seven discusses the concept of *wala'* (obedience). The authors stress that God, as the sovereign creator, is the one who should be followed and obeyed. The eighth section discusses the concept of *'ada'*, or the enemy, defined simply as the "oppressors."

Section nine, *ijtima'*, or, as used here, corporate activity, discusses the importance of organizing Muslims toward the pursuit of one goal, within one belief system or creed. The authors argue that Islam demands group activity, and they encourage conformity to Islamic codes of behavior. Even though there might be differences within the group, these must represent a variety of ideas limited by the overall Islamic *shari'a*. Persons whose ideas oppose those of the *Jama'a* cannot be part of the group, and it is noted that those who parted ways with Islam, the *Khawarij*, were killed by the Prophet Muhammad.

'Umar 'Abd al-Rahman reiterates the above discussion in other writings. He stresses that secular law, derived from Western thought, which is alien to the religion of Islam, must be eliminated and that the rulers of Egypt must be forced to see the folly of secular rule. In a 1988 publication he wrote that the ruler who has replaced God's law with constitutional law "must be fought until he returns to God's law . . . or he must be uprooted."[31]

Al-Jama'a al-Islamiyya also opposes foreign investment in Egypt and has declared war on tourism, the major source of hard currency for the state. In the *Jama'a*'s view, the monuments of the pharaohs to which tourists flock are condemned on two counts: first, they are pagan shrines unworthy of a Muslim people; second, they generate revenues that support a spiritually misguided state. All of the activity of the *Jama'a* is in line with this philosophy and demonstrates the determination to cripple the state.

The *Jama'a* has been connected with most of the political violence that has occurred in Egypt since 1981. Increasingly, much of the violence has been aimed directly at paralyzing the tourism industry. On 24 June 1992 militants carried out a grenade attack on a sound-and-light show in Luxor, Upper Egypt, and, also that summer, they shot at tour boats on the Nile. In October 1992 three Russian tourists were stabbed in Port Said. In 1993 communiqués urged foreign tourists and investors to leave the country, and foreigners in Upper Egypt who did not leave came under attack in tourist buses and on Nile River cruises. One of the most deadly attacks by far took place on 17 November 1997 in Luxor, Upper Egypt: gunmen burst into the courtyard of the thirty-four-hundred-year-old Hatshepsut Temple and fired bullets at tourists, killing at least sixty-six people, among them fifty-seven foreigners.[32]

Tourists in Cairo were not spared, with attacks on major tourist sites in the capital. Egypt's Cairo Museum was the target of a bomb attack in March 1993, and, just weeks later, a bomb went off in a pyramid outside Cairo. In December 1993 eight Austrian tourists were wounded on a bus in Cairo. In September 1997 two brothers, Sabir and Mahmud Farhat, bombed a tour bus in front of the Egyptian Museum in al-Tahrir Square; nine German tourists and their Egyptian driver were killed in the attack. On 30 October 1997 the two were sentenced to death by the Higher Military Court.

Egyptian intellectuals critical of the militant groups have also felt the wrath of the *Jama'a*. The group claimed responsibility for the assassination of secular writer Faraj Fuda, who was killed in June 1992 in Cairo for his open criticism of Islamist extremism.

Government Response

The assaults by Egypt's militant groups have compelled the Interior Ministry to crack down on Islamism with every method available, which, according to former Minister of Interior Hasan al-Alfi, have been greatly modernized.[33] Alfi notes that communications and transportation equipment have been improved, as have the methods for detecting the presence of explosives. The training method for security forces has been made tougher, and "some missions are sent abroad and technicians and experts have arrived from abroad to provide training."[34] Early in 1997 Egypt authorized the U.S. Federal Bureau of Investigation (FBI) to open an office in the U.S. Embassy in Cairo. Alfi argued that this did not violate Egyptian sovereignty because the fight against terrorism requires international cooperation and the United States has the right to protect its interests, particularly in light of the presence of Egyptian terrorists, such as 'Abd al-Rahman, on U.S. territory.[35] In October 1997 it was reported that the FBI office had "managed to collect important information about the armed Islamic groups in Egypt" and that, by working together with Egyptian security services, an attempt to bomb the U.S. Embassy in Cairo had been thwarted.[36]

The Interior Ministry is intent on ridding Egypt of the militant threat, and this often has meant the execution of militants by security forces during security sweeps and street battles. Security forces have become ruthless in their raids, especially in Upper Egypt, where they round up Islamists by the thousands. Alfi, in August 1994, suggested that approximately ten thousand detainees are held in Egypt's prisons.[37] In addition, the security forces have become more confrontational, firing live ammunition at suspects in an effort to break the will of the movement. On 9 March 1993 in a mosque in Aswan, police opened fire on what they said was a group of *Jama'a* members who had attacked them with bombs. The episode left seven Islamists dead and fourteen injured.

On 1 February 1994 security forces raided an *al-Jama'a al-Islamiyya* hideout in al-Zawya al-Hamra' in northern Cairo, killing seven of the group's senior members in an exchange of gunfire. The following day news agencies received faxes from the *Jama'a* warning that revenge would be taken on foreigners and advising tourists to leave the country. The clashes with the security forces set off even more violence, to which Minister of Interior Hasan al-Alfi reacted with vows to continue raids on the group. Tharwat al-Hajaj, alleged head of the *Jama'a*'s military wing in Cairo, and two other *Jama'a* members were killed by security forces in an ambush in southern Cairo on 14 February (during the holy month of Ramadan). True to its promise the *Jama'a* conducted numerous attacks in retribution. February and March 1994 saw the *Jama'a* attacking police officers, executing small bomb attacks against banks, and attacking tourist boats and trains passing through Asyut province, a major haven of the militant Islamists of Upper Egypt. Police officers were attacked for being the strong arm of the illegitimate state; banks for giving out and charging interest; and foreigners for their hard currency contributions to the state's coffers.

By 1994 the *Jama'a* seemed to have Egypt, particularly the governorate of Asyut, under seige, but the government was responding with equal severity. On 23 February "3,000 policemen accompanied by armored cars swept through Al Bedari [an island in Asyut] before dawn."[38] In the ensuing battle in the village of Tal Zayd, police, militants, and civilians were shot, and many suspected militants were arrested. Then, on the night of 27 February, the killing of a police recruit in Edfu, north of Aswan, touched off further clashes that left eight suspected Islamists and three police officers dead. In late April 1994 'Adil 'Awad Siyam, a military leader of the *Jihad* organization, was killed by police. Just days later a *Jama'a* military leader, Tal'at Yasin Hamam, was also killed. Hamam, born in 1963, was described in government announcements as "absolutely the most dangerous terrorist element," in charge of making plans for the *Jama'a*'s military wing and financing terrorist operations.[39] He had had a long history of antistate activities and arrests, beginning when he was an engineering student at Asyut University. First arrested (and found not guilty) following the Asyut riots of October 1981, most recently he had been held responsible for the assassination of high-level security officials in Upper Egypt and for issuing announcements on behalf of the *Jama'a*. Finally, at the end of January 1995, thirty people were killed during security operations against suspected Islamist militants in Upper Egypt.

The militants have been aided in their assaults by the camouflage provided by one of Upper Egypt's most profitable crops—sugar cane. Known as *mahsul al-jarima* ("the crop of crime"), sugar cane requires little water to grow to a height of two meters. Because it is easy to grow and brings in significant foreign exchange—one *feddan* (one and one-quarter acre) of sugar cane brings in £E 4,000 per year[40]— it is cultivated in every province in Upper Egypt. The crop covers vast territories across Upper Egypt and flanks both sides of the agricultural road that runs from Cairo to Asyut to Aswan, thus enabling violent extremists to attack those traveling through Upper Egypt and then hide in the dense fields from security forces. The latter have tried searching for the militants by helicopter, but the wind from the helicopters simply causes the plants to lean over, creating even more cover for those in hiding. Egypt's director of security in the province of Qina, Sa'd al-Jamal, complained that if it were not for sugar cane, the battle with the extremists would not have spread so extensively.[41]

In the mid-1990s, the Ministry of Agriculture began gradually replacing sugar cane with sugar beets, which grows much closer to the ground. In addition, the remaining sugar cane fields are being divided into smaller plots, which are then surrounded by lower vegetation. Security forces have destroyed many canefields, both purposely and inadvertently, during chases. Farmers resist the security policies because they bring a loss in their revenue, so the government reimburses any losses and proposes alternative income-generating projects.[42] Although the overall loss to the Egyptian economy is great, the government argues that the prohibitive cost to the state of pursuing the militants into the sugar cane forests justifies reducing cultivation of the crop of crime.

The government of President Hosni Mubarak has shown its resolve to battle the militant forces by any means, including storming a mosque in the heart of Upper Egypt, executing suspects without recourse to the courts, and conducting quick military trials that do not hesitate to mete out the death penalty. On 2 June 1996 six militants were hanged in accordance with a death sentence issued in January by a military court. The six belonged to *al-Jama'a al-Islamiyya*, and were convicted of plotting to smuggle weapons into Egypt across the Sudanese border and of planning to kill Egyptian officials and to bomb several targets.[43]

The line between militant Islamists and Islamist sympathizers has become blurred, with the government dealing harshly with nonviolent persons who in some way empathize with the militants. Muntasir al-Zayyat, for example, a defense lawyer for the militants on trial, has himself become a target of the Egyptian legal system; he was charged with "belonging to a secret group seeking to overthrow the government by force."[44] In addition, the government is trying to bring all mosques and *shaykh*s under the control of the *Waqf*, the Ministry of Endowments. Mubarak's regime has also embarked on a public relations battle with the militants: posters have gone up in Cairo pointing out the perils of militant Islamism; films and television programs testify to the "terrorist" nature of the militant groups; and government spokesmen often argue that Egypt is already an Islamic nation whose population consists predominantly of Muslims. Therefore, there is no need for Islam to play a political role in a country in which the people already practice their Islamic faith. Activists who profess that "Islam is the solution" seek only to impose their interpretation of Islam on already practicing and devout Muslims, and thus are a threat to the personal freedom of the population. The media offensive has successfully affected the perceptions of many on Egypt's streets. In the 1980s it was uncommon to find Egyptians referring to Islamists as "terrorists," but by the mid-1990s this had become a common label, although even many who use the term sympathize with the motives of the militant movement. Although the typical Egyptian abhors the violence and bloodletting in which militant groups engage, there is also pronounced disillusionment with the government.

Conclusion

All of the government's resolve to eliminate the militant *al-Tawaqquf wa al-Tabayyun* wing of the Islamist movement might simply be feeding an endless cycle of execution by the state and assassination by the *al-Jama'a al-Islamiyya* and *Jihad* organizations. It might also force the two groups to join their efforts in a united front against the state. Diya' Rashwan argues that this has already happened.[45] By 1993, it had become clear to Rashwan that the *Jihad* and *Jama'a* groups had agreed to the symbolic leadership of 'Abd al-Rahman over the entire militant wing, and that 'Abud al-Zumur, until then head of *Jihad*, became the leader of the military forces in the movement. As of this writing, however, it is unclear whether the two groups have indeed merged; on the contrary, *Jihad* and the *Jama'a* separately acknowledge responsibility for militant activities such as bombings and assassinations.

Nevertheless, there is much that the two groups agree upon, and state efforts might force them to unite in pursuit of their common objectives. Both the *Jama'a* and *Jihad* assert that society and all of its institutions have fallen prey to *jahiliyya* (pre-Islamic ignorance). Both groups are against the current secular laws and aim to achieve the *hakimiyya* (sovereignty) of God, condemning the system of rule by man over man rather than rule by God. In this regard, both groups reject democracy because they see it as an ideology that contradicts the *tawhid* (unity or oneness) of God. Both stress that democracy, as a system that gives sovereignty to the people, necessarily is at odds with the Islamic notion of sovereignty by none other than God. Al-Jama'a al-Islamiyya has also stated that the freedom to form parties is in opposition to *shari'a* in that it would allow non-Muslims to also have a political party, so that they might ultimately gain political power.[46] Both groups reject the slow pace of reform toward adopting *shari'a* and are doubtful that the state intends to implement Islamic law. Both groups charge the government with *kufr*. They agree that the leader of Egypt is a *kafir*, as is the entire political system. Both also agree that the use of violence is necessary to change the situation in Egypt and that the economy must be combatted as an extension of the state that gives it sustenance. *Thawra*, revolution, is necessary to uproot the evil system and replace it with an Islamic system.[47]

Even if the two groups remain separate, what they see as government oppression will continue to result in retribution by the groups. Even though the government's response has been harsh, it has not accomplished the ultimate task of eradicating the militants. A 1993 report noted that the extremists were still "a decentralized conglomeration of militant groups," numbering in the tens of thousands.[48] *Jama'a* leader Tal'at Qasim insists that the tactics of the security forces have resulted in more recruits for the group: "The Gama'a exists in 18 provinces, including tens of centers and hundreds of villages. . . . For every member killed, 20 join. Contrary to what some think, the power of the Gama'a is on the rise.[49]

Mamoun Fandy, who studies the separate identity of the south, stresses that the majority of those indicted for Sadat's assassination were either residents of the *Sa'id,* Upper Egypt, or lived in northern neighborhoods populated by *Sa'idis.*[50] According to some analysts, the *Sa'id* has a particular code of behavior that encourages retribution for harm done to one's family and village. In reference to Dayrut, the poorest district in Asyut province, an observer notes that "this corner of Egypt has well-established traditions of lawlessness and vendetta."[51] "Lawlessness" may be an external interpretation of the local *Sa'idis'* conflict resolution techniques, in that "southerners consider *tha'r* [vendetta] much more reliable than going through Egypt's slow and corrupt court system."[52] In addition, the central government in Cairo has "depended on the local notables [of the *Sa'id*] and their traditional authority to ensure order. This lack of penetration and the persistence of traditional institutions has enabled *Sa'idis* to use local customs in preference to civil law. In fact, southern villagers consider it shameful to involve the courts or police in their disputes."[53] In such a social climate it is difficult to establish law and order solely by use of oppressive force. It is particularly difficult to do so if the community sees little or no virtue in the institutions of the state, especially if compared with the many social services provided by the Islamist movement.

The October 1992 earthquake that struck Egypt was seen by the Islamists as a message from above. It was God's response to the rampant corruption plaguing the country. The ravages inflicted on Egypt's poor, whose dilapidated apartment buildings crumbled in the earthquake, were tended to by Islamist organizations that arrived on the scene ready to work and ahead of the government. Such social services and economic assistance programs are common among the Islamist groups, including the *al-Jama'a al-Islamiyya,* and fill a void created by the government's inability to meet the needs of its growing population. A major reason for the popularity of the Islamist groups is their services throughout both the poor districts of northern Egypt, where urbanization, population growth, and the elimination of government subsidies have left many families living in poverty, and southern Egypt, where the state historically has neglected the social needs of the population.[54]

In both regions, local notables and emergent groups have been forced to fill the social vacuum. The provision of services by locals stems from the oil boom in the Persian Gulf in the 1970s, which enabled both northern and southern Egyptians to earn previously unheard of wages. Their remittances back to Egypt often were invested in local projects that provided sorely needed social and community services: for instance, mosques became centers of medical and dental clinics that charged a nominal fee for services. And the state was increasingly viewed as incapable or unwilling of attending to the needs of the population. As Saad Eddin Ibrahim notes, "The Egyptian regime has not fully comprehended the multifaceted phenomenon of Islamic militancy, which reflects a profound social crisis compounded by simultaneous crises in the economy, the polity, and the culture."[55]

In such a climate, it is imperative that the government adopt a strategy that addresses the many concerns of the population. The state certainly cannot (and should not) be the provider to every member of the community, but it is essential that there be conditions under which people can meet their basic needs and can believe that the state has their interests at heart in the policies it enacts. Not only socioeconomic, but political channels must be opened to the public. A myriad of nongovernment associations and political parties have the potential to contribute positively and constructively to the political system, including such religious ones as the mosque-based NGOs and the Muslim Brotherhood. An unfettered civil society can mediate between the government and the people, mitigating the type of violence discussed in this chapter and reducing the appeal of the violent groups that have chosen to operate outside the bounds of civil society.

It is difficult for the central government to extend its control over the entire population, particularly to remote, southern areas that traditionally have been neglected by Cairo. The use of force by the state, in the absence of institutions and services that otherwise might legitimize the state's intrusion, is therefore seen not as law and order, but as lawlessness and oppression that require the locals to vindicate their honor by taking revenge on the oppressors. There is no doubt that the government must be firm with the militants and punish them for crimes committed; however, it must also draw a distinction between these criminals and other Islamists who do not espouse the same tactics. The government of Egypt should not penalize and paralyze civil society as a whole to punish the crimes of the few.

Notes

1. R. Hrair Dekmejian, *Islam in Revolution: Fundamentalism in the Arab World*, 2nd ed. (New York: Syracuse University Press, 1995), p. 82.

2. See, for example, Afaf Hussain, *Islamic Movements in Egypt, Pakistan and Iran* (London: Mansell Publishing, 1983), p. 13; Diya' Rashwan, "Al-Jama'at al-Islamiyya al-Misriyya wa al-Istiqrar al-Siyasi," *Al-Majalla*, 16 March 1993, pp. 24–28; and Ayman al-Sayyad, "'Ala Lisan Munsha'ayha wa Qadatha: Al-Tarikh al-Siri Li Jama'at 'al-Jihad' fi Misr," *Al-Majalla*, 14 May 1994, 26–33.

3. Ibid., Ayman al-Sayyad, "'Ala Lisan Munsha'ayha wa Qadatha."

4. Ibid., p. 30.

5. Ibid., p. 30.

6. Ali E. Hillal Dessouki, "The Resurgence of Islamic Organisations in Egypt: An Interpretation," in Alexander S. Cudsi and Ali E. Hillal Dessouki, eds. *Islam and Power* (Baltimore: Johns Hopkins University Press, 1981), p. 108. Dessouki notes, for example, that in 1978 Islamist candidates at Alexandria University won 60 out of 60 seats in the Faculty of Medicine, 60 out of 60 in the Faculty of Engineering, 47 out of 48 in the Faculty of Agriculture, 42 out of 48 in the Faculty of Pharmacy, 43 out of 60 in the Faculty of Science, and 44 out of 48 in the Faculty of Law.

7. *Qanun al-'Ayb*, the Law of Shame, was introduced in April 1980 by Sadat. The law stipulated the formation of the Court of Ethics to prosecute "antisocial" behavior. Such behavior includes inciting opposition to the state's economic, political, and social system, and disseminating false or extremist statements that damage national unity or social peace. See Keesing's Contemporary Archives, 21 November 1980, [30586]. The Court of Ethics is discussed in Nathan J. Brown, *The Rule of Law in the Arab World: Courts in Egypt and the Gulf* (Cambridge: Cambridge University Press, 1997).

8. Ayman al-Sayyad, "'Ala Lisan Munsha'ayha wa Qadatha," p. 32.

9. Rudolph Peters, "The Political Relevance of the Doctrine of *Jihad* in Sadat's Egypt," in Edward Ingram, ed., *National and International Politics in the Middle East: Essays in Honour of Elie Kedourie* (London: Frank Cass and Co., 1986), p. 256.

10. Gilles Kepel, *The Prophet and Pharaoh: Muslim Extremism in Egypt* (London: Al Saqi Books, 1985), p. 149.

11. Mahmud Mu'awwad Jami', quoted in Ayman al-Sayyad, "'Ala Lisan Munsha'ayha wa Qadatha," p. 33.

12. R. Hrair Dekmejian, *Islam in Revolution*, p. 83.

13. Diya' Rashwan, "Al-Jama'at al-Islamiyya," pp. 24–28.

14. Michael Youssef, *Revolt against Modernity* (Leiden: E. J. Brill, 1985), p. 78. This view is seconded in Al-Ahram Center for Political and Strategic Studies, "The Extra-Legal Forces," (in Arabic) in *The Arab Strategic Report*, 1986 (Cairo, 1987), pp. 396–398.

15. Kepel, *Muslim Extremism in Egypt*, p. 72. Ironically, it was Shukri Mustafa's release from prison in 1971, as part of Sadat's "rectification revolution" in which the new president renounced Nasser's concentration camps, that offered the occasion for founding the Society.

16. The word *takfir* approximates the Christian concept of "excommunication" more closely than "repentance," the usual (erroneous) translation given in discussions of the group. However, because there is no excommunication (i.e., expulsion from a church) in Islam, R. Hrair Dekmejian's choice of the word "denouncement" will be used here.

17. Kepel, *The Prophet and Pharaoh*, pp. 95–96.

18. Diya' Rashwan, "*Al-Jama'at al-Islamiyya*," pp. 24–28.

19. This discussion of the early years of the *Jihad* organization is based in part on the extensive analysis done by Hala Mustafa in *Al-Islam al-Siyasi fi Misr: Min Harakat al-Islah ila Jama'at al-'Unf* (Cairo: Center for Political and Strategic Studies, 1992).

20. This discussion is based on Muhammad 'Abd al-Salam Faraj, *Al-Jihad: Al-Farida al-Gha'iba* (Jerusalem: Maktabat al-Batal 'Iz al-Din al-Qassam, 1982); The book was translated into English by Michael Youssef in *Revolt against Modernity*, Appendix I, pp. 146–177.

21. Comprehensive details of the plot are reported in Youssef, *Revolt against Modernity*, pp. 102–106; and in Kepel, *The Prophet and Pharaoh*, pp. 191–215.

22. Hisham Mubarak, "What Does the *Gama'a Islamiyya* Want? An Interview with Tal'at Fu'ad Qasim," *Middle East Report*, (January-March 1996): 41.

23. As discussed in Chapter 1, the Salafiyya movement was a reform movement founded by Jamal al-Din al-Afghani and Muhammad Abduh.

24. Hisham Mubarak, "What Does the *Gama'a Islamiyya* Want?," p. 43.

25. Judith Miller, *God Has Ninety-Nine Names: Reporting from a Militant Middle East* (New York: Simon & Schuster, 1996), p. 53.

26. Hisham Mubarak, "What does the *Gama'a Islamiyya* want?," pp. 40–46.

27. Najih Ibrahim, 'Asim 'Abd al-Majid, and 'Isam al-Din Dirbala, under the supervision of 'Umar 'Abd al-Rahman, *Mithaq al-'Amal al-Watani* (Cairo: Maktabit Ibn Kathir, 1989), p. 55.

28. Ibid., p. 55.

29. Ibid., p. 78.

30. Ibid., pp. 80–81.

31. 'Umar 'Abd al-Rahman, *Al-Maw'itha al-Hasana [The Good Advice]* (Kuwait: Dar al-Siyasa, 1988), p. 92.

32. Mohamed El-Dakhakhny, "At Least 66 Dead in Egypt Attack," *The Associated Press*, 17 November 1997.

33. "Minister on 'Terrorism,' Muslim Brotherhood: Interview with Interior Minister Hasan al-Alfi," *Rose al-Yusuf*, 8 August 1994, pp. 10–15.

34. Ibid.

35. 'Abd al-Latif al-Minawi, "Egypt: Interior Minister al-Alfi on Security Issues—Interview with Egyptian Interior Minister Major General Hasan al-Alfi," *Al-Majalla*, 3 May 1997, pp. 26–30.

36. "Egypt: Attempt to Bomb US Embassy in Cairo Said Foiled," *Al-'Arabi*, 20 October 1997, p. 1, reported by *FBIS*, 28 October 1997.

37. "Minister on 'Terrorism,'" *Rose al-Yusuf*, 8 August 1994, pp. 10–15.

38. Details of the clashes between security forces and the *Jama'a* are given in "Militants Warn Foreigners' Lives at Risk," *Civil Society*, March 1994, pp. 5–7.

39. "Has There Been a Change in the *Jama'a*'s Strategy?" *Al-Majalla*, 14 May 1994, p. 25.

40. Hamdi Rizq, "The Sa'id of Egypt: The Game of Cat and Mouse in the Forests of Sugar Cane," *Al-Majalla*, 26 July 1997, p. 17.

41. Ibid., p. 19.

42. Ibid., pp. 16–20, for a discussion of government actions in this regard.

43. Dominic Evans, "Egypt Executes Six Moslem Militants," *Reuters World Service*, 3 June 1996.

44. "Egypt: Who Did It?" *The Economist*, 2 July 1994, p. 41.
45. Diya' Rashwan, "Al-Dawla Tata'amad Siyasit al-Qabda al-Hadidiyya [iron fist] lil Qada' 'ala al-Jama'at al-Mutatarrifa fi Misr," *Al-Majalla*, 30 March 1993, pp. 28–29.
46. Hala Mustafa, *Al-Islam al-Siyasi*, p. 172.
47. Ibid., p. 173.
48. Sarah Gauch, "Terror on the Nile," *Africa Report*, 38 (1993): 34.
49. Hisham Mubarak, "What Does the *Gama'a Islamiyya* want?" p. 44.
50. Mamoun Fandy, "Egypt's Islamic Group: Regional Revenge?" *The Middle East Journal* 48, no. 4 (1994): 607–608.
51. "Upper Egypt: The Battle Against the Leagues," *The Economist*, 4 July 1992, p. 38.
52. Fandy, "Egypt's Islamic Group," p. 621.
53. Fandy, "Egypt's Islamic Group," pp. 611–612.
54. Deborah Pugh, "Upper Egypt," *The Christian Science Monitor*, 4 May 1994, pp. 12–13.
55. Saad Eddin Ibrahim, "Reform and Frustration in Egypt," *Journal of Democracy* 7, no. 4 (1996): 127.

5

Gender, Islam, and Civil Society

Egyptian women, Muslim and Christian, have made significant contributions to social and political causes, especially in the past two centuries. Whether active in public or behind the scenes, women have advanced the causes of nationalism and independence, secularism and Islamism, and politics and governance, both in opposition to government and as part of the ruling party.

Feminists have won significant gains in the twentieth century. After decades of demanding the right to vote, women were granted suffrage in 1956. They won the right to hold public office, are now members of Parliament (*Majlis al-Sha'b*), and hold prominent political positions (e.g., cabinet seats and ambassadorships). The constitutions of 1956 and 1963 declared all Egyptians equal and forbade discrimination on the basis of gender. Law 14 of 1964 guaranteed both men and women public-sector jobs in return for a university education and gave women specific on-the-job rights.

We do not suggest that women fully share equal rights with men in Egypt, only that their struggle to attain those rights, along with the struggle of women and men for greater political freedoms, enriches the public sphere and civil society.

Egypt's Personal Status Laws, sometimes known as Family Laws, have been very problematic in the past two decades. Liberalized in 1979 by presidential decree, these became known as "Jehan's Laws" after their main supporter, the wife of President Anwar Sadat. But the reaction was so strong against these decreed changes that the state rescinded them in 1985, "only to restore [them] in diminished form."[1] Conservatives objected to the progressive nature of these laws; many feminists agonized over the fact that their improved legal status was the result of an autocrat's decree, and not achieved through an open, inclusive, democratic debate.

In the absence of a unified feminist movement, struggles against practices that injure[2] or inhibit women are less likely to be launched, let alone prove successful. There is a valid concern that, despite "fighting and winning the struggle for active participation in Egyptian political life, many Egyptian women feel that the 1980s and 1990s mark the beginning of their 'endangered rights.'"[3] This concern is one of warning, perhaps crisis, but not defeat. The achievements over the past century are great, the setbacks harmful, and the need still critical.

The net result of the intellectual debate and political activism on the part of women is their increased presence in the public arena, which was previously an exclusively male domain. Perhaps the greater achievements of women activists have been in promoting social, cultural, and economic development. These achievements easily translate into the development of the public sphere in Egypt.

In short, civil society in Egypt is richer, more broadly developed, and potentially more influential in political and policy terms than would be the case without women's involvement. Furthermore, the fact that Egyptian women have promoted causes that transcend those traditionally associated with women's issues has made them contributors to the development of civil society in general, and not just to "women's segments" of civil society.

In various arenas of civil society, the activities of Egyptian women appear to some as a contradiction: Egypt is known as the birthplace of the Arab women's feminist movement, a place where secular feminism remains active; it also is a society in which women are turning increasingly to Islamic symbols, dress, and political and social activism. The contradiction appears to be that many women and men are fighting to advance women's rights through a secular (and supposedly "modern") agenda, whereas many others appear to be seeking women's "return" to a traditional, subservient role (as supposedly prescribed by religion, both Islam and Christianity). Because women are involved in the latter movement, they are seen as helping to reproduce their inequality with men, reaffirming men's power over them. This is, however, no contradiction. Although the tensions between secular feminism and Islamism (or "Islamic feminism") may be a *challenge*, they also are reasons why women's activism, from various ideological perspectives, makes Egyptian civil society more vibrant. Just as *al-tayyar al-Islami* (the Islamic trend) is a multifaceted, heterogeneous set of movements in Egypt, there is a variety of feminisms[4] that seek to promote the liberation of women.[5]

To be sure, feminisms can be in conflict with each other. There is a vast array of women's NGOs working for social, educational, legal, and economic advancement for women and their families; these groups reflect the ideological differences in Egyptian society—from religious, conservative, and traditional to secular, liberal, and leftist. In addition to hundreds of women's NGOs (which are proscribed from political activity by Law 32), most of the thirteen or so political parties have a women's committee, *lajnat al-mar'a*.[6] Each committee reflects the views of (or differences within) the parties, which include Islamists (the Labor Party), economic liberals (*Wafd* and Liberal Parties), leftists (*Tajammu'* and Nasserists), and "opportunists" (the ruling National Democratic Party, which in particular seeks to embrace various, often conflicting, ideologies).

State Opposition to Women's Activism

The existence of different approaches to a similar objective (the liberation of women and advancement of their rights) is frequently manipulated by the state for its own purposes—dividing and conquering any opposition. One of the more prominent examples where the state used ostensibly competing feminisms to achieve blatant political ends is that of the Arab Women's Solidarity Association (AWSA), led by secular feminist, author, and opposition leader, Nawal el Saadawi.

AWSA was dissolved on 15 June 1991 although AWSA officials were not even informed about the order until July. AWSA members say they were given no specific reasons or justifications for the decision, although Saadawi suspects that AWSA's opposition to the 1991 Gulf War may have been a reason.[7] As is their custom, and as Egypt's Law 32 stipulates, Ministry of Social Affairs (MOSA) officials transferred AWSA's assets to another NGO nominally working in the same field, in this case the "Women of Islam" organization. This was a largely unknown Cairo-based NGO that, like hundreds of others, provides housing and social services to women (in this case, women from the provinces who come to Cairo to attend a university). It has not been active in promoting women's rights per se, as AWSA has been. What little is known of its ideology is conservative, very much at odds with the secular feminist approach of AWSA leaders.

Moreover, the director of Women of Islam was Faruq al-Fil, who also served as the director-general of social affairs in the Ma'adi district. The government appointed him as the legal liquidator of AWSA in the dissolution decree and granted al-Fil 10 percent of AWSA's assets as a liquidator's fee.[8] In other words, he was a government employee, working with MOSA, the agency charged with overseeing (i.e., controlling) NGO activity. This incident smacks of corruption, conflict of interest, suppression of free speech and association, and state manipulation of private interests, in this case feminist and opposition activities.

This was not the first time the government of Egypt had decreed the dissolution of a women's organization. In 1949, after the assassination of Hasan al-Banna, the government announced the dissolution of Zaynab al-Ghazali's Muslim Women's Association, an Islamist organization. The association took the matter to court, which resulted in a decision to reopen it. Then, on 15 September 1964, Nasser's government shut down the headquarters of the Muslim Women's Association. Thus, in the confrontation between civil society and the state, it has not been unusual for the state to ban organizations with which it disagrees, whether secular, as was AWSA, or religious, as was the Muslim Women's Association. Both met with the wrath of the government because their activities were seen as threatening to the regime in power.

Advancing Women's Rights: A Century of Feminism and Debate in Egypt

The debates involving gender as a factor in nationalism, Islamism, and opposition are not new in Egypt. One century ago, in 1899, the underlying debate on the role of women in society was raging as Qasim Amin, a respected Muslim lawyer and judge, published what has been called one of the first books on Egyptian feminism. In *Tahrir al-Mar'a (The Liberation of Women)*, Amin seemed to be moving away from his previous positions endorsing the exclusionary and otherwise inequitable gender practices of his society. In calling for the education of girls through elementary school, ending female seclusion, changing divorce and polygamy laws, and proposing an end to face veiling, Amin sounds like "the first male feminist" of nineteeth century Egypt. In reading his work, Egyptian conservatives felt they lost an ally, since only five years before Amin had supported gender separation, the seclusion of women, and veiling. Instead of a conversion, however, Amin may have just joined the ranks of other conservatives—in this case, external colonial powers—rather than the growing feminist movement led by Huda Sha'rawi (1879–1947) and Malak Hifni Nasif (1886–1918).

Amin's arguments resembled those of many British authors and colonial officials who saw in veiling (as a symbol of all that is "wrong" with Islam) proof of Islam's backwardness. Egyptians were enjoined to remove the veil, "liberate" girls through education and women through monogamy, and liberate Egyptian society in the process. For many Egyptian men veiling was and is a nationalist (as well as Islamist) issue. Men either resisted Western penetration into Egyptian society by preserving the veil or, like Amin, they felt that removing the veil would help Egypt emulate the progress of the more advanced West. Discourse concerning women, which should have emphasized a woman's right to select her own manner of dress, became a nationalist matter of interest to the men in society. In response to the call by male progressives (and, apparently, some conservatives) for unveiling, Malak Hifni Nasif "let it be known that women would decide for themselves when it was expedient to unveil. She insisted that the man 'should not be a tyrant in our liberation as he was a tyrant in our enslavement.'"[9]

Colonial leaders thus used the argument that "Islam oppresses women" as their "moral" justification to assault Islam as a religion and culture and to colonize the Muslim Middle East. Women and "the woman question" have been manipulated for political as well as cultural ends. It is no wonder, then, that feminism has been viewed quite negatively—when it is seen primarily as an external and imported ideology. However, we dissent from the notion "that feminism in Egypt began with men, that it was/is western, and that early feminism was restricted to upper-class women." Rather, we agree "that feminism began with women, that it has been indigenous" and that it cuts across class lines.[10]

There is no doubt among contemporary social scientists on the role played by the pioneers of Egyptian feminism: Malak Hifni Nasif, Huda Sha'rawi, Doria Shafik, among others.[11] There also is consensus that the feminist movement in Egypt was closely linked to the nationalist movement. Women were very active, in both urban and rural settings, in the 1919 national revolution and supported the political heirs to the revolution, primarily the Wafd Party. Indeed, feminism is said to have "started" in the 1880s,[12] a period of nationalist activism that set the stage for 1919.

Feminism and nationalism are also connected to "Islamism" (though the use of this term is not common when discussing the early part of the twentieth century). Margot Badran connects all three in her book, *Feminists, Islam, and Nation*.[13] Feminist pioneers balanced the three in their public lives.

Malak Hifni Nasif: Feminism with an Islamic Face

Malak Hifni Nasif (pen name: Bahithat al-Badiyya, or Searcher in the Desert), whose father, Muhammad Hifni Isma'il Nasif, studied with

Islamic reformist leader Muhammad Abduh (see Chapter 2), was a poet and writer, and became one of the most influential speakers at the Friday Women's Lectures at the Egyptian University. It was here that she met Huda Sha'rawi, founder of the Egyptian Feminist Union (*al-Ittihad al-Nisa'i al-Misri*). Malak Hifni Nasif reportedly was the first woman to present feminist demands in Egypt. In 1911, at the all-male Egyptian Congress, a male stand-in presented demands that Nasif had drafted to improve the condition of women. Among these were recommendations that women be allowed to pray in mosques; that education be made compulsory; that religion be taught to girls accurately and devoid of common misunderstandings; that Egyptian women be taught nursing; and that a medical school be established for women.[14] According to her biographer, Nasif "did not concern herself with politics."[15] Instead, she preferred to advance women's rights and improve the political system by working at the societal level and engaging in social work: in this manner, she believed she could reach a wide range of people without antagonizing those holding political power. Her writing argues for women's rights within the boundaries of Islamic teachings. She insists on the responsibility that men and women both have toward each other, and she asks women to assert themselves while maintaining their dignity and not transgressing the teachings of the Quran and Sunna.

Nasif *was* reluctant to call for unveiling. However, the assertion that Nasif "promot[ed] women's development within the system of sex segregation,"[16] must be compared with Nasif's many calls for women's education and women's employment, both of which would have led to decreased segregation of the sexes. In an address to fellow women, Nasif asked, "If I find no one to improve my education except a man, should I select ignorance or removal of the facial veil in front of that man in the company of [other female students]?"[17] Nasif admitted that she would in fact seek education through a man, although she reserved the right to keep her veil, while uncovering her eyes. After all, she asks rhetorically, are contemporary women more Muslim than the likes of prominent women from the Prophet Muhammad's family who would meet, in appropriate attire, with male *'ulama* and poets?[18]

Nasif's lectures to women, encouraging them to broaden and enrich their lives, consistently cautioned them to act within the limits of Islamic morality. Nasif encouraged women to attend school to gain an education that would enable them to work. She qualified this by saying: "I do not want to encourage women to leave their housework and stop raising their children in order to get an education in legal and judicial studies or in conducting locomotives; no, however, if there is among us [women] anyone who wants to work in any of these areas, her personal freedom is sufficient to keep others from stopping her."[19] In response to men who feared that women would compete with them for jobs, Nasif noted that men had initiated the competition in the first place by inventing machines that took jobs away from women. For example, women used to prepare wheat and make bread by hand; men invented machines to do this and made this a job for men. Women used to sew clothes for themselves and their families until men made sewing machines and hired male tailors. Nasif argued that the matter of work is a personal decision for each individual to make. One cannot impose a certain type of job on any individual, male or female. Since men invented machines that replaced women's work, Nasif asked, "Should we [women] kill time with laziness or should we search for work to keep us busy? It should be no surprise that we do the latter."[20]

Nasif's method was to promote a feminist agenda within the Islamic belief system of her generation. She did not demand removal of the physical veil. Instead, she demanded removal of the social veil, that is, the then-prevailing view that women should not be active outside the confines of their homes.

Huda Sha'rawi: Daring to Liberate Woman and Nation

When Huda Sha'rawi had to deliver a eulogy for her friend Malak, who died in 1918 at age thirty-two of influenza, it became one of Sha'rawi's first feminist public addresses. Perhaps more than any other person, Sha'rawi has become the face of Egyptian feminism. Her actions, thoughts, speeches, and writings justify this reknown. Probably the most enduring image of this feminist and nationalist leader, who led the movement from the founding of the Egyptian Feminist Union in 1923 until her death in 1947, is this:

> At Cairo station one spring day in 1923, a crowd of women with veils and long, black cloaks descended from their horse-drawn carriages to welcome home two friends returning from an international feminist meeting in Rome. Huda Shaarawi and Saiza Nabarawi stepped out on to the running board of the train. Suddenly Huda—followed by Saiza, the younger of the two—drew back the veil from her face. The waiting women broke into loud applause. Some imitated the act. Contemporary accounts observed how the eunuchs guarding the women frowned with displeasure. This daring act signalled the end of the harem system in Egypt.[21]
> At that moment, Huda stood between two halves of her life—one

conducted within the conventions of the harem system and the one she would lead at the head of a women's movement.[22]

Prior to this personal revolutionary act, Sha'rawi worked with Egyptian women across class lines to demonstrate against British occupation and to lead the Wafdist Women's Central Committee (WWCC).[23] Sha'rawi often worked within the social confines of her time even as she sought to transform Egypt socially and politically. Four years before her daring unveiling, she organized the 1919 "March of Veiled Women" in Cairo to protest British colonial rule and to foil "a British plan to exile four Egyptian nationalist leaders, including [her] husband."[24]

After Egypt gained nominal independence from Britain in 1922, Sha'rawi carried on her fight for women's rights, for instance by picketing the opening of the first Egyptian Parliament in 1924. She quit the WWCC that year out of frustration with its members' conciliatory stance toward the Wafd, which could do little about de facto British control over the country. She continued to lead the national feminist movement and extended the fight to other Arab countries. In 1945, two years before her death at age sixty-eight, Sha'rawi received the highest decoration from the Egyptian state, the *Nishan al-Kamal*, for services rendered to the country.[25] Yet, even as the state recognized Sha'rawi for her dual struggles for gender equality and national liberation, "it withheld from her political rights. It was a symbol of the contradictions with which she and other women had to live."[26]

Zaynab al-Ghazali: Islamist Feminist?

One of the most interesting actors in the struggle for greater freedom in both spheres of the sacred (the Islamic *umma*, or community of faith) and the profane (the social-political-economic structure known as Egypt) is Zaynab al-Ghazali al-Jubayli. Al-Ghazali began her feminist career working for Huda Sha'rawi at the Egyptian Feminist Union in 1935, at the age of 17. She left the following year and founded her own organization, the Muslim Women's Association.[27] Al-Ghazali felt that Sha'rawi's approach to feminism was a mistake, that it was "a grave error" to speak of the liberation of women in an Islamic society. Islam provided women with "everything—freedom, economic rights, political rights, social rights, public and private rights,"[28] even if these rights were not present in contemporary Islamic societies and polities. Al-Ghazali's association "helped women study Islam and carried out welfare activities, maintaining an orphanage, assisting poor families, and helping unemployed men and women to find useful employment."[29]

Zaynab al-Ghazali developed a strong relationship with the Muslim Brotherhood, beginning in 1937 when she delivered a lecture to the Muslim Sisters Association at the Brotherhood headquarters. Following the lecture, al-Banna, who founded the Muslim Sisters as a division of the Muslim Brotherhood, asked al-Ghazali to merge her organization with his.[30] Al-Ghazali consulted the board of her organization, and it declined the merger, preferring to maintain the independence of the Muslim Women's Association.[31] (After al-Banna's death in 1949, 'Abd al-Qadir 'Auda delivered a message to al-Ghazali on behalf of the Brothers: "It would please us if Zaynab al-Ghazali al-Jubayli were to become one of the Muslim Brotherhood," an invitation that she immediately accepted—as an individual, while maintaining a separate status for her organization.)[32] Al-Ghazali's ability to refuse the request of the leader of the Islamist movement speaks volumes about her independence, integrity, and commitment to her cause. "From the beginning [al-Ghazali] conceived of the Association as being equal to and equivalent with, yet deliberately separate from, the Muslim Brothers.... She must have known that had she accepted alliance any notion of equivalence and equality would certainly have degenerated into complementarity at best, subordination at worst."[33] While declining to merge her organization into (and under the control of) al-Banna's, al-Ghazali pledged her organization's and members' full cooperation with the leading Islamist organization and its leader. What is more, she took an oath pledging her personal efforts to the cause advanced by al-Banna. And she paid for this loyalty.

The government ordered the Muslim Women's Association disbanded in the late 1940s, in keeping with its campaign against Islamist groups, seen in the crackdown on the Muslim Brothers and the assassination of Hasan al-Banna in 1949. While she fought the government and won her case in court, persecution persisted. After al-Ghazali resisted repeated attempts by the government to co-opt her allegiance to the Brotherhood, President Nasser dissolved the association on 15 September 1964 and shut down their headquarters. In response, the Muslim Women's Association sent a letter of complaint to government agencies and to Nasser himself. According to al-Ghazali, the letter stated:

> The Muslim Women's Association was established in 1936 to spread the *da'wa* of God and to work towards the goal of a Muslim *umma*.

> ... The message [of the association] is a call to Islam, and the recruitment of men and women, young and old, ... to establish a state ruled by what God has revealed. ... And we, the Muslim Women's Association, reject the decision. The President of the Republic ... has no authority over us. ... Nor does the Ministry of Social Affairs. ... The government can confiscate assets but it cannot confiscate our creed.[34]

After the shutdown of the association's headquarters, members of the organization began to hold meetings in their homes, including al-Ghazali's. The government reacted by issuing warnings to the women, which resulted in fewer meetings and reduced their *da'wa* activities to the individual level.

Nasser then had al-Ghazali imprisoned and tortured for nearly seven years (1965–1972). She recounts in her memoirs the numerous attempts by her torturers to break her bond to the Brotherhood, Nasser's primary domestic opposition.

Before her imprisonment, throughout the development of building an independent nation in the 1940s and 1950s, al-Ghazali was a critical figure. She served as intermediary between her friends in the Islamist movement (the Brotherhood) and her friends in government, in particular Mustafa al-Nahhas, leader of the Wafd Party that controlled the government during this time.[35]

To one of many who have interviewed her, al-Ghazali recounted her life and her cause for women's rights within Islam. Women are, she said,

> a fundamental part of the Islamic call. ... They are the ones who build the kind of men that we need to fill the ranks of the Islamic call. So women must be well educated, cultured, knowing of the precepts of the Koran and sunna, informed about world politics, why we are backward, why we don't have technology. The Muslim woman must study all these things, and then raise her son in the conviction that he must possess the scientific tools of the age, and at the same time he must understand Islam, politics, geography, and current events. *He* must rebuild the Islamic nation.
>
> Islam does not forbid women to actively participate in public life. It does not prevent her from working, entering into politics, and expressing her opinion, or from being anything, as long as that does not interfere with her first duty as a mother, the one who first trains her children in the Islamic call. So her first, holy, and most important mission is to be a mother and wife. She cannot ignore this priority. If she then finds she has free time, she may participate in public activities. Islam does not forbid her.[36]

Al-Ghazali has been selective in practicing what she preaches. She has been prominent in Egypt's political and social arenas. Although her public statements emphasize that a woman's primary "mission" is to be a "wife and mother,"[37] her personal life demonstrates that, in practice, she has emphasized a public role in which women are encouraged to take part in actively spreading the Islamic *da'wa*. When al-Ghazali's first husband could not support her active role in the Islamic cause, the two were divorced. "She had stipulated before marrying him that her mission came first and that they would separate if there was any major disagreement between them."[38] Her stipulations before marriage were the same with her second husband, Muhammad Salim Salim:

> There is something in my life that you must know because you are going to be my husband. . . . I must tell you about it so that afterwards you will not ask me about it. I will not compromise on my demands with regard to this matter. I am the director of the Muslim Women's Association. . . . I believe in the message of the Muslim Brotherhood. . . . If [one day] your personal well-being and your economic work conflict with my Islamic work, and if I find that my marital life will get in the way of the *da'wa* and establishing an Islamic state, we will part roads. . . . It is my right to demand that you not prevent me from undertaking my *jihad* for God. And when responsibility places me in the ranks of the *mujahidin* [holy warriors], do not ask me what I am doing. . . . If the needs of marriage conflict with the *da'wa* for God, the marriage will end and the *da'wa* will remain.[39]

When her *da'wa* activitites raised Muhammad Salim's concern for her safety, al-Ghazali reminded him that he had agreed to these conditions before their marriage. She said: "Today I ask you to stand by your promise. Do not ask me whom I meet."[40]

Thus, although Zaynab al-Ghazali preaches that family responsibilities are important in a woman's life, her life's work does not suggest that a woman cannot simultaneously be a public figure and have a family. She explains that her public work did not lead to neglect of her "familial obligations" toward her husband.[41] Al-Ghazali asserted her independence before and after her marriage, and she placed her religious work above the marital obligations of which she often speaks. Her actions serve as a prominent example that women do not have to be relegated to a second class, subservient role in their marriages: the woman who is aware of her rights may stipulate conditions that her husband is then legally bound to uphold.

Al-Ghazali's second husband did support her ambitions, although he did not play an active role besides agreeing to serve as her "assistant." He facilitated her regular meetings at her home with other activists and allowed her to play a leading role in preparing new generations for the activism demanded by Hasan al-Banna. Her husband did not interfere in these activities, recognizing her right to work for the realization of an Islamic state. At no time did he suggest that her meetings with other men were improper. In the middle of the night, al-Ghazali writes, her husband would answer a knock at the door, admit one of her visitors, and then go back to bed, while al-Ghazali would join the visitor for a discussion. For this woman activist, there is no talk of female seclusion or segregation. Her role is similar to that of the veiled Islamist women described by Nilüfer Göle: "The prevailing image of a fatalist, passive, docile, and obedient traditional woman was replaced by that of an active, demanding, and, even, militant Muslim woman who is no longer confined to her home."[42]

Although al-Ghazali's work is not overtly feminist, the example she sets is that of a strong, independent woman who could not be held back either by her husband (who expressed concern for her safety) or by the state that tried to torture her into submission. She does not openly call for equality between men and women, but al-Ghazali's experiences demonstrate that the Islamist woman is not necessarily seeking to relegate women to the private sphere; on the contrary, in her activism against the secular state al-Ghazali shows strength, fortitude, and commitment to public change.

> By her own example, she emphasizes that women should be active in seeking to apply duties to God and the Islamic state above rights of individuals. This hierarchy allows her to use the Islamic legal system to empower herself. . . . She continues to use patriarchal discourse because like all women advocating radical reform in power relations she must hone her language so as to be heard. . . . Zaynab al-Ghazali may claim in interviews and write in Islamic journals that women should restrict themselves to the home, but in her life, and significantly, in writing her life, she marginalizes domesticity.[43]

In fact, in "writing her life" in her memoirs, al-Ghazali virtually avoids mention of a woman's responsibilities to her family. She does not seem to differentiate between her public role as a woman and that of a man. In her opinion both are equally responsible for upholding God's word. What is also noteworthy in al-Ghazali's memoirs is that she does not discuss women's rights, nor is she an advocate for women's causes. Rather, her advocacy is for an Islamic society that encompasses men and women alike. She calls not only on men to eliminate the *jahili* society but addresses both men and women, for the latter are also responsible for advancing the *da'wa* and building an Islamic society.

Islamist women's rights advocates (from various perspectives) abound in Egypt, including Safinaz Qasim, Ni'mat Fu'ad,[44] and Kariman Hamza,[45] though Zaynab al-Ghazali remains the best known and leading force in the women's Islamist movement through most of the 1990s.[46]

Women in Public and Private Spheres

The achievements of both Islamist and secular feminists have certainly been momentous, but women have a long way to go before becoming equal partners in Egypt's public realm. It is worth noting too that women's ventures into this "male domain" have been accompanied by an increased outward display of piety. As women attend college, hold down a job, and otherwise become public beings, they increasingly have opted to don the Islamic attire, *al-zay al-Islami*, which includes a head covering (*hijab*) and a long, modest dress. Thus rights have been won even though many women have consciously proclaimed themselves to be observant Muslims, demonstrating that women's rights and Islam are not incompatible. And Egypt's moderate Islamists agree. Indeed, they stress that women's rights are already well within the Islamic belief system. With regard to the role of women in society, al-Banna said:

> Woman is the half that influences the people's lives. She is the teacher who builds generations. . . . She is the primary influence on the lives of both the youth and men. Islam makes woman man's partner in rights and responsibilities, and Islam recognizes her complete personal, civil and political rights.[47]

The Muslim Brotherhood's Mustafa Mashhur argues that women should play a larger role in the *da'wa*. He cites specific methods that women should use, including holding private shows or bazaars that discuss Islamic issues and promoting awareness in schools. He also suggests that women should play a role in universities and syndicates, so long as this activity does not affect adversely a woman's responsibilities to her family. Mashhur stresses that a woman, as a good Muslim, should be active outside of the home:

> Some men have the false impression that a woman should have no work other than the home and they [men] stand in between her and participation [outside of the home]. This view must be corrected. There is nothing to prevent [a] woman from understanding what takes place around her in the Islamic realm. Whoever does not care about the condition of Muslims is not one of them.[48]

Similarly, Islamist Fahmi Huwaydi stresses the equality of man and woman before God, noting that man and woman were created from one spirit; both share responsibilities for one another; both are required to do good and avoid the forbidden; both must pray; both must pay *zakat;* and both must obey God and the Prophet. Thus, says Huwaydi, in Islam "there is equality between men and women in their rights and responsibilities in front of God and in front of the people."[49] Most Islamists discussing women's issues emphasize a woman's responsibility toward her family, but they are also quick to stress that a woman must also be active outside of the home. Huwaydi, for example, identifies raising a family as a woman's primary role. This notwithstanding, Huwaydi notes that for a woman

> this does not necessarily mean that she should not undertake another job, or that she must remain imprisoned in the home. The fact that motherhood is her primary job does not mean that it is her final job. Rather, there is nothing in the *Shari'a* or in the Islamic references to prevent a woman from taking another job alongside her familial responsibilities, whether this is participation in work in general, or in fulfillment of a hobby, or to deal with life's burdens. . . . [In Muslim history] . . . women participated in various activities, including politics and battle.[50]

Ma'mun al-Hudaybi, head of the Muslim Brotherhood delegation in the People's Assembly, argues that men and women are morally equal before God. According to Islam, woman and man both are commanded to seek knowledge. Since a woman must obey Islamic rules, al-Hudaybi asks, "how can she be held responsible for [obeying the rules] if she does not know and learn them? And how can she face the concerns of the era in which she lives if she does not have enough knowledge of the issues and condition of the era?"[51]

Islamists thus do not dispute that women should play a role in public affairs. They do, however, call on women to attend to their obligations to their families in addition to, and preferably in advance of, any public undertakings they might make. No doubt, the proliferation of Islamist organizations has had an impact on women's self-perceptions and their views on women's role in society. In accordance with the teachings of Hasan al-Banna and his followers, Islamists try to shape a new Muslim individual as the building block of a larger Muslim society, and they invariably influence society's views on gender relations.

Gender and Islam

Gender relations in contemporary Egyptian-Islamic society may be characterized as a combination of cooperation, indifference, and conflict.[52] In other words, they are more complex and nuanced than is thought by many. "The Western stereotype of relations between men and women in the Islamic world as the interaction of sheer power and abject obedience is quite inaccurate. Women are not passive victims, and they quite actively argue their case and seek to widen their opportunities when the chance is offered."[53] In analyzing gender relations in Egypt, it is helpful to examine various views concerning the status of women in Islam in general and to apply these "ideal-type" views to the Egyptian case. While allowing for the existence of other views, three perspectives tend to be dominant in Egyptian-Islamic society. Each perspective begins not with a view of gender relations or dynamics; rather, each tends to start with the position of "woman" in society, especially *woman* in *Islamic society*. "Gender," when it is discussed, flows from the centrality of *woman* in the debate over whether she is blessed or cursed (or both) in her situation in contemporary Egyptian society.[54]

One perspective argues that woman actually has a *preferred* status and position in Islam (in Egypt as throughout the *umma*), a better position than she has in secular society. This is the traditionalist or conservative perspective held by many Muslims, often to the bewilderment of those (in the West and the East) who criticize the subservience of Muslim women to men.

Many Islamists/traditionalists see the attempt to liberate woman as part of a "Western conspiracy" to undermine Islam. Some criticize reformist or progressive Muslims as dupes of the West, Crusaderism, and Zionism. And they are quick to point out that the model for reformists and the Arab feminist movement—"America"—is a morally bankrupt society characterized by, among other ills, violent crime; drugs; pornography; violence against children, women, and the family in general; and a rising number of illegitimate children. The accuracy of such a characterization, though close to caricature, adds weight to the traditionalist argument.

In contrast to the traditionalists' positive interpretation of woman's role in Muslim society is a negative view through which critics argue that traditionalists use the Quran to keep women subservient to men. These critics of the status of woman in Islam say that there is a duality here, that "fundamentalists" heap praise upon woman while humiliating and degrading her openly, in the name of Islam, but really for selfish, misogynist, or other ignorant reasons.

These critics include internationally acclaimed AWSA leader Nawal el Saadawi, whose organization's slogan is "Lifting the Veil from the Mind." Saadawi argues that most battles in the Arab region are religiously defined, thus reducing the multifaceted nature of Islam to a mere imposition of penalties that fall mostly upon the poor, and imposing the veil on women. . . . [The] economic reasons for expelling women from the wage-labour market and from public life are also concealed behind religious and moral appeals and claims. Thus, the challenge confronting Arab women becomes immense. It is women who must reveal these facts, must demonstrate that the particular Islamic sharia which the conservative movements have circulated is mostly based on distorted interpretations of Islam and other philosophies that emphasize the inevitability of fate. . . . The Arab woman must study religion, and interpret it with her own powers of rational intelligence, rather than seeing it through the minds of others.[55]

To Saadawi, Islam—its study and its active interpretation—can empower women. She represents, therefore, not a critic of *Islam* but of *conservatives* who incorrectly interpret Islam to the detriment, even "enslavement" of women.

Between the contrasting views of the role and status of women is a progressive, sensitive view of the potential for women's advancement in an Islamic discourse. Advocates of this view are understanding of the negative outlook and accept much of its critique of traditionalism. They do not disagree that Islam brought welcome reforms to the status of women in the Arab world. But they argue that the position of women in the early years of Islam, in the period during and immediately after the life of the Prophet Muhammad, was better than that which ensued under the increasingly patriarchal system that developed in subsequent years.

The progressives identify a difference between the religious injunctions introduced by Islam that, if properly interpreted, really can elevate the status of women, and the actual, male-dominated practices in Egypt (and elsewhere in the Islamic world) that, because of patriarchal interpretations by those in power, stress men's superiority over women. Therefore it is not Islam per se that is to blame for woman's position, but, rather, it is the conservative *interpretation* of Islam. Nawal el Saadawi "regards Islam as having progressive potential for women, and objects to conservative interpretations which cast women only in subordinated roles."[56]

Islam is not "owned" by any group; it is not limited to any ideology. Indeed, it is as much a part of conservatism as it is of progressivism. In the progressive sense Islam evokes a basic acceptance and accommodation of modernity. In returning to a genuine, legitimate, homegrown set of beliefs and values, Muslims can gain a sense of self-worth, independence of thought, and confidence on one hand and an acceptance of social, economic, scientific, political, and technological innovations on the other as their "Western" overtones are thrown off and these innovations are filtered through an authentic indigenous cultural screen.[57]

A Nonessentialist View of the Veil

The most visible outward display of the Islamic trend and of gender relations is Islamic attire, essentially that worn by women. The growing number of bearded men wearing white *jalabiyyas*, or other traditional gowns, is similarly an outward display of male piety. In its most common form, Islamic dress for women consists of a *hijab*, which is a head covering and not a facial veil, and a long, loose dress with long sleeves. Some women also wear a veil (*niqab*) across their face, and they might also wear gloves. Traditionalists stress the importance of Islamic attire for women, and they see its adoption as a demonstration of both increased religiosity and rejection of Western, alien norms. In contrast, critics of this view see the new trend toward Islamic attire as entirely retrogressive, wiping away the gains brought by decades of women's rights activism.

In a more practical mode, progressives look at the phenomenon of the *hijab* and see it not in stark revolutionary terms as do the two extremes. Veiling is seen to be appropriate if it is deemed useful by the woman who chooses it, and one cannot separate the return to the veil from the general increase in religious activity since the 1970s. After Egypt's defeat in 1967 at the hands of Israel, with the concomitant loss of the Sinai Peninsula, a general reexamination of politics and faith gave rise to a rejection of Nasser's version of socialism and Arab nationalism and to an embrace of traditionalism, including Islam.

Egyptian women, especially on college campuses, began to participate in a new veiling movement.[58] Also at this time, in addition to Egyptians' philosophical or psychological reexamination of lives, a much more practical reason for the adoption of the *hijab* developed: female students began to respond positively to efforts by the *jama'at Islamiyya*, the Islamic organizations at Egypt's universities. The *jama'at* were working to solve many of the problems of campus life— overcrowded classrooms, housing, and buses being primary. The *jama'at* also demanded and achieved segregation of the sexes by rows in the classrooms to alleviate the problem of having two or even three persons for each seat, a situation that often disturbed female students who had to choose between sitting in "mixed" company or enduring hours of instruction standing in equally mixed crowds. Similar embarrassment had to be endured on the daily journey to the campus in crowded public transportation. The *jama'at* responded to the latter problem by organizing a minibus service for the female students

> to preserve their dignity from the assaults to which they are subjected on public transport.... Its success was immediate. But since demand exceeded supply, it was first preferable, and later compulsory, for the women to dress in "Islamic style"—veil, long robe, gloves—if they wanted to use this means of transport.[59]

Thus, to many women students adherance to an Islamic dress code, which is easily justifiable in terms of local norms, practicality, and even emerging fashion, is a small price to pay to enjoy the special privileges fought for by the *jama'at*. Women have expressed many reasons for wearing Islamic attire:

- Religious. An act of obedience to the will of God
- Psychological. An affirmation of authenticity, a return to their roots and a rejection of Western norms
- Political. A sign of disenchantment with the prevailing political order
- Revolutionary. Identification with the Islamic revolutionary forces that affirm the necessity of the Islamization of society as the only means of its salvation
- Economic. A sign of affluence, of being a lady of leisure
- Practical. A means of reducing the amount to be spent on clothing (also an "economic" rationale, a class-based counterpoint to a sign of affluence)
- Cultural. A public affirmation of allegiance to chastity and modesty, of not being a sex object
- Domestic. A way to keep the peace, since males (husbands, fathers, brothers) in the family insist on it[60]

In our own research, we have found that alongside an increased religious awareness among some women, which results in their donning the *hijab*, Islamic attire is in many cases as much a statement of current fashion (*akhir moda*) as it is of convenience and of politics. In fact, the new Islamic attire differs from traditional dress in that it is much more fashionable. Women mix their messages: they don "Islamic" garb but wear makeup and dangling gold earrings—a combination that is inconsistent with prescribed Islamic attire. The clothing is of the latest style, often featuring sequins or other ornamentation, purchased in one of the "Islamic boutiques" located throughout Cairo and Alexandria, including in middle- and upper-class neighborhoods.

Whereas the point of Islamic attire is to hide the contours of the body, many of Egypt's new Islamic garments are form fitting and bear little similarity to the simple, loose Islamic garb of long ago. (President Sadat's criticism of this dress as akin to "tents" was not simply ignorant, it is now largely inaccurate.) An item of apparel accompanying many outfits—a matching hat adorned with sequins and sitting atop the *hijab*—differs significantly from the simple headdress worn in other parts of the Islamic world and suggests a sense of style and fashion as much as, if not more than, religious observance.

Some women wear traditional clothing one day yet switch back to more Western styles on other days. When asked whether they consider this inconsistent, respondents say no, that it is merely a matter of taste or mood—or, of course, purpose. Many women will dress conservatively in public to negotiate the crush of crowds, predominantly men. At home, however, the *hijab* readily comes off, even in the presence of men who are not close relatives—something that strict adherence to Islam dictates against.[61] All of this suggests less a concern about making a political or Islamic statement and more one of individual choice.

There was a similar pluralism in responses to a study carried out by Egypt's National Centre for Social and Criminological Studies. In the mid-1980s, the center found over 60 percent of their sample of educated Egyptian women wearing Islamic dress. "Of these, forty percent claim they wear it for reasons of modesty and cost, twenty-five percent because it is fashionable, ten percent to avoid going to a hair dresser, and five percent because they feel that men are less likely to molest a modestly dressed woman."[62]

As one respondent to an interview on this question put it to us, "I wear this traditional style to send a clear message to men in the streets [of Cairo] and especially on the metro [subway]. The message is, I'm a married woman, a mother, and a good Muslim. Don't bother me!"[63] This "20-something" woman made it clear she was not an Islamist or, as she put it, a "fundamentalist." She is as "modern" as many women who do not veil themselves, but the veil allows her to participate in the modern economy of Egypt.

Islamic attire remains a central component and prominent symbol of the larger debate regarding women's rights, role, and status in Muslim societies and polities:

> Some women argue that "modest dress" frees women to move around the streets and the workplace without harassment by men. Opponents argue that it is another form of male control and male definition of women's space. They further argue that it stigmatizes

those who do not conform and denies women the freedom to decide on their own appearance: personal morality should not be confused with external conformity to norms of dress. One consequence of this visual divide has been to put considerable pressure on young women to adopt modest dress, and many do so, for a variety of reasons which may have little to do with adherence to an Islamist group or even with personal piety.[64]

The *hijab* may be a symbol of social and political norms. It also may have nothing to do with such grand causes. For most Egyptian women, including traditional Christians who also dress conservatively, their attire is largely a matter of individual choice or negotiating behavior within the context of personal circumstances.

Conclusion

If there is a tentative conclusion about the debate over women's rights, role, and status in Muslim societies, it is that

> in all the discussions of the role and status of women one thing stands out. Regardless of ideological commitment, whether nationalist, socialist or Islamist, and regardless of the sex of the author, *the liberation of women is seen within the context of the liberation of the whole society, liberation essential in bringing about a virtuous order.*[65]

Women as a category indeed "are central to the process of the recreation of the community due to their role as symbolic 'cultural bearers' of national tradition." It is easy to see how this aspect of Islamist ideology (and/or Islamic theology) gets connected to the broader "issues of national identity, notions of citizenship as well as gender relations."[66]

As we have learned from Egyptian feminists over the past century, the struggles for Islam, women, nation, and identity (as well as education, development, and prosperity) need not be in isolation from or competition with one another.[67] These women and men have demonstrated that such struggles are more likely to succeed when collective and collaborative, not independently or in conflict. But when the state intervenes to "divide and conquer," it is quick to find obvious points of disagreement and turn them into divisive disputes. The state's interests are generally at variance with those of society and its various movements. Societal cooperation—for the cohesiveness it builds as well as for the improvement in collective lives—is thus a threat to state objectives (the regime's maintainenance of power being primary). Indeed, in the quest to perpetuate the political domination of a single political party with the state's president at its helm, Egypt, like many other states in the Arab world, has introduced policies of political democratization that allow only symbolic participation by citizens of either sex. Both men and women are denied their rights to engage fully in either the social or political arena. And, in the realm of women's social and political activity, both secular and Islamist women's organizations are penalized by the state if they transgress the threshold of tolerable opposition to the state.

> Arab democratic institutions have been created to enhance the legitimacy of precarious governments; they were not intended to invite men and women to express their needs and to participate in decision making.... Thus the roles of women were discouraged; they were seen as an inconvenience that could upset the delicate alliance between the ruling elite and the clerical establishment.[68]

The rulers of Egypt understand that Islam in and of itself is not the threat (witness, for instance, Sadat's use of Islam to build a constituency). Islam becomes a threat when it gets appropriated by societal groups seeking to pursue objectives that may challenge the state. In this regard, the promotion of women's rights through the discourse of Islam is very much the same as the promotion of Egyptian rights through that same discourse. Islamism, not Islam, may be considered a threat to the current political order.

Notes

1. Valentine Moghadam, *Modernizing Women: Gender and Social Change in the Middle East* (Boulder, Colo.: Lynne Rienner, 1993), p. 144. Under the title "Personal Status Laws and the Control of Women" Moghadam compares Egypt's laws with those of other Arab and Muslim polities.

2. One of the most troubling and culturally sensitive of these practices is female genital mutilation, more commonly and incorrectly known as female circumcision. This is not an Islamic practice, of course. It predates Islam and is practiced by Christians and Muslims alike in Egypt (and many other societies), primarily in the more traditional parts of Upper Egypt (the south of the country). The government has launched campaigns against this practice, a disturbing one to many in Egypt and elsewhere.

3. Azza M. Karam, *Women, Islamisms and the State* (New York: St. Martin's Press, 1998), p. 101.

4. Ibid., p. 234. Karam discusses three main feminisms: Islamist, Muslim, and secular (see Chapters 1 and 9). She uses feminism as "an identification technique to map out all the women [and men?] who acknowledge that women are oppressed by different means and in many ways, and who actively seek to rectify this injustice by diverse methods."

5. *The Liberation of Women (Tahrir al-Mar'a)* is the title of Qasim Amin's classic, first published in Arabic in 1899. See its translation, *The Liberation of Women: A Document in the History of Egyptian Feminism*, by Samiha Sidhom Peterson (Cairo: American University in Cairo Press, 1992).

6. Karam, *Women*, chapter 5.

7. Nawal el Saadawi, *The Nawal El Saadawi Reader* (London and New York: Zed Books, 1997), p. 7.

8. Middle East Watch, "Egyptian Government Moves to Dissolve Prominent Arab Women's Organization," September 1991, p. 4.

9. See Margot Badran, *Feminists, Islam and Nation: Gender and the Making of Modern Egypt* (Princeton: Princeton University Press, 1995), p. 67.

10. Margot Badran, "Independent Women: More than a Century of Feminism in Egypt," in Judith E. Tucker ed., *Arab Women: Old Boundaries, New Frontiers* (Bloomington: Indiana University Press, 1993), p. 129.

11. See especially Cynthia Nelson, *Doria Shafik, Egyptian Feminist: A Woman Apart* (Gainesville: University Press of Florida, 1996).

12. Karam, *Women*, p. 101. It may be difficult to pinpoint its birth, but feminism certainly was an important element in the 1880s when Egyptians fought against British colonial domination.

13. Badran, *Feminists*.

14. 'Abd al-Mut'al al-Jabri, *Al-Muslima al-'Asriyya 'Ind Bahithat al-Badiyya Malak Hifni Nasif [The Contemporary Muslim Woman According to the Searcher in the Desert Malak Hifni Nasif]* (Cairo: Dar al-Ansar, 1979), p. 9.

15. Ibid., p. 11.

16. Badran, "Independent Women," p. 134.

17. Al-Jabri, *Al-Muslima*, p. 54.

18. Ibid., p. 54.

19. Ibid., p. 35.

20. Ibid., p. 35.

21. The harem system was one of separation of women from men and the exclusion of men from their private space. In affluent homes, the portion of the home reserved for women (the harem) allowed women, unseen, to watch activities in the men's reception rooms from behind latticework windows. Evelyn A. Early, *Baladi Women of Cairo: Playing with an Egg and a Stone* (Boulder, Colo.: Lynne Rienner, 1993), p. 69.

22. Margot Badran, in Huda Shaarawi, *Harem Years: The Memoirs of an Egyptian Feminist (1879–1924)* (New York: The Feminist Press at the City University of New York, 1986).

23. The Wafd Party was the preeminent political force fighting British colonial rule and leading the country after nominal independence in 1922.

24. "Women," *Arab World Notebook*, unpublished manuscript, p. 74 (n.d.).

25. Badran, *Harem Years*, p. 136–137.

26. Ibid., p. 137.

27. Both "association" and "society" are used in English as translations of the Arabic word *jam'iyya*. Either is acceptable to speak of NGOs generally; but use of "society" often connotes political motivations. For example, the Society of Muslim Brothers, founded by al-Banna, or the Society of Muslims, founded by Shukri Mustafa (see Chapters 3 and 4).

28. Valerie J. Hoffman, "An Islamic Activist: Zeinab al-Ghazali," in Elizabeth Warnock Fernea, ed., *Women and the Family in the Middle East* (Austin: University of Texas Press, 1985); cited in Leila Ahmed, *Women and Gender in Islam* (Yale University Press, 1992), p. 198.

29. Ibid., Ahmed, p. 197.

30. The establishment of the Muslim Sisters Association is discussed by Layla Salim in "Al-Mar'a fi Da'wat wa Fikr Hasan al-Banna: Bayn al-Madi wa al-Hadir [Woman in the Call and Thought of Hasan al-Banna: Between the Past and Present]," *Liwa' al-Islam,* January 1990, p. 52.

31. Al-Ghazali's relationship with Hasan al-Banna is discussed in her prison memoirs: Zaynab al-Ghazali, *Ayam min Hayati [Days of My Life]* (Cairo: Dar al-Shuruq, n.d.).

32. Al-Ghazali, *Ayam min Hayati,* p. 25.

33. Miriam Cooke, "Zaynab al-Ghazali: Saint or Subversive?" *Die Welt des Islams* 34 (1994), p. 2.

34. Al-Ghazali, *Ayam min Hayati,* pp. 14–15.

35. Hoffman, "An Islamic Activist," pp. 197–198.

36. Ibid., pp. 236–237; see also Ahmed, p. 199. Emphasis added.

37. See al-Ghazali's regular column in *Liwa' al-Islam* for the advice she gives to Muslim women.

38. Ahmed, "Women," p. 200.

39. Al-Ghazali, *Ayam min Hayati,* pp. 34–35.

40. Ibid., p. 35.

41. Ibid., p. 33.

42. Nilüfer Göle, *The Forbidden Modern: Civilization and Veiling* (Ann Arbor: University of Michigan Press, 1996), p. 84.

43. Cooke, "Zaynab al-Ghazali," p. 20.

44. For discussions of Fu'ad and Qasim, as well as detailed analysis of the views and life work of Zaynab al-Ghazali, see Sherifa Zuhur, *Revealing Reveiling: Islamist Gender Ideology in Contemporary Egypt* (Albany: SUNY Press, 1992).

45. On Hamza, see Fedwa Malti-Douglas, *A Woman and Her Sufis,* the Kareema Khoury Annual Distinguished Lecture in Arab Studies. Published by Georgetown University's Center for Contemporary Arab Studies, 1995. Malti-Douglas examines Hamza's autobiographical *My Journey from Unveiling to Veiling,* which "recounts the dramatic story of a born-again young woman who travels from a secular to a religious lifestyle" (p. 3).

46. See Elizabeth Warnock Fernea, *In Search of Islamic Feminism: One Woman's Global Journey* (New York: Doubleday, 1997) for a discussion of Islamic women's movements in comparative perspective, including the Egyptian case.

47. Salim, "Al-Mar'a," p. 52.

48. Ibid., p. 52.

49. Fahmi Huwaydi, "Twenty-Four Conditions in Which Woman Inherits the Same as Man, and Sometimes More than Him!" (in Arabic) *Al-Majalla,* 25 October 1997, p. 32.

50. Ibid., p. 32.

51. Asma al-Husayni, "Interview with Ma'mun al-Hudaybi," *Liwa' al-Islam,* August 1990, p. 50.

52. For a discussion of *baladi* (traditional) gender relations, see Early, *Baladi Women of Cairo*; put in the *sha'bi* (popular) context, see Diane Singerman, *Avenues of Participation: Family, Politics, and Networks in Urban Quarters of Cairo* (Princeton, N.J.: Princeton University Press, 1995).

53. Arlene Elowe Macleod, *Accommodating Protest: Working Women, the New Veiling, and Change in Cairo* (New York: Columbia University Press, 1991), p. 41.

54. For an account of how gender is portrayed (or neglected) in Egyptian literature see Nadje Sadig Al-Ali, *Gender Writing/Writing Gender: The Representation of Women in a Selection of Modern Egyptian Literature* (Cairo: American University in Cairo Press, 1994).

55. Nawal El Saadawi, trans. Marilyn Booth, "The Political Challenges Facing Arab Women at the End of the 20th Century," in Nahid Toubia, ed., *Women of the Arab World* (London: Zed Books, 1988), p. 19.

56. Sarah Graham-Brown, "Women and Politics in the Middle East," in Suha Sabbagh, ed., *Arab Women: Between Defiance and Restraint* (New York: Olive Branch Press, 1996), p. 7.

57. Louis J. Cantori, "The Islamic Revival as Conservatism and as Progress in Contemporary Egypt" in Emile Sahliyeh, ed., *Religious Resurgence and Politics in the Contemporary World* (Albany: SUNY Press, 1990), p. 192.

58. Macleod, *Accommodating Protest*, p. 103.

59. Gilles Kepel, trans. Jon Rothschild, *Muslim Extremism in Egypt* (London: Al-Saqi Books, 1985). See especially his section, *Prima la Donna*, in chapter 5; the quote is from this section, p. 143.

60. In creating this list, we borrow heavily from Yvonne Yazbeck Haddad, "Islam, Women and Revolution in Twentieth-Century Arab Thought," in Y. Y. Haddad and E. B. Findly, eds., *Women, Religion and Social Change* (Albany: State University of New York Press, 1985). Our own research and interviews in Egypt and elsewhere corroborate Haddad's findings.

61. Denis Sullivan, interview with health insurance agency administrator, al-Marg, April 1991.

62. Andrea Rugh, *Reveal and Conceal: Dress in Contemporary Egypt* (Syracuse, N.Y.: Syracuse University Press, 1986), p. 149.

63. Denis Sullivan, interview with cashier in a large grocery store in Digla region of Cairo, May 1991.

64. Sarah Graham-Brown, "Women and Politics in the Middle East," second pamphlet in MERIP's series on women in the Middle East (n.d.). pp. 7–8.

65. Haddad, "Islam," p. 279 (emphasis added).

66. Hala Shukrallah, "The Impact of the Islamic Movement in Egypt," *Feminist Review*, no. 47 (Summer 1994), p.16.

67. See, for instance, Denis J. Sullivan, *Private Voluntary Organizations in Egypt: Islamic Development, Private Initiative, and State Control* (Gainesville: University Press of Florida, 1994).

68. As'ad AbuKhalil, "Gender Boundaries and Sexual Categories in the Arab World," *Feminist Issues* 15, nos. 1–2 (1997): 100.

6

State and Civil Society in Conflict

Often thought of as being one of the more tolerant, liberal, and secure of Arab states, Egypt has a political structure that is in fact an authoritarian, dominant-party system supported by a military and security establishment that severely restricts the political, social, and economic activities—and rights—of its citizens. While there has been a steady movement over the past two decades by both grassroots and elite organizations[1] to promote greater freedoms in all of these activities, Egypt's political leaders have successfully stifled progress on these fronts. With some notable exceptions,[2] Egyptian society in general and its resilient civil society in particular do exhibit the traits of tolerance and civility.[3] Still, Egypt's political overlords have failed to take advantage of this situation, which they might have used to develop the open political and economic system many in the West think the nation has already. Indeed, Egypt's leaders have squandered decades of political successes—stability, regime maintenance, international backing, and relative social order—with a series of self-inflicted wounds, largely in the form of legal "reforms" initiated by the executive and rubber-stamped by a parliament controlled by President Hosni Mubarak's ruling National Democratic Party (NDP). Even though it is correct to say that in Egypt "the state has permitted a degree of autonomy for societal actors," it is even more the case that there are no effective "limitations on arbitrary exercise of state authority."[4]

This concluding chapter analyzes the last point and suggests that, although the intolerance that is demonstrated so violently by militant Islamist groups has been a significant issue throughout the 1990s,[5] the overall crisis atmosphere in state-society relations in Egypt is due primarily to the policies and intolerant attitudes of Egyptian government officials. The best demonstration of these policies is the state's crackdown on Islamists from 1992 onward, a crackdown that has targeted militant as well as nonviolent Islamists; further, the state has not hesitated to detain and interrogate members of Islamists' families in pursuing its security measures. This political and policing method of dealing with Islamist opponents "will prove counter-productive in the long run—and even in the short run. . . . [President Mubarak's] regime spares no effort to antagonize the masses and alienate the elite. Ordinary Egyptians already endure economic crisis and structural adjustment. They require no further harassment in the form of increasing police brutality."[6]

In addition to its campaign of violence against political challengers, the government has embarked on promulgating a string of laws and other actions to strengthen the control it already has over Egyptian society. This chapter examines the most significant of these many laws and analyzes their collective impact, which is to restrict individual and collective efforts of Egyptian citizens, their professional and community associations, and their political and other ideological organizations. These laws and other acts include the following:

- Law 32 of 1964, the Law of Associations (see Chapter 2)
- Emergency Law, in effect continuously since 1981
- Law 97, the Antiterrorism Law of 1992
- 1992 executive order aimed at "nationalizing" private mosques
- Syndicates Law of 1993
- Manipulation of elections (local and national)
- Use of military courts to expedite trials and executions of accused terrorists
- Law 93, the Press Law of 1995

These actions, coupled with increased government repression and torture, have diminished what little popular support the political system previously had. Still, this government is not in danger of losing power to a resurgent society: that is, Islamist revolution is unlikely in Egypt and the secular opposition is likewise unable to transform the system.

This assessment is at odds with reports, the details of which were denied by several intelligence officials interviewed for this book,[7] that "American intelligence analysts believe that President Hosni Mubarak of Egypt is in grave danger of being overthrown by Islamic fundamentalists."[8] Although the Egyptian government demonstrates numerous deficiencies and weak spots, the *system* (i.e., the regime) has long had the ability to survive, by pluck or luck, and to thwart any competition or threat to its existence (e.g., Islamist violence, foreign invasion, economic crises, social unrest, internal division, and drift). Such survivability is due to the continued strength and general loyalty of the armed forces, central security forces (*al-amn al-markazy*), and secret police (*mukhabarat*). And whether or not Mubarak remains, the regime that he runs (like Sadat before him) is what will survive for many years to come.

The foiled assassination attempt on Mubarak in Addis Ababa, Ethiopia, in June 1995 (one of many attempts) has become a cause the government uses to demonstrate the effectiveness of its security forces, the indispensability of Mubarak to stability in Egypt, the necessity of continued vigilance against terrorism, and the government's supposed commitment to continued democratic reform.[9] This incident plus two other occurrences—(1) continuing violence between Islamist militants and police and (2) parliamentary elections in November and December 1995 (criticized widely for their apparent unfairness and "irregularities")—seem to have emboldened the government in its ongoing campaign to crush nonviolent opponents of the regime *as well as* violent groups and to prevent the development of a more free and open civil society. There is at present no alternative that can challenge, or act as a check on, the power of the state.

The most apparent alternative is the Muslim Brotherhood, the group considered to have the most effective organization, the largest following, and the longest record of electoral success against the ruling party. In addition to the Brotherhood's electoral success as an indication of popular support for the group, the *Ikhwan* is popular because of its ability to mobilize financial and human resources for the benefit of the poor and neglected across the country. The Brotherhood's social services and economic enterprises have given hope and concrete benefits to millions of Egyptians. The Brotherhood has been both a social-economic organization and a political movement since its founding. It has been joined in the social-economic realm in the past two decades by hundreds of other Islamic NGOs that also can mobilize resources to respond to the needs of the poor and neglected in villages, towns, and districts of major urban centers throughout Egypt. This latter amalgamation of disparate organizations, however, has not been centrally coordinated or nationally connected enough to insert itself into the political realm, as has the Brotherhood.

The Brotherhood might actually benefit from this. As it and the disparate groups serve thousands of communities nationally, they become a collective challenge to the state that has largely failed those same communities. If such a challenge to the state is to be used for electoral gain, it is the nationally organized Brotherhood that can undertake the necessary mobilization. Similarly, if the state sees that this challenge is credible, it will be the Brotherhood that will suffer the consequences of a "defensive" authoritarian regime.

Perhaps it is no coincidence that after the popular show of support for Mubarak upon his safe return to Cairo from Ethiopia in 1995 and as parliamentary elections approached, the government accelerated a massive campaign against the previously tolerated Brotherhood, which espouses nonviolence and a willingness to play by the rules of Egyptian politics. The government claims to have found a "paper trail" linking the Brotherhood with the outlawed Islamic militant groups *al-Jihad* and *al-Jama'a al-Islamiyy*a. It imprisoned over two hundred mainly young members of the Brotherhood in July 1995. Fahmi Huwaydi, a prominent Islamist columnist for the semiofficial *Al-Ahram* Arabic daily, compares this move with the mistakes made by Algeria's government when it cracked down on the Islamic Salvation Front in January 1992,[10] sending that country into military dictatorship and chaos. Egypt is far from falling into such chaos, but the fear among many in Egypt is that without any limits on government dictates, this could be the direction in which the country is heading. For now the government remains powerful and effective at stifling dissent from both the militant minority and the nonviolent mainstream opposition.

Islam . . . "Resurgent"?[11]

Manageable though they might be, domestic instability and Islamist militancy—attacks on police, other government officials, innocent bystanders, and tourists—are arguably manifestations of severe economic dislocation: consistently high unemployment; overpopulation (mainly in urban areas); bank failures (primarily Islamic investment companies); and the inadequacy of transportation, housing, education, and health services.[12] Authoritarian politics of exclusion is an equally important factor explaining the continuing conflict between state and society in Egypt. Such exclusion limits the outlets of expression of dissatisfaction, anger, and frustration. In these circumstances, the growing popularity of Islamist groups (primarily the mainstream Muslim Brotherhood but not necessarily the militant groups such as *al-Jihad* and *al-Jama'a al-Islamiyy*a) is understandable.[13]

Such popularity is not due to some inevitable return to the traditionalism long sought by most Egyptians. Indeed, *Islam* is not necessarily "resurgent" in Egypt; this religion and way of life has been maintained for centuries as the dominant factor throughout society. Fouad Ajami indicated in 1981 that

> phrases like "the resurgence of Islam" are so powerfully evocative that they make us lose sight of the real struggles that [people] are engaged in. . . . People summon the spirits of the past to help them achieve very precise goals. . . . In some cases, the spirits are summoned simply because people are trying to find something with which to combat remote, smug, or oppressive state elites. The balance between state and society has been fundamentally disrupted in the Arab-Muslim order. . . . The popular culture finds no more effective weapon of resistance than Islam.[14]

Edward Said, in a general look at the Islamist trend in the Arab world, agrees. He criticizes the Western tendency to misrepresent the current crisis in the Arab world, especially Egypt, and denounces the idea that "fundamentalism is a sudden and therefore entirely new eruption from within. For at least a hundred years, the Arab nationalist movement and the Islamic reform movement have been intertwined."[15]

Whether Egyptians are more or less "Islamic" today than ten or twenty years ago is perhaps an unanswerable question; given the authoritarian nature of Egypt's government throughout this timeframe plus the built-in inadequacies of attempting to conduct survey research in such a setting, the question is not measurable at any rate. What is demonstrable (and measurable) and worthy of attention is the rising popularity of the various Islamic *institutions,* political and nonpolitical, violent and nonviolent.

Egyptian intellectuals see the increase in Islamism as being related both to political and socioeconomic deficiencies. Isma'il Sabri 'Abdallah, minister of planning under Sadat, links the growth in militancy to economic problems and to "the normative vacuum of Egyptian society," by which he means the lack of national goals and beliefs.[16] Feminist psychiatrist Nawal el Saadawi finds the popularity of Islamism rooted in socioeconomic frustrations, including unemployment and lack of affordable housing. Such frustration, she notes, leads either to violence or to increased submission to God.[17] We find the increase in Islamist activity to indeed be related to both sets of national deficiencies—the political and the economic.

The increase in Islamist organizational activity is due to the ability of Islamist individuals, groups, and their organizations to recognize the problems of ordinary Egyptians, to mobilize resources, and to help solve many such problems (e.g., health care, education, job training, access to credit facilities and legal services). Even when these groups cannot actually solve some problems (e.g., unemployment), the fact that they recognize socioeconomic ills and are addressing them in a proactive manner tells the ordinary Egyptian that these people, from their own communities, are at least concerned about their plight. In contrast, they view the government mainly as a corrupt and lazy bureaucracy[18]—a government (especially its powerful and effective security apparatuses) that does not care, is not trying to help, and is in fact making matters worse.

Government Attacks

Many analysts in Egypt are placing blame for the continuing instability on the government itself. Even though President Mubarak admitted to one journalist from *The New Yorker* that "we are in a mess," he blames the Western media for scaring off tourists (one of Egypt's primary sources of revenues and foreign exchange);[19] and as some in the semiofficial Egyptian press likewise blast Western media "propaganda," other Egyptian journalists say it is the government itself that has exaggerated the power of Islamist militants. Muhammad Hassanein Heikal, a close confidant of President Nasser, criticizes the massive government assault on the Cairo slum district of Imbaba in December 1992: this act gave the militants a "bonus of strength" they did not really have. It frightened away would-be visitors to Egypt and "killed" tourism.[20]

Six months before this particular government assault, in June, the security forces were sent into another poor Cairo suburb after the assassination of Faraj Fuda, a liberal Muslim intellectual, leader in the human rights and democracy movements, and strong critic of Islamist fundamentalists and militants. His murderers, one of whom was caught immediately, are said to be from the outlawed *Jihad* organization, the group associated with the assassination of Anwar Sadat in 1981. In the aftermath of Fuda's murder, progovernment journalists were warning of the dangers should the government overreact. Hasan Rajab, of *Al-Akhbar*, said that these militants/terrorists "love to be martyrs and they want to move the government toward confrontation. And the more repressive the government becomes, the more unstable it becomes. If the government takes away civil liberties, the extremists have succeeded."[21] The distinguished columnist Mustafa Amin similarly warned that the extremists "are strong when you hit them—weak when you argue with them."[22]

The government, however, does not heed this advice from its own highly respected social commentators. Instead, it has taken the opposite course of action: it strikes hard, and it avoids accommodation. A report by the Lawyers Committee for Human Rights finds that, "Tens, if not hundreds, of thousands of Egyptians have been detained without charge or trial under the Emergency Law since 1981. Most detainees are released after a month or two in prison without charge or trial. They emerge having suffered some rough treatment, and bearing a grudge against the authorities."[23] The Egyptian Organization for Human Rights and Human Rights Watch/Middle East have documented hundreds of cases of torture by government officers, primarily against Islamists.[24]

In 1993 the U.S. Department of State also acknowledged that "there is convincing evidence that police and security forces systematically practice torture. . . . Most torture is perpetrated by officers of the Interior Ministry's GDSSI (General Directorate for State Security Investigations]."[25] By 1995 the State Department was even more direct in noting that "there continued to be widespread human rights violations in 1994. . . . Security forces committed human rights abuses in their campaign against terrorist groups, but frequently victimized noncombatants as well."[26] The government is relentless in pursuing and eliminating any challengers. The history and continuation of torture demonstrate the lengths government agents go to "defend" themselves—and torture is not limited to suspected militants but extends to family members and legal counsel as well.[27] Egyptian and international human rights reports document not only the abuse of human rights but the failure of the government of Egypt "to punish those responsible for torture."[28]

Laws of the Land

The Emergency Law has been in effect continuously since Sadat's assassination in 1981. First promulgated in 1958 and then in 1967, it was resurrected in the state of emergency that accompanied Sadat's murder. The law gives the government sweeping authority and control over societal activities and authorizes censorship of printed materials, restrictions on meetings and gatherings, and arrests on the basis of suspicion.[29] It has been supplemented with a series of new laws and at least one old one. Law 32 of 1964 restricts freedom of association and governs (monitors, controls, and limits) private, nonprofit activities. The 1992 Antiterrorism Law allows government to (judicially) kill people just for belonging to a "terrorist" group. The 1993 Syndicate Law makes it nearly certain that the government will appoint the boards of syndicates (unions) in an attempt to break Islamist control of professional associations. In its campaign against militants, the government has shifted the trials of suspected militants to military courts to ensure conviction, hasten execution, and avoid appeals.

In November 1992 the government announced its intention to "nationalize" private mosques, numbering some 140,000 in Egypt, in order to dictate sermons to Muslims attending Friday prayers and to better monitor the activities of militant organizations. "Nationalizing" meant putting these 140,000 mosques under the direct supervision of the Ministry of Religious Endowments (*Awqaf*). The Minister of Awqaf, Muhammad 'Ali Mahjub, justified the government's actions by claiming that mosques had a "duty . . . to be a source of security and stability for the country. . . . They should not be allowed to become centres for extremist activities."[30]

This action is reported to have been decided in the wake of a clash between security forces and Islamist militants around a private mosque in Asyut.[31] The Muslim Brotherhood was among the first to denounce the government's plan as a violation of freedom of expression. Ma'mun al-Hudaybi, spokesman for the Brotherhood, said that freedom of expression in Friday sermons is as vital to society as the freedom to deliver speeches or publish one's viewpoint in newspapers or books. He suggested that the government's action "would further promote extremism and violence among young people."[32] The mosque "nationalization" law came under criticism from various government officials, who claim that it will only push militants further underground and that the government could have continued to monitor their activities as it had done previously.[33]

This critique of the Egyptian government and its manipulation of the legislative process is not to suggest that the regime is teetering on the brink. In fact, state security apparatuses are relatively effective in uncovering threats, preventing them, and/or retaliating against groups and individuals who sponsor them. Such effectiveness, however, might be the problem. The strength of its security and police apparatuses and their combined disregard for human rights and civil liberties mean that the government can indeed control Egyptian society but the methods it uses remove its legitimacy to govern. Egyptians have long tolerated the authoritarian, undemocratic rule established by Nasser but only as long as their basic economic needs were met and so long as their personal and social liberties have remained *relatively* unencumbered by political processes. This was the "social contract" established under Nasser and maintained, with some major violations, by his successors.

As the government of Egypt has failed in its economic programs and has expanded its control over and restriction of political activities, societal tolerance of state practices has begun to be reconsidered, to say the least. For many Egyptians, the current regime is illegitimate, always has been, and always will be. Michael Hudson pointed out in 1977 that "the Egyptian political system today faces a serious legitimacy problem."[34] How much worse did this legitimacy problem become after Camp David and the failure by Sadat to secure the peace dividend he promised? And how worse still with the increasingly authoritarian nature of the regime and the low-level civil strife evident throughout the country?

For the majority of Egyptians, legitimacy is not the key issue: the government has long had very little of it. Instead, tolerance is the key. Whatever the institutions (be they Islamic, Coptic Christian, capitalist, feminist, labor, other government, or nongovernmental) that *do not hinder* a person, her or his family, and community, those institutions will be tolerated. Institutions that *do hinder* individuals and families will not be. Most important, whatever institutions *help* people and their families are to be supported, given allegiance, and bestowed with legitimacy.

This is the danger for the Egyptian government. It surely will remain in power (for the medium term at least); but if it loses acceptance and/or legitimacy in the eyes of the majority of Egyptians, its tenure will remain tentative and unstable. Therefore the chance remains that it could collapse, either within the existing system, from some invigorated democratic impulse, or from some as yet unseen Islamist organization that is much stronger and more unified than the existing groupings. The key for the government's stability is not just to offset obvious threats and establish security, though these are necessary prerequisites. The government must win the acceptance and support of the increasingly less silent majority that is fed up with the two faces of the Egyptian government: first, the *ineffective face* of economic planners and managers and their bureaucratic inertia, red tape, neglect, and disrespect; and, second, the *effective face* of security forces that demonstrate their power to force compliance, control private organizations, prohibit formation of political parties and numerous other groups, and restrict the supposedly guaranteed freedoms of speech and assembly.

The Egyptian government says these prohibitions are necessary given the security situation, a situation that threatens not only the government but also its citizens generally (Christians and Muslims) and its guests (resident foreigners, tourists, diplomats). Former Prime Minister 'Atif Sidki called the Antiterrorism Law of July 1992 "the minimum required" to confront the danger of "terrorist groups whose aim is to topple the government, suspend the constitution, and sabotage the economy."[35] The dominant voice of the internally divided Egyptian government maintains that democratic principles, as with economic reform, must be pursued and attained gradually, step by step, and this approach is an understandable argument. Still, the *pressure* to move down the liberal path—for both economic and political liberalization—must be maintained, primarily from within and only subtly from outside Egypt.

Government Confronts the Press

In one case where the government attempted to severely restrict freedom of expression via legislative action, internal liberal voices were heard and forced the government to back away from its plans. This case is that of Law 93 of 1995, the new Press Law, which would have made the publication of "false" news deemed detrimental to national interest punishable by imprisonment for five years plus a £E 20,000 (approximately $6,500) fine. After the Press Syndicate threatened a one-day work stoppage and their chairman, Ibrahim Nafie, who otherwise supports Mubarak's government, denounced the proposed law, Mubarak all but withdrew the bill and promised no further action until after the parliamentary elections in November. This issue returned to prominence in early 1996 as the legislature passed a watered-down version of this bill that still restricts freedom of the press and other publications. Despite the apparent backing down by Mubarak's government, opposition journalists in mid-1996 were still charged with "crimes" related to criticizing the president and/or his family.

Society Resurgent

What these laws indicate is a government that is out of touch with its citizenry even as society does what it can to help itself. The manifestation of this self-help is found in a widespread and diverse phenomenon, reemerging especially since the 1980s, whose roots date back to over a century ago in Egypt. That phenomenon is of Islamic, Christian, and secular NGOs operating as an important developmental and political community; indeed, they are a primary component of civil society. The NGOs are responding primarily to the needs of individuals and communities suffering from government mismanagement of the largely state-run economy and from state control of social and political activities. Many NGOs are inevitably involved in both socioeconomic development and political activism (the latter being specificly illegal under Law 32 of 1964; see Chapter 2).

As discussed in Chapter 2, through Law 32 the government has maintained a great degree of control over Islamic, Christian, and secular NGOs, even as an increasing number of academics, people in business, development specialists, and political and social activists have sought a reform of this law.[36] The government does not appear to be moving toward any type of accommodation with the above disparate groups, and, indeed, it may not have to.

By 1997 the informal amalgam of groups—whose views were supported by Americans working at the U.S. Agency for International Development (USAID)—became divided over whether to continue to push for reform of Law 32. For instance, some felt the government was no longer relying on this law to control NGOs. And many human rights advocates found ways around this law and registered their organizations under the commercial code; their efforts continue to be focused on how best to promote human rights and not on how to get "legally" registered. However, others felt that if they were to fight for the rule of law in Egypt, they must still focus on reforming this law. They continue to worry that the government would still have this law in its arsenal and could "dust it off" at any time to crack down on otherwise legal civil society institutions trying to promote social, political, and economic development.

USAID officials have been attempting for several years to encourage the government of Egypt to amend Law 32, to allow greater autonomy to community organizations (NGOs, community development organizations, and foundations). Reforming this one law would do as much to promote the development of civil society in Egypt as just about any other legal reform. Ending the Emergency Law, in effect since 1981, would send an even stronger message to Egyptians that a change is coming.

Elections

Another way the government strengthens its control over society is through manipulation of various types of elections, both public and private. For years, there has been a clear indication of a decline in support for the government and a growth of support for Islamists and their programs. This indication is found in the contrasting results of elections for public office and those for professional, "private" office. (Nominally independent, professional unions are of course part of the state corporatist structure.)[37] In the public domain, where the government has the advantage with its ruling NDP and power to restrict participation and count the votes, the government wins these contests overwhelmingly.

The results of the two-round (November 29 and December 6) 1995 parliamentary elections demonstrate this point. Amid violence (forty dead and many more injured) and numerous claims of abuse by the government against voters and opposition parties, Mubarak's ruling NDP swept the elections.[38] The NDP won 317 of the 444 seats directly, and ninety-nine nominal "independents" joined the NDP after the second round. Opposition parties and candidates won a total of thirteen seats. It is little wonder, given the Muslim Brotherhood's consistent popularity with the Egyptian electorate, that the government feared that organization's untrammeled participation in the elections.

In the months leading up to the elections, the Egyptian police arrested scores of mainstream Brotherhood members who were, not coincidentally, candidates for parliamentary seats. Many senior members of the Brotherhood were also arrested, and a senior Al-Azhar University cleric, Shaykh Sayyid 'Askar, was detained in July. In September, the president transferred the jurisdiction over the prosecution of dozens of Muslim Brethren to a military court, which, it has been observed, holds trials that "fall short of minimum internationally agreed upon fair trial standards."[39] Mubarak's decision drew criticism even from secular political parties that did not support the Brotherhood, including the Nasserists, the New Wafd, and the *Tajammu'*. On 23 November 1995, six days before the elections began,

> Egypt's Supreme Military Court sentenced 54 leading members of the Muslim Brotherhood to prison terms ranging from 3 to 5 years with hard labor. The trial marked the culmination of a turbulent four-year period which witnessed a deterioration of the state's tolerance for the outlawed Brotherhood. [And it] represents the first prosecution of members of the organization by a military court since 1965, when Nasser . . . sought to crush the Brotherhood.[40]

In addition, the military court ordered the closing of the Brotherhood's headquarters in Cairo. On the eve of the elections more than one thousand Brotherhood members were arrested, including hundreds who were scheduled to monitor the elections.

The local elections of 3 November 1992 are another case in point. The ruling NDP swept the municipal council elections, electing 2,370 slates plus winning 2,232 independent seats compared to 55 slates and 16 independent seats for the Islamic Alliance of the Socialist Labor Party (SLP) and the outlawed Muslim Brotherhood and 29 slates and 115 independent seats for the New Wafd Party. *Al-Sha'b*, the newspaper of the Islamic Alliance, cried foul. They claimed to have won at least 79 slates and 43 independent seats. Hilmi Murad, SLP deputy chairman, told *Al-Ahram* newspaper that the NDP had "definitely rigged the vote." Fu'ad Badawi of the Wafd agreed. The party paper, *Al-Wafd*, described the elections as the "funeral of democracy. . . . Our candidates and their representatives were subjected to the assaults of the thugs of the NDP. . . . The NDP attempted to disqualify our candidates and our supporters were intimidated."[41]

On 10 April 1994, the government intensified its control over local politics by passing a law abolishing local elections for village mayors. It decreed that henceforth, the Ministry of the Interior (responsible for security) would have the power to appoint the mayors, or *'umda*s. Thus, another serious blow was dealt to the democratization process, setting Egypt further back toward authoritarianism.

Even though the government continues to dominate public elections, through legal and extralegal means, elections for officers in the professional syndicates (*niqabat*, or unions of, for example, doctors, lawyers, journalists, and engineers) continue to be won by Islamist candidates (Muslim Brethren primarily). Unlike local and national elections for town councils or Parliament, syndicate elections were more free of government interference—until the government imposed a new syndicate law in February 1993. The victory of the Islamists in the election for the executive board of the Lawyers' Syndicate in September 1992 was "shocking" to many analysts. The lawyers' union is seen as one of the more liberal syndicates with many Western-educated and/or westernized members. The Islamists still do not do well in the commerce and teachers' (the largest) syndicates.

Because of the Islamists' successes and the related inability of the government to control syndicate elections, Parliament, in February 1993, enacted the law requiring that syndicate elections have at least 50 percent of *registered* members vote in the first round or 33 percent in the second round for election results to be honored. If a sufficient turnout is not attained, the government appoints municipal judges and old-guard syndicate leaders to the board. Backers of the law suggest that the government is not denying any group anything; rather, the government's action ensures that minimal levels of participation will be attained in syndicate elections. Critics say that the whole point of the law is to dislodge the Islamists and that these new levels required by the government are unattainable by any group.

Some syndicates have hundreds of thousands of members registered, and most elections generally experience an 8–12 percent voter turnout—extremely low and perhaps unrepresentative of the entire group. However, participation rates as high as 30 percent had been reached in the 1992 doctors' syndicate elections, which the Islamists won handily. The act of 1993 is obviously an attempt to extend government control over nominally independent organizations and to curtail the popularity of Islamist groups in these important syndicates.

Such government action might set a dangerous precedent and come back to haunt this same government. Given that public elections also experience very low voter turnout, setting a minimum—and a very high minimum in a country where voter apathy is itself extremely high—for "private" elections might suggest to society as a whole that its publicly elected officials are not legitimately elected. There is already a low opinion of Parliament as a body beholden to the ruling party, placed in office by that party, and generally unable to effect change in opposition to the NDP. When opposition parties (except for *Tajammu'*) boycotted the 1990 elections, popular attitudes toward the secular opposition groups, already bad to begin with, became even more negative.

The Potential for State-Society Cooperation

In the midst of such popular disapproval of both government and official opposition, coupled with increasingly favorable views of local groups, that is, the Islamic, Christian, and other NGOs, the government has continued its attack on Islamic institutions—at least those outside its control. A prime example is the ill-conceived and half-hearted attempt to "nationalize" 140,000 private mosques, announced in 1992 and recently revived.

The result of such tight control over social and political activities, plus a limited liberalization of the economy, is a continuing authoritarian political system dominated by a single political party and backed by the national security organs (as well as being financially, politically, and/or militarily supported by the United States, Saudi Arabia, Kuwait, the World Bank, the European Union, and Japan, among others). Rather than encouraging the generally peaceful and pluralistic organizations of civil society to function unfettered, and thus facilitating a peaceful channel for the venting of social and political grievances, the government strives to restrict and circumvent potentially participatory institutions. The remaining "space" left for civil society institutions and energetic entrepreneurs (of a political, social, or economic bent) is limited at best, ephemeral at worst.[42] But this space is not nonexistent.

Civil society exists in Egypt, but it is severely restricted and ever under siege by a government concerned first and foremost with its own survival, not the political and social enrichment of the society. *Economic* development is certainly a government goal, because this would help the government in its efforts to maintain itself by removing the constant and primary source of social instability. This regime simply has not listened to the voices of a minority in its own government calling for social and political liberalization, which is seen by members of that minority as essential to promoting their own economic development goals. Leaders of civil society institutions continue to wage their campaign to loosen the restrictions, limitations, and controls on their activities so that they might solidify the gains they have made over the past several decades. As the chairman of Egypt's Ibn Khaldun Center for Development Studies sees it, Egypt has undergone promising starts that then get bogged down. "What is left is the unfinished business of a blocked society, a thwarted democracy, and an almost-but-not-quite-reformed economy. The key to breaking out of this pattern is to create the kind of free environment that will invigorate civil society and increase the pace of democratization."[43]

The government of Egypt must be convinced, either by its own liberal voices or by "friendly donors" (e.g., the United States, Japan, France, Britain, the Netherlands, Canada), that only by working with such civil society leaders can the bottom-line goals of economic development and social stability be achieved. If such a cooperative regime were established, the frictions between "state" and "society" (Islamic, secular, or otherwise) would be lessened considerably. Peaceful channels for airing dissent would minimize the perceived need to use underground, often violent, methods of political opposition. As Fahmi Huwaydi puts it, "If the doors of participation were to be opened to those calling for change, and if the possibility of bringing about peaceful change were to appear before them, they would cease thinking of using violence as a means for change."[44] Huwaydi does not condone the use of violence by extremist groups, and, indeed, refers to violence as a "plague" that has infected the Arab world. He does, however, insist that "the solution to the problem is democracy."[45] Plenty of other problems—among them poverty, unemployment, pollution, population, urban blight—will remain, but perhaps the vast resources of the Islamist movements could be joined with those of the government to move toward a more coordinated, complementary development effort. Given the nature of this regime and its resistance to cooperation with societal oganizations, however, there is little room for optimism.

Notes

1. *Al-Nida' al-Jadid* and the Egyptian Businessmen's Association are two such elite groups. Made up of the intellectual and business community, both aim at promoting mainly economic liberalization, and members in each see political liberalization as important to that process.

2. These include such militant groups as *al-Jama'a al-Islamiyya, Jihad,* and the Society of Muslims (*al-Takfir wa al-Hijra*).

3. For an impressive analysis of Egyptian society and the political significance of the informal sector, especially that of the popular class (*al-sha'b*) in Cairo, see Diane Singerman, *Avenues of Participation: Family, Politics, and Networks in Urban Quarters of Cairo* (Princeton, N.J.: Princeton University Press, 1995). For an equally impressive analysis of the formal side of Egyptian political activity and activism, see Raymond William Baker, *Sadat and After: Struggles for Egypt's Political Soul* (Cambridge, Mass.: Harvard University Press, 1990).

4. Mustapha K. Al-Sayyid, "A Civil Society in Egypt?" *Middle East Journal* 47, no. 2 (Spring 1993): 229, 230.

5. For a "liberal Islamist" criticism of militant Islam, see Muhammad Sa'id al-'Ashmawi, *Al-Islam al-Siyasi* (Cairo, 1987). For a "liberal Muslim" critique, see many of the works by Faraj Fuda, including *al-Haqiqa Al-Gha'iba* (The Absent Reality) (Cairo: Dar al-Fikr, 1988).

6. Ahmed Abdalla, "Egypt's Islamists and the State: From Complicity to Confrontation," *Middle East Report* 23, no. 4 (July-August 1993): 29.

7. Interviews with U.S. intelligence and State Department officials, Washington, D.C., May 1995.

8. James Adams, "Mubarak at Grave Risk of Being Overthrown by March of Islam," *The Sunday Times,* 20 February 1994. Quoted in Muslim Student Association Internet news service, msanews@magnus.acs.ohio-state.edu, Ohio State University, 25 February 1994.

9. For example, in its first issue after the attack on Mubarak, Egypt's *Al-Ahram Weekly* newspaper celebrated his survival with the following headlines: "Towards Greater Reforms: No Fear for Democracy"; "Confronting Terrorism Beyond Egypt's Borders"; "United We Stand"; "Egypt Able to Oust Bashir" (Bashir being the military leader of the Sudan, accused by Egypt of encouraging or planning the attempt); "Marchers Celebrate Mubarak's Safety." 29 June–5 July 1995, pp. 1–3.

10. James Whittington, "Egypt's Islamists: Proscribed or Provoked?" *Financial Times,* 9 August 1995.

11. For an excellent discussion of Islamist activity in Lebanon, one that provides an interesting comparison with the Egyptian case, see A. Nizar Hamzeh, "Lebanon's Hizbullah: From Islamic Revolution to Parliamentary Accommodation," *Third World Quarterly* 14, no. 2 (1993): 321–337. Hamzeh notes that the "rise of Islamic revivalist movements in general and Hizbullah in particular has been tied to the crises conditions" in Lebanon and the Middle East, including "Arab defeats by Israel, the failure to achieve balanced socioeconomic development, the pervasiveness of political oppression, gross maldistribution of wealth, and the disorienting psychocultural impact of Westernization." Most of these crises are similar to those from which the Egyptian population suffers.

12. See Hala Mustafa, *Al-Islam al-Siyasi fi Misr: Min Harakat al-Islah ila Jama'at al-'Unf. (Political Islam in Egypt: From the Movement of Reform to Associations of Violence)* (Cairo: Al-Ahram Center for Strategic Studies, 1992). Also, Raouf Abbas Hamed, "Factors Behind the Political Islamic Movement in Egypt" (Paper presented at Middle East Studies Association annual meeting, San Antonio, Tex., November 1990).

13. One of the earlier works describing the popularity of Islamist organizations on Egyptian campuses is Gilles Kepel, *Muslim Extremism in Egypt* (London: Al-Saqi Books, 1985). For an impressive analysis of postgraduate Islamist activity and popularity in professional syndicates, see Carrie Rosefsky Wickham, "Islamic Mobilization and Political Change: The Islamist Trend in Egypt's Professional Associations," Joel Beinin, ed., *Political Islam: A MERIP Reader*, University of California Press; and see Wickham, Ph.D. dissertation, Princeton University.

14. Fouad Ajami, *The Arab Predicament: Arab Political Thought and Practice Since 1967* (Cambridge and New York: Cambridge University Press, 1981), pp. 177–178.

15. Edward W. Said, *The Politics of Dispossession* (New York: Random House, 1994), p. 389.

16. Sana Abed-Kotob, interview with Isma'il Sabri 'Abdallah at Third World Forum, Cairo, 1991.

17. Sana Abed-Kotob, interview with Nawal el Saadawi at the Arab Women's Solidarity Association, Cairo, 1991.

18. One study, which has developed a legendary status, conducted in the late 1980s by the Al-Ahram Center in Cairo determined that the average bureaucrat works 23 minutes per day. For a systematic treatment of Egypt's bureaucracy, see Monte Palmer, Ali Leila, and El Sayed Yassin, *The Egyptian Bureaucracy* (Syracuse, N.Y.: Syracuse University Press, 1988).

19. See Mary Anne Weaver, "The Novelist and the Sheikh," *The New Yorker*, January 30, 1995, p. 69.

20. As reported in James Napoli, *Washington Report on Middle East Affairs* (December 1992–January 1993): 41.

21. Ibid.

22. Ibid.

23. Lawyers Committee for Human Rights, *Escalating Attacks on Human Rights Protection in Egypt* (New York, September 1995), p. 1.

24. The following are all from Middle East Watch: *Behind Closed Doors: Torture and Detention in Egypt* (New York: Human Rights Watch, 1992); "Egypt: Hostage-Taking and Intimidation by Security Forces," January 1995; "Egypt: Trials of Civilians in Military Courts Violate International Law," July 1993; and "Egyptian Authorities Clamp Down on Dissent," 13 February 1991.

25. U.S. Department of State, *Country Report on Human Rights Practices for 1992* (Report submitted to Committee on Foreign Relations, U.S. Senate, and Committee on Foreign Affairs, U.S. House of Representatives, February 1993), p. 991.

26. U.S. Department of State (Annual human rights report presented to U.S. Congress on February 1, 1995). The quote is from page 1 of a document acquired directly from the State Department.

27. On April 30, 1994, Abdel-Harith Madani, a lawyer defending Islamists charged with terrorism, was reported by the Egyptian Bar Association to have been tortured to death in police custody. The government, calling him a "terrorist," said he died of asthma.

28. U.S. Department of State, February 1, 1995.
29. For more information, see Egyptian Organization for Human Rights, "Freedom of Opinion and Expression in Egypt" (Mohandessin, Giza: EOHR, 27 June 1990).
30. *Al-Ahram Weekly,* 12–18 November 1993.
31. *Middle East Economic Digest,* 20 November 1992, p. 11.
32. *Al-Ahram Weekly,* 4–10 March 1993, p. 2.
33. FBIS-NES, "Officials Comment on Government Control of Mosques," 24 February 1993, p. 10.
34. Michael Hudson, *Arab Politics: The Search for Legitimacy* (New Haven, Conn.: Yale University Press, 1977) p. 234.
35. Economist Intelligence Unit, *Egypt,* August 1992, p. 10.
36. For example, see Mona Makram Ebeid's maiden speech in Egypt's Majlis al-Sha'b (Parliament). *Madhbata* [Minutes] of Majlis al-Sha'b, 11 March 1991.
37. See Robert Bianchi, *Unruly Corporatism: Associational Life in Twentieth-Century Egypt* (New York: Oxford University Press, 1989).
38. James Whittington, "Radicals Frustrated by Egyptian Poll: Many Feel Disputed Election Confirmed Limits of Democracy," *Financial Times,* 13 December 1995, p. 4.
39. Lawyers Committee for Human Rights, *Escalating Attacks on Human Rights Protection in Egypt* (New York, September 1995), p. 2.
40. Joel Campagna, "From Accommodation to Confrontation: The Muslim Brotherhood in the Mubarak Years," *Journal of International Affairs* 50, no. 1 (Summer 1996): 278.
41. *Al-Ahram Weekly,* 12–18 November 1992.
42. Tolerance for opposing viewpoints is necessary for the inclusion of NGOs in the discourse within civil society; likewise, such tolerance on the part of the state is vital for social and political stability. A plurality of political voices, including those representing a peaceful Islamist movement, can contribute to a healthy debate that propels the state toward more democratic, civic interaction. Scholarly emphasis on civil society thus needs to expand its parameters to include the requisite civility of government.
43. Saad Eddin Ibrahim, "Reform and Frustration in Egypt," *Journal of Democracy* 7, no. 4 (October 1996), p. 135.
44. FBIS 12/11/94 (FBIS-NES-95–033). Translation of Fahmi Huwaydi, "Article Examines Extremism, Democracy," *Al-Majallah,* 11 December 1994, pp. 42–43.
45. Ibid.

Bibliography

Abaza, Mona, *The Changing Image of Women in Rural Egypt.* Cairo: American University in Cairo Press, 1987.

Abdalla, Ahmed, "Egypt's Islamists and the State: From Complicity to Confrontation," *Middle East Report* 23, no. 4 (July-August 1993): 29–31.

'Abd al-Maqsud, Salah, "Ten Charges Against the Society [Muslim Brotherhood]," (in Arabic) *Liwa' al-Islam* (February 1989): 12–16.

'Abd al-Rahman, 'Umar, *Al-Maw'itha al-Hasana* [The Good Advice]. Kuwait: Dar al-Siyasa, 1988.

'Abduh, Al-Sadiq, "What Has the Muslim Brotherhood Offered?" (in Arabic) *Liwa' al-Islam* (September 1987): 12–14.

———, "President Mubarak and the Islamic Movement After Six years," (in Arabic) *Liwa' al-Islam* (September 1987): 10–11, 27.

Abu al-Nasr, Muhammad Hamid, "Editorial: Liberties, Between Application and Slogans," (in Arabic) *Liwa' al-Islam* (August 1988): 4–5.

———, "Editorial: Valuable Freedom," (in Arabic) *Liwa' al-Islam* (July 1990): 4–5.

———, "Communique Regarding the Minya and Asyut Incidents," (in Arabic) *Liwa' al-Islam* (March 1990): 7.

Abu al-Sa'ud, Mahmud, *The Islamic Movement: Future Vision and Papers on Self Criticism* (in Arabic). Cairo: Madbuli Library, 1989.

AbuKhalil, As'ad, "Gender Boundaries and Sexual Categories in the Arab World," *Feminist Issues* 15, nos. 1–2 (1997): 91–104.

Abu-Lughod, Lila, "Islam and Public Culture: The Politics of Egyptian Television Serials," *Middle East Report* 23, no. 10 (1993): 25–30.

Adams, Charles C., *Islam and Modernism in Egypt.* New York: Russell & Russell, 1968.

Adams, James, "Mubarak at Grave Risk of Being Overthrown by March of Islam," *The Sunday Times*, 20 February 1994.

Afshar, Haleh, *Women in the Middle East: Perceptions, Realities and Struggles for Liberation.* New York: St. Martin's, 1993.

Ahmed, Leila, *Women and Gender in Islam.* New Haven: Yale University Press, 1992.

Al-Ahram Center for Political and Strategic Studies, "The Extra-Legal Forces," (in Arabic). In *Arab Strategic Report 1986.* Cairo: Al-Ahram Center for Political and Strategic Studies, 1987, pp. 389–408.

———, "Parties and Political Power," *Arab Strategic Report: 1992*. Cairo: Al-Ahram Center for Political and Strategic Studies, 1993.

———, "Parties and Political Power," *Arab Strategic Report: 1993*. Cairo: Al-Ahram Center for Political and Strategic Studies, 1994.

Ajami, Fouad, *The Arab Predicament: Arab Political Thought and Practice Since 1967*. Cambridge and New York: Cambridge University Press, 1981.

Al-Ali, Nadje Sadig, *Gender Writing/Writing Gender: The Representation of Women in a Selection of Modern Egyptian Literature*. Cairo: American University in Cairo Press, 1994.

"An Alternative Response to Foda's Assassination," *Al-Ahram Weekly*, June 18–24, 1992, p. 6.

'Amara, Dr. Muhammad, *Islam and Human Rights: Necessities . . . Not Rights* (in Arabic). Cairo: Dar Al-Sharuq, 1989.

Amin, Osman, "The Modernist Movement in Egypt." In *Islam and the West*, ed. Richard N. Frye. The Hague: Mouton & Co., 1957.

Amnesty International, *Egypt: Ten Years of Torture*. London, 23 October 1991.

Anderson, Lisa, "The State in the Middle East and North Africa," *Comparative Politics* 20, no. 1 (1986): 1–18.

———, "Policy Making and Theory Building: American Political Science and the Islamic Middle East." In *Theory, Politics and the Arab World: Critical Responses*, edited by Hisham Sharabi. New York: Routledge, 1990.

Ansari, Hamied, "The Islamic Militants in Egyptian Politics," *International Journal of Middle East Studies* 16, no. 1 (1984): 123–144.

———, "Sectarian Conflict in Egypt and the Political Expediency of Religion," *Middle East Journal* 38, no. 3 (1984): 397–418.

———, *Egypt: The Stalled Society*. Albany: SUNY Press, 1986.

Al-'Ashmawi, Muhammad Sai'd, *Al-Islam al-Siyasi*. Cairo, 1987.

"Associations of Religion, Violence and Despair," *Al-Ahram Weekly*, June 18–24, 1992, p. 7.

Auda, Gehad, "The Islamic Movement and Resource Mobilization in Egypt: A Political Culture Perspective." In *Political Culture and Democracy in Developing Countries*, edited by Larry Diamond. Boulder, Colo.: Lynne Rienner, 1993.

Ayubi, Nazih N., "Government and the State in Egypt Today." In *Egypt under Mubarak*, edited by Charles Tripp and Roger Owen. London and New York: Routledge, 1989.

———, *Political Islam: Religion and Politics in the Arab World*. London: Routledge, 1991.

Azer, Mona Amin, "Egyptian Women Have Secured a Lot of Rights, in Theory!," *Ru'ya/Vision* 2 (1992): 4.

Badawi, M. A. Zaki, *The Reformers of Egypt*. London: Croom Helm, 1978.

Badran, Margot, "Introduction" and "Epilogue." In *Harem Years: The Memoirs of an Egyptian Feminist (1879–1924)*, by Huda Shaarawi. New York: The Feminist Press at the City University of New York, 1986.

———, "Independent Women: More than a Century of Feminism in Egypt." In *Arab Women: Old Boundaries, New Frontiers*, edited by Judith E. Tucker. Bloomington: Indiana University Press, 1993.

———, *Feminists, Islam and Nation: Gender and the Making of Modern Egypt*. Princeton, N.J.: Princeton University Press, 1995.

Baker, Raymond William, *Sadat and After: Struggles for Egypt's Political Soul*. Cambridge, Mass.: Harvard University Press, 1990.

———, "Afraid for Islam: Egypt's Muslim Centrists Between Pharaohs and Fundamentalists," *Daedalus* 120, no. 3 (1991): 41–68.
Al-Banna, Hasan, *Five Tracts of Hasan al-Banna 1906–1949: A Selection from the Majmuʻat Rasaʼil al-Imam al-Shahid Hasan al-Banna*, translated and annotated by Charles Wendell. Berkeley: University of California Press, 1978.
———, *The Muslim Woman and Her Duties* (in Arabic). Cairo: Dar al-Daʻwa.
Baron, Beth, *The Women's Awakening in Egypt: Culture, Society and the Press*. Berkeley: University of California Press, 1994.
Beinin, Joel, "Aspects of Egyptian Civil Resistance," *Middle East Report* 179 (November–December 1992), pp. 38–39.
Bellin, Eva, "Civil Society: Effective Tool of Analysis for Middle East Politics?" *PS* (September 1994).
Ben Nefissa-Paris, Sarah, "L'etat egyptien et le monde associatif," *Egypt/Monde Arabe* 8 (4eme trimestre 1991): 107–124.
———, "Zakat officielle et zakat non officielle aujourd'hui," *Egypt/Monde Arabe* 7 (3eme trimestre 1991): 105–120.
Berger, Morroe, *Islam in Egypt Today: Social and Political Aspects of Popular Religion*. Cambridge: Cambridge University Press, 1970.
Bianchi, Robert, *Unruly Corporatism: Associational Life in Twentieth-Century Egypt*. New York: Oxford University Press, 1989.
Bibars, Iman M. Diaa El Din, "Women's Political Interest Groups in Egypt," Master of Arts Thesis, Number 751, American University in Cairo, 1987.
Binder, Leonard, *Islamic Liberalism*. Chicago: University of Chicago Press, 1988.
"The Brotherhood Denies the Lies of the Minister of the Interior," *Al-Shaʻb*, February 11, 1992, pp. 1–11.
Brown, Nathan J. *The Rule of Law in the Arab World: Courts in Egypt and the Gulf*. Cambridge: Cambridge University Press, 1997.
Burgat, Francois, "Les Islamists et la transition democratique: Jalons pour une recherche," *Egypt/Monde Arabe* 4 (1990), pp. 129–140.
———, and William Dowell, *The Islamic Movement in North Africa*. Austin: Center for Middle Eastern Studies, University of Texas, 1993.
Butterworth, Charles, "Prudence versus Legitimacy: The Persistent Theme in Islamic Political Thought," in *Islamic Resurgence in the Arab World*, ed. Ali E. Hillal Dessouki. New York: Praeger Publishers, 1982.
Cairo Institute for Human Rights Studies, "Setting Civil Society Free: A Draft Law on Civil Associations and Institutions." Cairo, 1998.
Calhoun, Craig, ed., *Habermas and the Public Sphere*. Cambridge: MIT Press, 1992.
"A Call to Muslims: Islamic Hospital Project," (in Arabic) *Al-Daʻwa* (February 1980).
Campagna, Joel, "From Accommodation to Confrontation: The Muslim Brotherhood in the Mubarak Years," *Journal of International Affairs* 50, no. 1 (1996).
Cantori, Louis J., "The Islamic Revival as Conservatism and as Progress in Contemporary Egypt." In *Religious Resurgence and Politics in the Contemporary World*, edited by Emile Sahliyeh. Albany: SUNY Press, 1990.
Cassandra, "The Impending Crisis in Egypt," *Middle East Journal* 49, no. 1 (1995): 9–27.
Chatterjee, Partha, "A Response to Taylor's 'Modes of Civil Society,'" *Public Culture* 3, no. 1 (1990).

Cooke, Miriam, "Zaynab al-Ghazali: Saint or Subversive?" *Die Welt des Islams* 34 (1994): 1–20.
Cox, Harvey, *Religion in the Secular City: Toward a Postmodern Theology.* New York: Simon & Schuster, 1984.
Cudsi, Alexander S. and Ali E. Hillal Dessouki, eds., *Islam and Power.* Baltimore: Johns Hopkins University Press, 1981.
El-Dakhakhny, Mohamed, "At Least 66 Dead in Egypt Attack," The Associated Press, 17 November 1997.
Davis, Eric, "Ideology, Social Class and Islamic Radicalism in Modern Egypt," in *From Nationalism to Revolutionary Islam*, ed. Amir Arjomand. Albany: SUNY Press, 1984.
Dekmejian, R. Hrair, *Islam in Revolution: Fundamentalism in the Arab World*, 2nd ed. New York: Syracuse University Press, 1995.
Denoeux, Guilain, *Urban Unrest in the Middle East: A Comparative Study of Informal Networks in Egypt, Iran and Lebanon.* New York: SUNY Press, 1993.
Dessouki, Ali E. Hillal, "The Resurgence of Islamic Organisations in Egypt: An Interpretation." In *Islam and Power*, edited by Alexander S. Cudsi and Ali E. Hillal Dessouki. Baltimore: Johns Hopkins University Press, 1981.
———, ed., *Islamic Resurgence in the Arab World.* New York: Praeger Publishers, 1982.
"Dialogue Between Ma'mun al-Hudaybi and Hasan Abu-Basha," (in Arabic) *Liwa' al-Islam* (January 1991): 24–26.
Diamond, Larry, "Introduction: Political Culture and Democracy." In *Political Culture and Democracy in Developing Countries.* Boulder: Lynne Rienner, 1993.
———, ed., *Political Culture and Democracy in Developing Countries.* Boulder: Lynne Rienner, 1993.
Donahue, John J. and John L. Esposito, eds., *Islam in Transition: Muslim Perspectives.* New York: Oxford University Press, 1982.
Early, Evelyn A., *Baladi Women of Cairo: Playing with an Egg and a Stone.* Boulder, Colo.: Lynne Rienner, 1993.
Ebeid, Mona Makram, "Maiden Speech in Egypt's Majlis al-Sha'b [Parliament]," in *Madhbata* (Minutes) of Majlis al-Sha'b, 11 March 1991.
Eccel, A. Chris, *Egypt, Islam, and Social Change: Al-Azhar in Conflict and Accommodation.* Berlin: Klaus Schwarz Verlag, 1984.
Economist Intelligence Unit, *Egypt* (August 1992): 10.
"Egypt: Attempt to Bomb US Embassy in Cairo Said Foiled," *Al-'Arabi*, October 20, 1997, reported by *FBIS*, October 28, 1997.
"Egypt: Who Did It?," *The Economist*, July 2, 1994, p. 41.
"The Egyptian Official," *Al-Jarida Newspaper*, March 16, 1909.
Egyptian Organization for Human Rights, "Freedom of Opinion and Expression in Egypt." Mohandessin, Giza: EOHR, 27 June 1990.
"The Elections of the Doctors Syndicate: A Vision from Inside," (in Arabic), *Al-Sha'b*, April 21, 1992, p. 6.
Eley, Geoff, "Nations, Publics, and Political Cultures: Placing Habermas in the Nineteenth Century," in *Habermas and the Public Sphere*, ed. Craig Calhoun. Cambridge, Mass.: MIT Press, 1992.
Emam, Samah, "Civil Society in Egypt . . . A Reminder," *Civil Society* 10 (October 1992): 4–6.
Esposito, John L., *Islam: The Straight Path.* New York: Oxford University Press, 1991.

———, *The Islamic Threat: Myth or Reality?* New York: Oxford University Press, 1992.

———, and James P. Piscatori, "Democratization and Islam," *The Middle East Journal* 45, no. 3 (1991): 427–440.

———, and John O. Voll, eds., *Islam and Democracy.* New York: Oxford University Press, 1996.

Evans, Dominic, "Egypt Executes Six Moslem Militants," Reuters World Service, 3 June 1996.

Fandy, Mamoun, "Egypt's Islamic Group: Regional Revenge?" *Middle East Journal* 48, no. 4 (1994): 607–625.

Faraj, Muhammad 'Abd al-Salam, *Al-Jihad: Al-Farida al-Gha'iba.* Jerusalem: Maktabat al-Batal 'Iz al-Din al-Qassam, 1982.

FBIS-NES, "Officials Comment on Government Control of Mosques," 24 February 1993: p. 10.

Fernea, Elizabeth Warnock, *In Search of Islamic Feminism: One Woman's Global Journey.* New York: Doubleday, 1997.

———, ed., *Women and the Family in the Middle East: New Voices of Change.* Austin: University of Texas Press, 1985.

Flores, Alexander, "Secularism, Integralism and Political Islam: The Egyptian Debate," *Middle East Report* 23, no. 4 (1993): 32–38.

Fuda, Faraj, *Al-Haqiqa al-Gha'iba* [*The Absent Reality*], (Cairo).

———, *Al-Irhab* [The Terror] (Cairo, 1988).

Fuller, Graham E., "Islamic Fundamentalism: No Long-Term Threat," *Washington Post,* 3 January 1992.

Gauch, Sarah, "Terror on the Nile," *Africa Report* 38 (1993): 34.

Gellner, Ernest, "Civil Society in Historical Context," *International Social Science Journal* 129 (August 1991): 495–510.

Al-Ghazali, Zaynab, *Ayam min Hayati* [*Days of My Life*]. Cairo: Dar al-Shuruq, n.d.

———, "Complete Joy at the Return of *al-Da'wa,*" *Al-Da'wa,* May 6, 1993, p. 38.

Gilsenan, Michael, *Saint and Sufi in Modern Egypt.* Oxford: Clarendon Press, 1973.

Gocek, Fatma Muge and Shiva Balaghi, eds., *Reconstructing Gender in the Middle East.* New York: Columbia University Press, 1995.

Göle, Nilüfer, *The Forbidden Modern: Civilization and Veiling.* Ann Arbor: University of Michigan Press, 1996.

Gomaa, Salwa Sha'rawi, Ken Menkhaus, and Denis J. Sullivan, "Egyptian Public Opinion During the Gulf War." Unpublished research, 1991.

Graham-Brown, Sarah, "Women and Politics in the Middle East." In *Arab Women: Between Defiance and Restraint,* edited by Suha Sabbagh. New York: Olive Branch Press, 1996.

———, "Women and Politics in the Middle East." Second pamphlet in MERIP series on women in the Middle East, n.d. pp. 7–8.

Guenena, Nemat, *Cairo Papers in Social Science: Vol. 9, Monograph 2. The Jihad: An Islamic Alternative in Egypt.* Cairo: American University in Cairo Press, 1986.

———, "The Islamic Alternative in Egypt Today" mimeo, n.d.

Haddad, Yvonne Yazbeck, "Islam, Women and Revolution in Twentieth-Century Arab Thought." In *Women, Religion and Social Change,* edited by Y. Y. Haddad and E. B. Findly. Albany: SUNY Press, 1985.

Haggag, Karim, "A Civil Society in the Arab World?," *Civil Society* 6 (June 1992): 11–18.

Al-Hakim, Sulayman, *'Abd al-Nasir wa al-Islam* ['Abd al- Nasir and Islam]. Cairo: Dar al-Kutub, 1988.

Hamed, Raouf Abbas, "Factors Behind the Political Islamic Movement in Egypt." Middle East Studies Association annual conference, San Antonio, Texas, November 1990.

Hammady, Iman Roushdy, "Religious Medical Centers in Egypt." Master's thesis at American University in Cairo, 1990.

Hamzeh, A. Nizar, "Lebanon's Hizbullah: From Islamic Revolution to Parliamentary Accommodation," *Third World Quarterly* 14, no. 2 (1993): 321–337.

Harik, Iliya, *Economic Reform in Egypt*. Gainesville, Fla.: University Press of Florida, 1997.

"Has There Been a Change in the *Jama'a*'s Strategy?," *Al-Majalla*, May 14, 1994, p. 25.

Hatem, Mervat F., "The 'Secularist and Islamist Gendered Faces' of Political Liberalization in the Arab World," Paper presented at the Conference on Political Liberalization and Democratization in the Arab World, McGill University and University of Montreal, Montreal, May 7–8, 1993.

Heikal, Muhammad Hassanein, *Misr wa al-Qarn al-Wahid wa al-'Ishrun* [Egypt and the 21st Century]. Cairo: Dar al-Shuruq, 1995.

Hinnebusch, Raymond A., Jr., "Children of the Elite: Political Attitudes of the Westernized Bourgeoisie in Contemporary Egypt," *Middle East Journal* 36, no. 4 (1982): 535–561.

———. *Egyptian Politics under Sadat: The Post Populist Development of an Authoritarian-Modernizing State* (updated edition) (Boulder, Colo.: Lynne Rienner, 1988.

Hoffman, Valerie J., "An Islamic Activist: Zeinab al-Ghazali." In *Women and the Family in the Middle East,* ed. Elizabeth Warnock Fernea. Austin: University of Texas Press, 1985.

———, "Polemics on the Modesty and Segregation of Women in Contemporary Egypt," *International Journal of Middle East Studies* 19 (1987): 23–50.

Hourani, Albert, *Arabic Thought in the Liberal Age, 1798–1939*. New York: Oxford University Press, 1970.

Al-Hudaybi, Ma'mun, "Muslim Brotherhood Condemns the Assassination of Dr. 'Ala' Mohi al-Din" (in Arabic), *Liwa' al-Islam* (September 1990): 41.

Hudson, Michael C., *Arab Politics: The Search for Legitimacy*. New Haven, Conn.: Yale University Press, 1977.

Al-Husayni, Asma', "Interview with Ma'mun al-Hudaybi" (in Arabic), *Liwa' al-Islam* (August 1990): 50–51.

Hussain, Afaf, *Islamic Movements in Egypt, Pakistan and Iran*. London: Mansell Publishing, 1983.

Hussain, Freda, ed., *Muslim Women*. New York: St. Martin's Press, 1984.

Hussein, Aziza, "Recent Amendments to Egypt's Personal Status Law." In *Women and the Family in the Middle East,* ed. E. W. Fernea. Austin: University of Texas Press, 1985.

Huwaydi, Fahmi, *The Quran and Power: Contemporary Islamic Concerns* (in Arabic), 3rd ed. Cairo: Dar al-Shuruq, 1991.

———, "Twenty-Four Conditions in Which Woman Inherits the Same as Man, and Sometimes More than Him!" (in Arabic), *Al-Majalla*, 25 October 1997, pp. 32–33.

Ibrahim, Barbara Lethem, "Indigenous Philanthropy in the Arab World: Contrasting Cases from Egypt and Palestine." In *The Non-Profit Sector in the Global Community*, ed. Kathleen D. McCarthy et al. San Francisco: Jossey-Bass, 1992.

Ibrahim, Najih, 'Asim 'Abd al-Majid, 'Isam al-Din Dirbala, and 'Umar 'Abd al-Rahman, *Mithaq al-'Amal al-Watani*. Cairo: Maktabit Ibn Kathir, 1989.

Ibrahim, Saad Eddin, "Anatomy of Egypt's Militant Islamic Groups: Methodological Note and Preliminary Findings," *International Journal of Middle East Studies* 12 (1980): 423–453.

———, "Egypt's Islamic Militants," *MERIP Reports* (February 1982): 5–14.

———, "An Islamic Alternative in Egypt: The Muslim Brotherhood and Sadat," *Arab Studies Quarterly* 4, 1–2 (Spring 1982): 75–93.

———, "Egypt's Islamic Activism in the 1980s" *Third World Quarterly* 10, no. 2 (1988): 632–657.

———, "Islamic Activists Take Over Egypt's Fortress of Liberalism," *Civil Society* 10 (October 1992): 2.

———, "Reform and Frustration in Egypt," *Journal of Democracy* 7, no. 4 (1996): 127–135.

Ingram, Edward, ed., *National and International Politics in the Middle East: Essays in Honour of Elie Kedourie*. London: Frank Cass, 1986.

Istiphan, Isis, *Directory of Social Agencies in Cairo*. Cairo: American University in Cairo Press, 1956.

Al-Jabri,'Abd al-Mut'al, *Al-Muslima al-'Asriyya 'Ind Bahithat al-Badiyya Malak Hifni Nasif (The Contemporary Muslim Woman According to the Searcher in the Desert Malak Hifni Nasif)*. Cairo: Dar al-Ansar, 1979.

Karam, Azza M. *Women, Islamisms and the State*. New York: St. Martin's Press, 1998.

Keesing's Contemporary Archives, November, 21 1980, [30586].

Keddie, Nikki R. and Beth Baron, *Women in Middle Eastern History: Shifting Boundaries in Sex and Gender*. Berkeley: University of California Press, 1992.

Kedourie, Elie, *Democracy and Arab Political Culture*. London: Frank Cass, 1994.

Kepel, Gilles, *Muslim Extremism in Egypt: The Prophet and Pharaoh*, translated by Jon Rothschild. Berkeley: University of California Press, 1985.

Al-Khatib, Muhammad 'Abdallah, "Al-Ifta' [Legal Opinion]," *Liwa' al-Islam* (January 1990): 60–61.

Khouri-Dagher, Nadia, "The Answers of Civil Society to a Defaulting State: A Case Study around the Food Question in Egypt," Middle East Studies Association Annual Meeting, Baltimore, November 14–17, 1987.

Khoury, Nabil F. and Valentine Moghadam, *Gender & Development in the Arab World: Women's Economic Participation—Patterns and Policies*. London: Zed Books, 1995.

Kupferschmidt, Uri M. "Reformist and Militant Islam in Urban and Rural Egypt," *Middle Eastern Studies* 23, no. 4 (1987): 403–420.

Al-Kurdi, Jihad, "The Muslim Brotherhood and Democracy: Conference Transformed to Confrontation" (in Arabic), *Liwa' al-Islam* (October 1990): 15.

LaTowsky, Robert, "Building Capacity for Self-Help and Community Action among the Poor: Priority Support for CDAs in Egypt," a strategy paper prepared for Catholic Relief Services—Egypt, February 1990.

Lawrence, Bruce B., *Defenders of God: The Fundamentalist Revolt Against the Modern Age*. San Francisco: Harper & Row, 1989.

Lawyers Committee for Human Rights, *Escalating Attacks on Human Rights Protection in Egypt*. New York: September 1995.

Leenders, Reinoud, "The Struggle of State and Civil Society in Egypt: Professional Organizations and Egypt's Careful Steps towards Democracy," *Middle East Research Associates,* Occasional Papers, no. 26 (April 1996).

Lesch, Ann M., "The Muslim Brotherhood in Egypt: Reform or Revolution?" In *The Religious Challenge to the State,* edited by Matthew C. Moen and Lowell S. Gustafason. Philadelphia: Temple University Press, 1992.

Macleod, Arlene Elowe, *Accommodating Protest: Working Women, the New Veiling, and Change in Cairo.* New York: Columbia University Press, 1991.

Mahmud, Mustafa, "Islam vs. Marxism and Capitalism," in *Islam in Transition: Muslim Perspectives,* edited by John J. Donohue and John L. Esposito. New York: Oxford University Press, 1982.

Makram-Ebeid, Mona, "Political Opposition in Egypt: Democratic Myth or Reality?" *Middle East Journal* 143, no. 3 (1989): 423–436.

Al-Malt, Ahmad, "How Can We Stop the Chain of Violence?," (in Arabic), *Al-Da'wa,* May 6, 1993, pp. 18–21.

Malti-Douglas, Fedwa, *A Woman and Her Sufis.* Occasional papers, Center for Contemporary Arab Studies. Washington, D.C.: Georgetown University, 1995.

Marsot, Afaf Lutfi al-Sayyid, *A Short History of Modern Egypt.* Cambridge: Cambridge University Press, 1985.

———, "Popular Attitudes Towards Authority in Egypt," *Journal of Arab Affairs* 7, no. 2 (1988): 174–198.

Marty, Martin E. and R. Scott Appleby, eds., *Fundamentalisms Observed.* Chicago: University of Chicago Press, 1991.

Mashhur, Mustafa, "Elections: On the Road to the Call," (in Arabic), *Liwa' al-Islam* (June 1987): 10–11.

———, "Who Are the Terrorists? And Who Are Their Accusers?" (in Arabic), *Al-Sha'b,* 3 September 1991: 5.

———, "Islam Calls Us to Unite the Egyptian Nation," (in Arabic), *Al-Sha'b,* 1 October 1991, p. 5.

Mernissi, Fatima, *Beyond the Veil: Male-Female Dynamics in a Modern Muslim Society.* New York: Schenkman Publishing, 1975.

Middle East Watch, "Egypt: Hostage-Taking and Intimidation by Security Forces". New York: Human Rights Watch, January 1995.

Middle East Watch, *Egyptian Authorities Clamp Down on Dissent.* New York: Human Rights Watch, February 1991.

———, *Egyptian Government Moves to Dissolve Prominent Arab Women's Organization.* New York: Human Rights Watch, September 1991.

———, *Egypt: Court Upholds Closure of Women's Organization.* New York: Human Rights Watch, June 1992.

———, *Behind Closed Doors: Torture and Detention in Egypt.* New York: Human Rights Watch, 1992.

———, *Egypt: Trials of Civilians in Military Courts Violate International Law.* New York: Human Rights Watch, July 1993.

Migdal, Joel, *Strong Societies and Weak States: State-Society Relations and State Capabilities in the Third World.* Princeton, N.J.: Princeton University Press, 1988.

"Militants Warn Foreigners' Lives at Risk," *Civil Society* (March 1994): 5–7.

Miller, Judith, *God Has Ninety-Nine Names: Reporting from a Militant Middle East.* New York: Simon & Schuster, 1996.

Al-Minawi, 'Abd al-Latif, "Egypt: Interior Minister al-Alfi on Security Issues—Interview with Egyptian Interior Minister Major General Hasan al-Alfi," (in Arabic), *Al-Majalla,* May 3, 1997, pp. 26–30.

"Minister on 'Terrorism,' Muslim Brotherhood: Interview with Interior Minister Hasan al-Alfi," (in Arabic), *Rose al-Yusuf,* August 8, 1994, pp. 10–15.
Ministry of Social Affairs, Egypt, *Law No. 32 of 1964: Concerning Private Associations and Establishments* (mimeo, n.d.).
Mitchell, Richard P., *The Society of the Muslim Brothers.* London: Oxford University Press, 1969.
Moen, Matthew C. and Lowell S. Gustafason, eds., *The Religious Challenge to the State.* Philadelphia: Temple University Press, 1992.
Moghadam, Valentine, *Modernizing Women: Gender and Social Change in the Middle East.* Boulder, Colo.: Lynne Rienner, 1993.
Moussalli, Ahmad S., *Sayyid Qutb: The Ideologist of Islamic Fundamentalism.* Abstract from *Al-Abhath,* vol. XXXVIII (1990).
Mubarak, Hisham, "What Does the Gama'a Islamiyya Want? An Interview with Tal'at Fu'ad Qasim," *Middle East Report* (1996): 41–44.
Muslim Student Association internet news service, Ohio State University, February 25, 1994: msanews@magnus.acs.ohiostate.edu.
Mustafa, Hala, *Al-Islam al-Siyasi fi Misr: Min Harakat al-Islah ila Jama'at al-'Unf (Political Islam in Egypt: From the Movement of Reform to Associations of Violence).* Cairo: Center for Political and Strategic Studies, 1992.
Mustafa, Majdi, "The Muslim Brotherhood in the People's Assembly: Trial and Results; Dialogue with Ma'mun al-Hudaybi" (in Arabic), *Liwa' al-Islam* (June 1990): 24–25.
Najjar, Fauzi M., "The Application of Shari'a Laws in Egypt," *Middle East Policy* 1, no. 3 (1992): 72–73.
Napoli, James, *Washington Report on Middle East Affairs,* December 1992–January 1993.
Nelson, Cynthia, *Doria Shafik, Egyptian Feminist: A Woman Apart.* Gainesville: University Press of Florida, 1996.
The Network of Egyptian Professional Women, *Egyptian Women in Social Development: A Resource Guide.* Cairo: American University in Cairo Press, 1988.
Norton, Augustus Richard, ed., *Civil Society in the Middle East,* vol. 1. Leiden: E. J. Brill, 1995.
———, "Introduction." In *Civil Society in the Middle East,* vol. 1. Leiden: E. J. Brill, 1995.
Palmer, Monte et al., *The Egyptian Bureaucracy.* Syracuse, N.Y.: Syracuse University Press, 1988.
Perlmutter, Amos, "Wishful Thinking About Islamic Fundamentalism," *Washington Post* (19 January 1992).
Peters, Rudolph, "The Political Relevance of the Doctrine of Jihad in Sadat's Egypt." In *National and International Politics in the Middle East: Essays in Honour of Elie Kedourie,* edited by Edward Ingram. London: Frank Cass, 1986.
Peterson, Samiha Sidhom, *The Liberation of Women: A Document in the History of Egyptian Feminism.* Cairo: American University in Cairo Press, 1992.
Pugh, Deborah, "Upper Egypt," *Christian Science Monitor,* 4 May 1994, pp. 12–13.
Qutb, Sayyid, *Ma'alim fi al-Tariq.* Cairo: Dar al-Shuruq, 1980.
Al-Rahman, 'Umar 'Abd, *Al-Maw'itha al-Hasana.* Kuwait: Dar al-Siyasa, 1988.
Ramadan, 'Abdel 'Azim, "Fundamentalist Influence in Egypt: The Strategies of the Muslim Brotherhood and the Takfir Groups." In *Fundamentalisms and the State: Remaking Polities, Economies, and Militance,* edited by Martin

E. Marty and R. Scott Appleby. Chicago: University of Chicago Press, 1991.

Rasheed, B.S. et al., *The Egyptian Feminist Union: Now the Hoda Sha'arawi Association.* Cairo: Anglo-Egyptian Bookshop, 1973.

Rashwan, Diya', "Al-Jama'at al-Islamiyya al-Misriyya wa al-Istiqrar al-Siyasi [Egyptian Islamist Groups and Political Stability]," *Al-Majalla,* March 16, 1993, pp. 24–28.

———, "Al-Dawla Tata'amad Siyasit al-Qabda al-Hadidiyya lil Qada' 'Ala al-Jama'at al-Mutatarrifa fi Misr [The State Uses an Iron Fist Policy to Eliminate Radical Groups in Egypt]," *Al-Majalla,* March 30, 1993, pp. 28–29.

"Representatives of the Muslim Brotherhood Respond to the Government's Report," (in Arabic), *Liwa' al-Islam* (February 1989): 28–31.

Rizq, Hamdi, "The *Sa'id* of Egypt: The Game of Cat and Mouse in the Forests of Sugar Cane," (in Arabic), *Al-Majalla,* 26 July 1997, pp. 16–20.

Rizq, Jabir, "Egypt Between the Terror of Governments and the Terror of Groups" (in Arabic), *Liwa' al-Islam* (June 1987): 4–5.

Rugh, Andrea, *Family in Contemporary Egypt.* Syracuse, NY: Syracuse University Press, 1984.

———, *Reveal and Conceal: Dress in Contemporary Egypt.* Syracuse, NY: Syracuse University Press, 1986.

El-Saadawi, Nawal, *The Hidden Face of Eve.* Boston: Beacon Press, 1982.

———, *God Dies by the Nile.* London: Zed Books, 1985.

———, "The Political Challenges Facing Arab Women at the End of the 20th Century," translated by Marilyn Booth. In *Women of the Arab World,* edited by Nahid Toubia. London: Zed Books, 1988.

———, *Memoirs from Women's Prison.* Berkeley: University of California Press, 1994.

———, *The Nawal El Saadawi Reader.* London and New York: Zed Books, 1997.

Said, Edward W., *The Politics of Dispossession.* New York: Random House, 1994.

Salim, Layla, "Al-Mar'a fi Da'wat wa Fikr Hasan al-Banna: Bayn al-Madi wa al-Hadir" (Woman in the Call and Thought of Hasan al-Banna: Between the Past and Present), *Liwa' al-Islam* (January 1990): 52.

Al-Sayyad, Ayman, "'Ala Lisan Munsha'ayha wa Qadatha: Al-Tarikh al-Siri Li Jama'at 'al-Jihad 'fi Misr" (In the Words of Its Founders and Judges: The Secret History of the Jihad Organization in Egypt), *Al-Majalla,* 14 May 1994, pp. 26–33.

Al-Sayyid, Mustapha K., "A Civil Society in Egypt?" *Middle East Journal* 47, no. 2 (1993): 228–242.

Shaarawi, Huda, *Harem Years, the Memoirs of an Egyptian Feminist, 1879–1924.* London: Zed Books, 1987.

Shahrough, Akhavi, "The Clergy's Concepts of Rule in Egypt and Iran," ANNALS 524 (1992): 92–102.

Sharabi, Hisham, ed., *Theory, Politics and the Arab World: Critical Responses.* New York: Routledge, 1990.

Shukrallah, Hala, "The Impact of the Islamic Movement in Egypt," *Feminist Review,* no. 47 (1994).

Singerman, Diane, *Avenues of Participation: Family, Politics and Networks in Urban Quarters of Cairo.* Princeton, N.J.: Princeton University Press, 1995.

Sivan, Emmanuel, *Radical Islam: Medieval Theology and Modern Politics.* New Haven, Conn.: Yale University Press, 1985.

Smith, Brian H., *More Than Altruism: The Politics of Private Foreign Aid*. Princeton, N.J.: Princeton University Press, 1990.
De Soto, Hernando, *The Other Path: The Invisible Revolution in the Third World*. New York: Harper & Row, 1989.
Springborg, Robert, *Mubarak's Egypt: Fragmentation of the Political Order*. Boulder: Westview Press, 1989.
Starrett, Gregory, "Our Children and Our Youth: Religious Education and Political Authority in Mubarak's Egypt." Mimeo, 1993.
———, *Putting Islam to Work: Education, Politics, and Religious Transformation in Egypt*. Berkeley: University of California Press, 1998.
Sullivan, Denis J., *Private Voluntary Organizations in Egypt: Islamic Development, Private Initiative, and State Control*. Gainesville: University Press of Florida, 1994.
———, "State and Civil Society in Conflict in Egypt," *Middle East Affairs Journal* 3, nos. 1–2 (1997): 67–86.
Sullivan, Earl L. and Karima Korayem, *Cairo Papers in Social Science* 4, no. 4: *Women and Work in the Arab World*. Cairo: American University in Cairo Press, 1981.
Tahtawi, Rifa'a, *Manahij al-Albab al-Misriyya fi Mabahij al-Adab al-'Asriyya*. Cairo, 1912.
Taylor, Charles, "Modes of Civil Society," *Public Culture* 3, no. 1 (1990).
Tibi, Bassam, *Islam and the Cultural Accommodation of Social Change*. Translated by Clare Krojzl. Boulder, Colo.: Westview Press, 1991.
———, "Culture and Knowledge: The Politics of Islamization of Knowledge as a Postmodern Project? The Fundamentalist Claim to De-Westernization," *Theory, Culture & Society* 12 (1995): 1–24.
Al-Tilmisani, 'Umar, "Do the Missionaries for God Have a Program?" (in Arabic), *Liwa' al-Islam* (June 1987): 6–8.
Toubia, Nahid, ed., *Women of the Arab World*. London: Zed Books, 1988.
Tripp, Charles and Roger Owen, eds., *Egypt under Mubarak*. London and New York: Routledge, 1989.
Tucker, Judith E., *Women in Nineteenth Century Egypt*. Cambridge and New York: Cambridge University Press, 1985.
"Upper Egypt: The Battle Against the Leagues," *The Economist*, July 4, 1992: 38.
U.S. Department of State, *Country Report on Human Rights Practices for 1992*. Report submitted to Committee on Foreign Relations, U.S. Senate and Committee on Foreign Affairs, U.S. House of Representatives, February 1993.
———. Annual human rights report to U.S. Congress, 1 February 1995.
Voll, John O., "Fundamentalism in the Sunni Arab World," in *Fundamentalisms Observed*, ed. Martin E. Marty and R. Scott Appleby. Chicago: University of Chicago Press, 1991.
Walsh, James, "The Sword of Islam," *Time International*, 15 June 1992: 18–22.
Waterbury, John, *The Egypt of Nasser and Sadat: The Political Economy of Two Regimes*. Princeton, N.J.: Princeton University Press, 1983.
Weaver, Mary Ann, "The Novelist and the Sheikh," *The New Yorker*, 30 January 1995: 69.
Wendell, Charles, *The Evolution of the Egyptian National Image*. Berkeley: University of California Press, 1972.
White, Louise G., "Urban Community Organizations and Local Government: Exploring Relationships and Roles," *Public Administration and Political Development* 6 (1986): 239–253.

Whittington, James, "Egypt's Islamists: Proscribed or Provoked?" *Financial Times* 9 August 1995, p. 4.
———, "Radicals Frustrated by Egyptian Poll: Many Feel Disputed Election Confirmed Limits of Democracy," *Financial Times*, 13 December 1995, p. 4.
Wickham, Carrie Rosefsky, "Are the Islamists in Egypt Part of Civil Society?" American Political Science Association annual meeting, Washington, D.C. (September 2–5, 1993).
———, "Beyond Democratization: Political Change in the Arab World," *PS* (September 1994): 507–508.
Youssef, Michael, *Revolt Against Modernity*. Leiden: E. J. Brill, 1985.
Zubaida, Sami, *Islam: The People and the State*. London: Routledge, 1989.
———, "Islam, the State, and Democracy: Contrasting Conceptions of Society in Egypt," *Middle East Report* 22, no. 6 (1992): 2–10.
———, "The Politics of the Islamic Investment Companies in Egypt," *Bulletin—British Society for Middle Eastern Studies* 17, no. 2 (1990): 152–161.
Zuhur, Sherifa, *Revealing Reveiling: Islamist Gender Ideology in Contemporary Egypt*. Albany: SUNY Press, 1992.

Arabic Newspapers and Periodicals

Al-Ahram
Al-Ahram Weekly
Al-Da'wa
Liwa' al-Islam
Al-Majalla
Rose al-Yusuf
Al-Sha'b

Index

'Abdallah, Isma'il Sabri, 125
'Abduh, Al-Sadiq, 48
Abduh, Muhammad, 6, 9–10, 21, 102
Abu al-Nasr, Muhammad Hamid, 49, 56
al-Afghani, Jamal al-Din, 9
Ahmad, Makram Muhammad, 82
Al-Ahram (newspaper), 133, 136*n9*
al-Alfi, Hasan, 53, 62, 86, 87
Algeria, 11, 124
Ali, Muhammad, 8, 15*n30*
Alim Muhammad, 9
Almsgiving, 50
Amin, Mustafa, 126
Amin, Qasim, 100
Antiterrorism Law (1992), 122, 127, 129
Arab-Israeli War (1967), 20, 44, 45
Arab(s): conservative regimes, 20; identity, 8, 15*n25;* leadership, 20; relations with Israel, 20, 44, 45, 72
Arab Women's Solidarity Association, 25, 36, 99
al-'Aryan, 'Isam, 48, 62, 82
al-'As, Amr ibn, 8
al-'Asal, Ahmad, 44
al-Ashmawi, Muhammad Said, 6, 15*n17*
'Askar, Sayyid, 132
Assassinations: attempts, 61, 62, 67*n8*, 81, 82, 88, 123; al-Dhahabi, Muhammad, 61, 78; al-Mahjub, Rif'at, 82; al-Nuqrashi, Mahmud Fahmi, 42, 60; Sadat, Anwar, 22, 75, 81, 83, 91, 126, 127
Associations, 118*n27. See also* Syndicates; athletic, 45; autonomous, 4; centralized, 34; charitable, 27; in civil society, 2; community development, 25, 27–28, 36; Islamic, 26–27; political, 45; private, 26–27, 34; professional, 54, 55; state control of, 4; student, 21, 23, 55, 73, 74, 82; voluntary, 35
Authoritarianism, 4, 23, 128, 133, 134
AWSA. *See* Arab Women's Solidarity Association
Ayyubi dynasty, 8, 9

Badawi, Fu'ad, 133
al-Badiyya, Bahithat, 101
Banking, 51, 71, 87, 124
al-Banna, Hasan, 10, 11, 21, 41, 42, 43, 47, 48, 54, 60, 63, 79, 80, 100, 105, 107, 109, 118*n27*
al-Banna, Sayf al-Islam Hasan, 48, 55
Banner of Islam (newspaper), 47
Basha, Hasan Abu, 61, 81
Ba'thist Party (Syria), 20
Bey, Qait, 8
al-Bis, Ahmad, 59
Bonaparte, Napoleon, 9

Cairo Institute for Human Rights Studies, 15*n23*

The Call (magazine), 44, 62
Camp David Accords, 74
Canada, 135
Capitalism, 22, 45
Change: from within, 12; constitutional, 52–57; gradual, 12; political, 4; revolutionary, 12, 80, 81
Christianity, 6, 20, 24, 73, 80
Colonialism, 7, 9, 41, 100, 101, 104, 118*n12*, 118*n23*
Community, 3, 25, 27–28, 36; of believers, 77–78; Islamic, 46; services, 92; virtuous, 46
Conventions of Islamic Action (Ibrahim), 84
Corporatism, 4
Corruption, 23, 99; in non-governmental organizations, 35–36
Cosmopolitanism, 1
Court of Ethics, 93*n6*
Cultural: development, 98; hegemony, 15*n20*; imperialism, 5; organizations, 45; values, 57
Culture: of activism, 4; Islamic, 41; maintainance of, 6; political, 6, 15*n21*

Al-Da'wa (magazine), 44, 62, 67*n1*
Democracy: civil society in, 2–3; Islamic, 47–50, 66; progress toward, 13; spread of, 49
Denouncement and Holy Flight. *See* al-Takfir wa al-Hijra
Development: community, 25, 27–28, 36; cultural, 98; economic, 51, 98, 135; "Islamic," 28; political, 3; programs, 22; public sphere, 98; social, 98
al-Dhahabi, Muhammad, 61, 78
al-Din, Muhi, 82
al-Din, Salah, 8
Dirbala, 'Isam al-Din, 83, 84
Divorce, 100, 107
Dogmatism, 1, 14*n2*
Du'ah la Quday (al-Hudaybi), 63

Economic: activities, 4; development, 51, 98, 135; liberalization, 130, 134, 136*n1*;
occupation, 15*n24*; policy, 15*n24*; productivity, 51; reform, 12, 58
Education, 124; and non-governmental organizations, 27; private, 10; reform attempts, 9; of women, 100, 102
Egypt: Arabization of, 8; as authoritarian state, 4, 23, 128, 133, 134; British rule in, 9, 10, 16*n39*, 104, 118*n23*; Christianity in, 6, 7, 20, 24; civil society in, 1–13, 121–135; democratization in, 3, 4; dynasties in, 8; economic crises, 128–129; economic occupation of, 15*n24*; Islam in, 1–13, 19–37; monarchy in, 10–11, 16*n38*; national identity in, 6, 7, 8, 10–12; overthrow of government in, 42–43; political evolution in, 5; political occupation of, 6–7; political structure, 121; population figures, 19–20; relations with Israel, 20, 44, 45, 73, 74; secularism in, 19–20; socialism in, 21
Egyptian Businessmen's Association, 136*n1*
Egyptian Feminist Union, 102, 103, 104
Egyptian Organization for Human Rights, 15*n23*, 38*n15*, 127
Elections, 131–134; abolishment of, 133; boycotts, 56, 61; local, 53, 56, 122, 132–133; manipulation of, 122, 131–134; parliamentary, 132; People's Assembly, 48, 52, 56, 61; syndicate, 55, 133; union, 22; validation of, 55
Emergency Law (1981), 122, 127
European Union, 134

Family Laws, 97
Faraj, Muhammad 'Abd al-Salam, 78, 79, 80, 83
Faruq (King of Egypt), 21, 42
Fatimid dynasty, 8
al-Fil, Faruq, 99
France, 135
Free Officers' coup, 10–11, 42–43
Friday Gathering (magazine), 34
Fu'ad, Ni'mat, 108

Fuda, Faraj, 6, 83, 126
al-Futuh, 'Abd al-Mun'im Abu, 82

Ghanouchi, Rachid, 11
al-Ghazali, Zaynab, 100, 104–109
God's Troops. *See* Jund Allah
Great Britain, 9, 10, 16*n39*, 104, 118*n23*, 135
Group for Democratic Development, 15*n23*

Habib, Kamal al-Sa'id, 78
al-Hajaj, Tharwat, 87
Halawi, Hasan, 78
Hamam, Tal'at Yasin, 88
Hamza, Kariman, 108
Al-Haqiqa (newspaper), 56
Harem system, 103, 118*n21*
Hasanayn, Ahmad, 60, 61
Health care, 92, 124; Fath Complex, 30–31; by Islamist associations, 28–32; by Muslim Brotherhood, 22; non-governmental organization provisions, 24, 28–32
Heikal, Muhammad Hassanein, 126
Hilmi, 'Abd al-Qadir, 44
Hizb al-Tahrir al-Islami, 22, 61, 75, 76
Hizb al-Wasat, 54
Hizbullah, 136*n11*
Holy War: The Neglected Duty (Faraj), 79
Huda and Nur, 35
al-Hudaybi, Hasan, 48
al-Hudaybi, Muhammad Ma'mun, 48, 54, 57, 58, 61, 63, 110, 128
Human Rights Watch, 26, 127
Hussein (King of Jordan), 37*n3*
Huwaydi, Fahmi, 48, 109, 124, 135

Ibrahim, Najih, 83, 84
Identity: Arabic, 8, 15*n25*; national, 6, 7, 8, 10–12; self, 15*n25*
al-Ikhwan al-Muslimun. *See* Muslim Brotherhood
Infidels, 77, 80
Infitah, 51
International Monetary Fund, 15*n24*
Iran, 11; revolution in, 20, 74
Islam: antipolitical, 6; chauvinistic, 6, 14*n2*; codes of conduct, 63, 85; comprehensiveness of, 58–59; contemporary, 1; diversity in, 1, 19–37; Egyptian, 1–13; fundamentalism in, 15*n20*, 37*n8*, 125; individual accountability in, 63, 65–66; opposition to West, 41, 42, 85, 136*n11*; pluralism of, 1, 19–37, 47–50, 62, 67; and political legitimacy, 20; political manipulation of, 21; in political realm, 45–51, 89; promulgation of message of, 57–59; research on, 2–5, 14*n6*; resurgence of, 9–10, 12, 14*n4*, 24–25, 45, 113, 136*n11*; and science, 10, 28; secular, 6, 9; shari'a in, 9, 10, 42, 43, 46, 65, 74, 80, 90; Shi'ite, 8, 20; and socioeconomic justice, 50–51; state-sponsored, 19; Sunni, 8, 20; women in, 47, 73, 97–117
al-Islambuli, Khalid, 75
al-Islambuli, Muhammad Shawqi, 75
Islamic Alliance of the Socialist Labor Party, 132–133
Islamic Liberation Army. *See* Hizb al-Tahrir al-Islam
Islamic Medical Association, 59
Islamic Medical Society, 30
Islamic Salvation Front, 124
Islamic Vanguards, 75
Islamist(s): associations, 26–27; defining, 14*n1*; dress, 100, 101, 102, 104, 109; economic activities, 4; institutions, 124; liberal, 6, 15*n17*; militant, 14*n2*, 20, 21, 22–24, 38*n13*, 53, 71–92; morality, 73–74; nationalism, 11; political activities, 4; revolution, 63, 80, 81; social activities, 4, 91; society, 77–78; student organizations, 21; values, 42; voluntarism, 24
Isma'il, 'Ali 'Abdu, 76
Isma'il, Muhammad Nabawi, 81
Israel, 20, 44, 45, 73, 74, 136*n11*
al-Ittihad al-Nisa'i al-Misri, 102
'Izbat Zayn (community association), 27–28

al-Jama'a al-Islamiyya, 6, 20, 23, 34, 53, 73, 74, 75, 82–86, 124, 136*n2*
Jama'at al-Faniyya al-'Askariyya, 76

Jama'at al-Muslimin, 75, 77
al-Jamal, Sa'd, 88
Jami', Mahmud Mu'awwad, 44, 73
al-Jam'iyya al-Shar'iyya, 34
Jam'iyyat al-'Ashira al-Muhammadiyya, 34
Jam'iyyat al-Muhafitha 'ala al-Quran al-Karim, 34
Jam'iyyat al-Shaban al-Muslimin. *See* Young Men's Muslim Association
Jam'iyyat al-Tabligh, 22, 38*n10*
Japan, 134, 135
al-Jazzar, Hilmi, 73, 82
"Jehan's Laws," 97
Jihad, 6, 20, 22, 43, 45, 53, 60, 63, 65, 75, 76, 79, 80, 81, 82, 83, 85, 88, 90, 124, 126, 136*n2*
al-Jubayli, Zaynab al-Ghazali, 47
Jund Allah, 22, 75
Justice, social, 50–51, 65, 73

al-Khatib, Muhammad 'Abdallah, 47
Khomeini, Ayatollah Ruhollah, 11
Kuwait, 134

Labor Party, 52, 53, 56, 99
Law 14 (1964), 97
Law 32, Law of Association (1964), 15*n23*, 25–26, 38*n15*, 39*n26*, 99, 122, 127
Law 93, Press Law (1995), 122, 130
Law 97, Antiterrorism Law (1992), 122, 127, 129
Law of Association (1964), 15*n23*, 25–26, 38*n15*, 39*n26*, 99, 122, 127
Law of Shame, 74, 93*n6*
Lawyers Committee for Human Rights, 127
Lebanon, 136*n11*
Liberalization: economic, 130, 134, 136*n1*; political, 56, 130, 135; social, 135
Liberal Party, 52, 56, 99
Liberation of Women, The (Amin), 100
Liwa' al-Islam (newspaper), 47, 67*n1*

Ma'alim fi al-Tariq (Qutb), 43, 44
Madani, Abdel-Harith, 137*n27*
Madi, Abu al-'Ala, 54, 62, 82
Mahjub, Muhammad 'Ali, 128
al-Mahjub, Rif'at, 82

Mahmud, Mustafa, 28
Majallat "al-Jum'a" (magazine), 34
Majallat "I'tisam" (magazine), 34
al-Majid, 'Asim 'Abd, 83
Majlis al-Sha'b. *See* Parliament; People's Assembly
Majlis al-Shura, 79, 83
al-Malt, Ahmad, 58–59, 60
Mamluk dynasty, 8, 9
"March of Veiled Women," 104
Mashhur, 'Abd al-Mun'im, 44
Mashhur, Mustafa, 54, 58, 62, 109–110
Media relations, 130
Middle East Watch, 64, 127
Military Technical Academy Group, 76
Ministry of Agriculture, 88
Ministry of Endowments, 89
Ministry of Interior, 81–82, 85–86, 87, 127
Ministry of Religious Endowments, 128
Ministry of Social Affairs, 25–26, 30, 34, 35, 99
Missionaries, Not Judges (al-Hudaybi), 63
Mithaq al-'Amal al-Islami (Ibrahim), 84
MOSA. *See* Ministry of Social Affairs
Mosques, 34, 92, 102, 122, 128
Movements: army, 16*n38*; conservative, 10; evolution, 1; historical perspectives on, 19–21; Islamic companies, 35; lack of knowledge of, 13; pluralism of, 13, 19–37, 47–50, 62, 67; secular-feminist, 13, 98, 99, 117*n4*, 118*n12*; uniform categorization of, 12, 13
Mubarak, Hosni, 21, 22, 23, 41, 48, 49, 53, 57, 75, 81, 83, 89, 121, 122, 123, 124, 126, 130, 132, 136*n9*
Muhammadan Family Association, 34
Muhammad (Prophet), 45, 68*n13*, 72
Murad, Hilmi, 133
Al-Musawwir (magazine), 82
Muslim Benevolent Society, 10
Muslim Brotherhood, 1, 8, 12, 13,

34, 36, 41–67, 82, 105, 106, 107, 118n27, 123, 124, 128, 132; accomodationist stance, 6, 20, 45, 51–57; associational activities, 54–55; criticisms of, 56; evolution of, 41–45; General Guides of, 45, 46, 48, 49, 54, 56, 63; goals, 36–37, 41, 45–47, 52–57; membership, 42; in Nasser era, 42–44; nonviolence affirmation of, 59–65; in People's Assembly, 48, 52, 56, 57, 58; in political elections, 52, 132; political involvement, 22; political role, 48, 49, 50, 52–57; relations with state, 42–45, 123–124; in Sadat era, 44–45; social justice beliefs, 50–51; social welfare activities, 22, 123; state opposition to, 22, 36, 52–57; strategies, 41, 52–57; in union elections, 22

Muslim Sisters Association, 105
Muslim Women's Association, 104, 105, 106, 107
Mustafa, Shukri Ahmad, 20, 61, 77, 78, 80, 93n15, 118n27
Mustafa Mahmud Society, 28–29
al-Mustashfa Sayyida Zaynab (hospital), 28–29

Nabarawi, Saiza, 103
Nafie, Ibrahim, 130
Naguib, Muhammad, 42
al-Nahhas, Mustafa, 106
al-Najun min al-Nar, 82
Nasif, Malak Hifni, 100, 101–103
Nasif, Muhammad Hifni Isma'il, 101
al-Nasr, Abu, 61
Nasser, Gamal Abdel, 10, 19, 20, 21, 41, 42, 43, 44, 60, 67n8, 72, 76, 93n15, 105, 106, 126, 128
Nasserist Party, 53, 54, 99, 132
National Democratic Party, 22, 50, 58, 67, 99, 121, 132, 133
Nationalism, 7, 9, 10–12, 101; Arab, 11; Islamist, 11; secular, 11, 23; and women, 97, 101
National Unity Law, 74
Netherlands, 135
New Wafd Party, 22, 52, 53, 132

NGOs. See Non-governmental organizations
Al-Nida' al-Jadid, 136n1
Nijm, Salim, 44
Nishan al-Kamal, 104
Non-governmental organizations, 118n27, 123, 130–131; autonomous, 33; corruption in, 35–36; as "cover," 31–32; government-oriented, 25; human rights, 15n23; Islamic, 26–27, 33–35, 39n26; laws controlling, 15n23; and legal reform, 5; national, 29, 33–35; provision of services by, 24, 27, 28–32; registered, 24–25; relation to state, 25, 27, 36; secular, 24; superiority of services, 32–33; urban, 28–29; women's, 98–99
al-Nuqrashi, Mahmud Fahmi, 42, 60

October War (1973), 68n13, 72
Operation Badr, 68n13, 72
Opposition: political, 74; to state, 11, 13, 41–67, 71–92
Organizations: charitable, 38n15; community, 24–25; corruption in, 35–36; cultural, 45; dependence on government, 25; educational, 45; feminist, 25; grass roots, 38n10, 55; Islamic, 124; militant, 71–92; non-governmental, 5, 15n23, 24, 25; pyramid schemes in, 35; student, 21

Pahlavi, Shah Riza, 20, 74
Palestine, 11
Pan-Islamism, 11
Party of the Center, 54
Patriotism, 7; excessive, 14n2
People's Assembly, 21, 48, 52, 56, 61
Personal Status Laws, 97
Policy: economic, 15n24; foreign, 74; making, 4; public, 4; restrictive, 61; state, 74
Political: activism, 14n1, 20, 25; activities, 4; associations, 45; change, 4, 15n21; culture, 6, 15n21; development, 3; evolution, 5; exclusion, 23; legitimacy, 20, 129; liberalization, 56, 130, 135;

occupation, 6–7; opposition, 74; oppression, 136n11; participation, 58, 62; parties, 43, 52, 54, 56, 74, 132, 134; protests, 74; reform, 12, 43, 58; restriction, 128–129; stability, 12, 66–67, 71, 75, 138n42; subcultures, 1, 14n3; violence, 59, 85–86
Polygamy, 100
Preservation Inheritance (magazine), 34
Press Law (1995), 122, 130
Press Syndicate, 130
Privatization, 51

Qalawun, 8
Qasim, Safinaz, 108
Qasim, Tal'at Fu'ad, 82, 83, 90
al-Qirdawi, Jusif, 44
Qutb, Sayyid, 43, 46, 63, 67n8, 76, 77, 79

al-Rahhal, Salim, 78
al-Rahman, 'Umar 'Abd, 79, 83, 84, 85, 86–87, 90
Rajab, Hasan, 126
Raqiq, Salih Abu, 44
Reform: accomodationist, 6, 45; economic, 12, 58; educational, 9; Islamic efforts, 5; legal, 5, 43; political, 12, 43, 58; social, 12, 47; system, 45
Relations: gender, 110–113; media, 130; state-society, 1, 2, 3, 64, 86–89, 121–135
Repression, 5, 11, 23, 43, 49, 50, 122, 123; relation to violence, 13
Rida, Rashid, 9, 10
Rights: abuse of, 13, 127; equal, 110; human, 5, 13, 15n23, 26, 38n15, 127; legal, 4; monitoring groups, 25; recognition of, 62; respect for, 5; women's, 97, 99, 100–101, 104, 108, 109, 115–116
Rizq, Jabir, 64

el-Saadawi, Nawal, 25, 99, 111–112, 124
Sadat, Anwar, 10, 20, 21, 22, 23, 41, 44, 45, 51, 66, 72–75, 81, 83, 91, 93n6, 93n15, 115, 126, 127

Salifiyya movement, 8, 10, 21
Salim, Muhammad Salim, 107
Saudi Arabia, 20, 134
al-Sayyid, Ahmad Lutfi, 6, 7
Science, and religion, 10, 28
Searcher in the Desert, 101
Sector, informal, 39n26
Sector, private, 51; state control in, 5
Sector, public, 51
Secularism, 4, 13, 42, 74, 80, 82, 85, 108; cosmopolitan, 6; Egyptian, 19–20; nationalistic, 11, 23; opposition to, 10
Al-Sha'b (newspaper), 62, 67n1, 132–133
Shafik, Doria, 101
Sha'rawi, Huda, 100, 101, 102, 103–104
Shari'a, 9, 10, 38n10, 42, 43, 46, 65, 74, 80, 90
al-Sharif, 'Ali, 83
al-Sharif, Safwat, 62
al-Shawqiyyun, 6, 78
Shenouda III (Pope), 75
Sidki, 'Atif, 128–129
Signs Along the Path (Qutb), 43, 44
Siriyya, Salih, 61, 76
Siyam, 'Adil 'Awad, 88
Smuggling, 89
Social: activism, 14n1, 98; activities, 4, 27–32, 91; contract, 128; crises, 92; development, 98; evolution, 5; justice, 50–51, 65, 73; liberalization, 135; philosophy, 3; programs, 22; reform, 12, 47; security, 50; services, 24, 92, 99, 123; stability, 135; welfare, 22, 27–32, 91
Socialism, 21, 44, 45, 51
Socialist Labor Party, 22
Society, civil, 1–13; associations in, 2; autonomy in, 4; community organizations in, 24–25; conflict with state, 1, 2, 6, 19, 121–135; defining, 2–3; in democracies, 2–3; evolution of, 3; Islamist role in, 1; noninvolvement in politics in, 8; participation in, 4–5; research on, 2–5, 14n6; resurgence of, 130–131; syndicates in, 2; tolerance in, 3, 4, 59, 129,

138*n42;* as Western notion, 3, 4; women in, 13, 97–117
Society for the Preservation of the Quran, 34
Society of Denunciation. *See* Jam'iyyat al-Tabligh
Society of Fulfilling One's Mission. *See* Jam'iyyat al-Tabligh
Society of Muslims, 118*n27*, 136*n2*
Society of Repudiation and Renunciation, 75
Soldiers of God, 22, 75
State: antimilitant stance of, 13, 21, 53, 72, 86–89; authoritarian, 4, 23, 128, 133, 134; conflict with society, 1, 2, 6, 19, 64, 86–89, 121–135; control, 2, 5, 52–53, 121–135; Islamic, 45–47, 51–65, 89; legitimacy of, 76, 129; militancy against, 6, 20, 22–24, 38*n13*, 71–92; opposition to, 11, 13, 41–67, 71–92, 121–135; opposition to women's activism, 99–100; policy, 74; and religion, 42, 45–51, 67; repression, 5, 11, 23, 43, 49, 50, 122, 123; secularism, 74; subsidies, 91
Sudan, 11
Sufism, 6, 8, 20, 21
Syndicate Law (1993), 55, 122, 127, 133
Syndicates, 55; in civil society, 2, 133; professional, 62
Syria, 20

Tablighi Jamaat, 38*n10*
Tahrir al-Mar'a (Amin), 100
Tahtawi, Rifa'a, 7
Tajammu', 53, 132
al-Takfir wa al-Hijra, 6, 20, 21, 22, 61, 63, 75, 77–78, 136*n2*
Tanzim al-Jihad, 75, 78–82
al-Tawaqquf wa al-Tabayyun, 75–77, 89
al-Tayyar al-Islami, 14*n4*
Terrorism, 67*n8;* as justification for repression, 11; state-sponsored, 63–64
Those Saved From the Fire, 75, 82
al-Tilmisani, 'Umar, 45, 46, 51

Tolerance: in civil society, 3, 4, 59, 129, 138*n42;* as Muslim Brotherhood tenet, 59
Torture, 5, 48, 64, 76, 122, 127, 137*n27*
Tourism, 23, 71, 85, 87, 126
Turabi, Hasan, 11

'Umar, Ahmad, 82
'Umara, Muhammad, 49
'Umar (Caliph), 8
Unemployment, 124
United States, 134, 135; Department of State, 127; Federal Bureau of Investigation, 86–87
Universalism, 11
'Urabi, Ahmad, 10, 16*n38*
'Urabi Revolt (1882), 9
Al-'Usra al-'Arabiyya (Newspaper), 56

Veiling, 100, 101, 102, 104, 113–116
Violence: alternatives to, 67; attempts to stop, 23; electoral, 132; lack of support for, 23, 48, 59–65, 89; political, 59, 62, 71–92, 85–86, 132; religious justification for, 79; sectarian, 73; state-society, 13, 22–24, 71–92; against tourists, 23, 38*n13*, 71, 85, 87, 126
Voluntarism, 24

Wafdist Women's Central Committee, 104
Al-Wafd (newspaper), 133
Wafd Party, 16*n39*, 101, 106, 118*n23*
Wahba, Shaykh, 34
Waqf, 89
Williams, Dennis, 82
Women: access to credit, 25; in civil society, 13, 97–117; dress and veiling, 100, 101, 102, 104, 109, 113–116; education for, 100, 102; feminist movements, 13, 25, 97–117, 117*n4*, 118*n12;* genital mutilation, 117*n2;* in Islam, 47, 73, 97–117; in politics, 99; public participation of, 106, 107, 109–110; rights of, 97, 99, 100–101, 104, 108, 109, 115–116;

role in society, 109–113; seclusion rules, 100; services for, 73, 99–100, 113, 114; state opposition to activism of, 99–100; suffrage, 97
Women of Islam, 25, 36, 99
World Bank, 15*n24*, 134

Yassin, Ahmed, 11

Young Men's Muslim Association, 24, 29–30; Cultural and Social Club, 29

Zaghlul, Sa'd, 10, 16*n39*
al-Zayyat, Muntasir, 89
Zionism, 11, 80
Zuhdi, Karam Muhammad, 79, 83
al-Zumur, 'Abbud 'Abd al-Latif, 79, 80–81, 90

About the Book

This unusually accessible book provides a comprehensive picture of Islam in contemporary Egyptian politics and society, emphasizing its diversity and heterogeneity.

Tracing the development of Islam as a social, political, and economic force in Egypt, Sullivan and Abed-Kotob analyze the role it plays in governance and opposition to political authority, in social relations, and in the often-ignored areas of social and economic development. They also discuss Muslim-Christian relations and women in Islam. They conclude with a consideration of the future impact of Islam on state-society relations in Egypt and on the legitimacy of the secular regime.

Denis J. Sullivan is associate professor of political science at Northeastern University and affiliate in research at Harvard University's Center for Middle Eastern Studies. He is coeditor (with Iliya Harik) of *Privatization and Liberalization in the Middle East* and author of *Private Voluntary Organizations in Egypt*. **Sana Abed-Kotob** is associate editor of the Middle East Journal and director of publications for the Middle East Institute.